Early Indian Religions

A HALSTED PRESS BOOK

EARLY INDIAN RELIGIONS

P. BANERJEE

JOHN WILEY & SONS
NEW YORK • TORONTO

VIKAS PUBLISHING HOUSE PVT LTD
5 Daryaganj, Ansari Road, Delhi-6
Savoy Chambers, 5 Wallace Street, Bombay-1
10 First Main Road, Gandhi Nagar, Bangalore-9
80 Canning Road, Kanpur
17/19 High Street, Harlesden, London N.W. 10

Library of Congress Cataloging in Publication Data

Banerjee, P
Early Indian religions.

"A Halsted Press book."
Bibliography: p.
1. India—Religion—History. 1. Title
BL2001.2.B3 1973 294'.09 73-5869
ISBN 0-470-04670-8

Published in the U.S.A., Canada and Latin America
by Halsted Press, a Division of John Wiley & Sons, Inc.,
New York

Printed in India

Foreword

The religious history of India is probably the most vital factor in determining the trends of history itself, particularly in the ancient period. The great vitality of the Vedic religion is such that it has survived through the ages upto the present day in one form or the other. The various sacrifices that were enjoined and in the performance of which even the kings of a later day took pride, have been significantly praised by *arthavādas* as Śāyaṇa would explain it. In refuting the objection that impossible statements occur in the *Veda*, as for instance, the animals performing sacrifice, the ready reply is that this is just an *arthavāda.* If even animals and reptiles could derive benefit from the performance of the sacrifices, how much more the humans. The Bhāraśivas, Vākāṭakas, Pallavas, long after the Śuṅgas, had performed various sacrifices like *ukthyā*, *shoḍaśī*, *atirātra, vāja-peya* and so on. This Vedic faith spread even in far off islands, and the Kutei inscriptions in Borneo mention *bahusuvarṇa* sacrifice performed by Mūlavarman. Among the earliest Pāṇḍyas of about the beginning of the Christian era, one is named Palyākaśālai, who was mostly in the sacrificial hall. Kālidāsa mentions *dīrghasatra* or a year-long sacrifice performed by even Varuṇa. Even in the epic period, the highest place was given to the *Veda* and the Brāhmaṇas who kept up the study of the *Veda.* That is why there is a story of a sage who demonstrated that his value was equal to a cow implying that the cow and the *rishi* were of the same importance. The *Mahābhārata* makes it clear in the verse, *brāhmaṇānām gavām chaiva kulam ekam dvidhā kṛitam ekatra vedās tishṭhanti havir anyatra tishṭhati* (*Mahā-bhārata*). All the *saṁskāras* are even today according to the Vedic *mantras*. *Daśapūrṇamāsa* sacrifice and the annual sacrifices like *paśubandha* are not altogether given up even now. The *Smritis*, *Gṛihyasūtras*, *Dharmaśāstras* all ultimately proclaim their Vedic source and give the highest place to the *Veda*. *Veda* is considered a *prabhu* that commands as it gives directions. But strangely enough, even as a *brahmachārī* performs *samidādhāna* and the householder (*gṛihastha*) *aupāsana*, and even as a *prāyaśchitta* is done at last on the *śrāddha* days, repenting for the non-performance of the daily *homas* like *aupāsana*, there has been greater stress laid on the personal predilection for deities like Śiva, Skanda, Nārāyaṇa, Sūrya, Ambikā and Gaṇapati. But even this *pañchāyatanapūjā*, that was given a definite shape by Śaṅkara, is only secondary to *sandhyā* and *gāyatrī*. In fact, the sculpture at Mahābalipuram shows the *rishis* in penance in the highest communion born of Upanishadic thought, but the *Ṛishikumāras* are engaged in *sandyā* and *gāyatrī*, *dikpradakshiṇa* and looking at Sūrya through the aperture in the fingers in *yamapāśamudrā*. There are *vratas*, fasts, feasts and Vedic ceremonies all going together. Bhagavān Nārāyaṇa Vishṇu as Vāsudeva along with Saṅkarshaṇa and with the expanded *Vyūha* has so caught the popular imagination that while honouring *jñānayoga*, *bhaktiyoga* has practically drowned the masses in its depth. It is, therefore, *nāmasaṅkīrtanas*, *bhajanas* and such other modes of addressing a personal god in the shape of Kṛishṇa and Rāma that have come to stay, but along with Vedic practices that go hand in hand.

Jainism, with its great stress on *ahimsā*, has to a great extent in an unnoticed and even unobtrusive manner completely changed the ideology, outlook, and even the mode of life of at least portions of India by a total abhorrence of carnivorous food.

Buddhism has had the greatest influence in India for several centuries with people equally adoring the *stūpa* and the temple as recorded in an eleventh century inscription at Amarāvatī where Amareśvara and Buddha were equally adored by princesses. There was a strange but wonderful sprit of toleration where members of the same family could profess different religions and all of them respect the faith of the other. Prabhākaravardhana was a *Saura*, Rājyavardhana a *Saugata* and Harshavardhana a *Māheśvara*. Even in the Vijayanagara period, sectarian quarrels were set at rest by the emperor who was impartial towards all faiths. Emperor Rājarāja's sister, Kundavai, herself a great devotee of Śiva, built Jaina temples, and Rājarāja richly endowed the Buddhist monastery at Nāgapaṭṭinam. Narasiṁha, the great devotee of Sūrya, who built the temple at Koṇārak is shown in a sculpture adoring Śiva, Jagannātha and Mahisha-mardinī Durgā, for whom temples were constructed by his ancestors in Bhubaneśvar, Purī and Jājpur respectively. The Kushāṇa kings issued coins with different deities imprinted like Vāyu, Chandra, Śiva, Buddha and so forth. Buddha himself was recognised as an *avatāra* of Vishṇu and Jayadeva sings of him as such. It is this spirit of assimilation that has given great vitality to the Brahmanical faith. Epigraphical, numismatic, literary, sculptural and pictorial evidences are quite abundant in India to illustrate the history of the growth and development of religious thought.

Dr Priyatosh Banerjee has given me the greatest joy as I read through his book. Dr Banerjee has dealt with the subject with an objective outlook, wonderfully marshalling facts, and differing from even the best known authors, and trying to maintain his position by cogent arguments, thoroughly documented with epigraphic, literary, numismatic and other evidences. The introductory chapter is, as it, were, the base on which the entire book rests, and Dr Banerjee has thoroughly discussed and shown how the Vedic thoughts and trends have not ceased to be by the end of the Vedic period, but have continued to exercise their influence even up to the present day, all the more in early India which is the period of his study. Śaivism, Bhāgavatism, the Nāga Cult, the survival of Vedic elements in Neo-Brāhmanism, and separate appraisals in Jainism and Buddhism and their reactions on Brāhmanism and vice versa are all studied, discussed and presented with a rare vitality that makes the book a most inviting one. I must congratulate Dr Banerjee, for whom I have always had a high regard as a scholar, on this brilliant performance.

New Delhi
January 1973

C. SIVARAMAMURTI
Director, National Museum

Preface

The book aims at presenting a historical account of some aspects of India's religious life of the post-Mauryan period, i. e. 185 B. C. to A. D. 300. Indian civilisation is of great antiquity and has a continuous development. Every religio-philosophic idea has a traceable history of several centuries. As such, while dealing with the religious history of the above period, I have found it necessary also to provide the genesis or the earlier phases or stages of developments of the religious cults discussed in this volume.

The chapters are based upon a comprehensive and critical study of contemporary archaeological, numismatic and epigraphic materials. Traditions and evidence of literature have been properly utilised to supplement the archaeological studies and link up the narrative as it was necessary.

The treatise is divided into seven chapters. The first or the introductory chapter is devoted mainly to the study of the origin, growth and nature of Neo-Brahmanism which is ordinarily known as Hinduism. Neo-Brahmanism is characterised by profound catholicity and receptivity. It is a synthesis of polygenous religious ideas, historical and popular, Vedic and non-Vedic, a compromise between the speculation of the intellectual and emotionalism of the masses. A clear-cut discussion of the theme in this chapter makes it easy to understand the multiform characters of Neo-Brahmanic cults. Further, this chapter sets the background for the rise and popularity of the dissenting faiths, such as Jainism and Buddhism.

Chapter II deals with the history of Śaivism. Śaivism is not a single cult but a bundle of cults, which is amply testified to by the varied and manifold characteristics attributed to Rudra-Śiva in Vedic and post-Vedic literature.

A few other points of interest in this chapter are concerned with the discussion of (*i*) the historical development of the Rudra-Śiva cult, (*ii*) the wide popularity of this cult among all sections of people, native and foreign, and (*iii*) Liṅga-worship and its association with Śaivism, etc.

Chapters III and IV are devoted respectively to a detailed study of Bhāgavatism and Nāga worship during the period.

In Chapter V an attempt has been made to indicate that there was a continuity of orthodox practices in the framework of Neo-Brahmanism, notwithstanding the overwhelming popularity of the sectarian cults. The historic and popular forms of worship are so intimately mixed up that they can be separated only by an act of abstraction.

Chapters VI and VII describe the history of Jainism and Buddhism during the period. The popularity of these two religious sects is amply illustrated by a large number of contemporary inscriptions and architectural remains pointing to their activities throughout the length and breadth of the Indian subcontinent.

The religious history of India is a fascinating but complicated study and this has not received much attention by Indian scholars except a few. In these chapters I have made a humble attempt to present an exhaustive treatment of the topics on the basis of both literary and archaeological sources. In spite of this, it is quite possible that some points have been left unexplained or inadequately explained for which I crave the indulgence of the generous reader. I will, however, consider my labour amply rewarded if the book stimulates further studies in the field.

In the writing of the first six chapters of the book, I received generous guidance from the late Dr Subimal Chandra Sarkar, formerly Principal of the Patna College, Patna. I enormously benefited from his profound knowledge of Indian history and culture. I take this opportunity of paying my respectful homage to his sacred memory.

My sincere thanks are also due to Dr K. K. Datta, Retired Vice-Chancellor, Patna University, Patna, Shri A. Ghosh (Retired Director-General of Archaeology in India), and Shri C. Sivaramamurti, Director, National Museum, New Delhi, who have taken a keen interest in my work and have helped me in various ways in the preparation of this book and have thus placed me under a deep debt of gratitude.

January 1973

P. BANERJEE

Contents

Dedicated to the sacred memory of my father

I. Introductory

One of the main aspects of the religious history of the post-Mauryan period is the gradual emergence of Neo-Brahmanism more or less in the form in which we know it in later periods or even now. Neo-Brahmanism, as we know, is a mass of beliefs, opinions, usages, religious creeds and observances derived from manifold sources, hieratic or popular, Vedic or non-Vedic, native or foreign, Aryan or non-Aryan, orthodox or dissenting. In short, it is a synthesis, the process of which stretches over a long period, though it assumes a tangible shape in the epic literature. Diversity is its very essence. One of its peculiar manifestations, however, is the devotional monotheistic worship of personal gods within various sectaries. This monotheistic form of worship is, however, one of the diverse forms of worship prevailing in this period. It is well known to the students of Indian mythology that polytheism, pantheism, and theism mix and coexist throughout in Indian religious thought. As early as the earlier *Saṁhita* period, side by side with external and polytheistic forms of worship, there was the idea of a personal god, and also an attempt towards reaching a unity of godhead. The idea of grace, mercy, and intimate fellowship between god and the worshipper which characterize the Bhakti movement of Krishṇa-Vāsudeva are present also in the cult of Varuṇa of the *Rigveda.* Varuṇa is looked upon as an upholder of moral order and the hymns addressed to him are ethical and devout in tone.[1] While he punishes those who transgress his ordinances, he is gracious to the penitent as is apparent from the following Rigvedic verse.

[1] *Rigveda,* I. 25, 16 ff.

Oh thou strong and mighty god, through want of strength I went astray. Be gracious, mighty lord, have mercy.[2] Whatever wrong we men commit against the heavenly host, O Varuṇa, whatever law of thine we break through thoughtlessness, for that iniquity chastise us not, O god.[3]

While belief in many gods existed, the practice of extolling one god as the greatest when he is the subject of adoration (called monotheism or kathenotheism by Max Müller) led to the idea that the functions of creation, preservation, and rulership of the world may be predicated of a single divinity giving rise to the conception of Prajāpati or Viśvakarman.[4]

Further, some of the events and personages that are the subject of religious speculation in the epic literature also figure in and are coeval with the later Vedic period. Thus, Krishṇa-Vāsudeva himself is a scholar and follower of the Brahmanical theology as mentioned in the *Chhāndogya Upanishad.*[5] It may also be stated that the early Upanishads themselves reveal here and there the monotheistic, personal, and devotional attitude of some of the Upanishadic thinkers, though their theme was the rational idealism of the Ātman-Brahman doctrine.[6] These arguments make it clear that personal deities and theistic forms of worship (whatever may be their origin) were quite well known to the intellectual classes in the Vedic and Upanishadic periods though they came to possess mass appeal through larger religious movements by popular leaders and preachers of subsequent times as revealed in the epic composition. Their prominence in our time may be due to the fact that the other forms of worship were either too archaic, esoteric, or too intellectual to appeal to any but few.

Though like the reform movement of Gautam Buddha, the origin of the sectarian monotheistic cults as revealed in the

[2]*Ibid.*, VII. 89, 3; see also Hopkins, *Religions of India* (Boston, 1895), p. 17.

[3]*Ibid.*, VII., 89, 5.

[4]Macdonell, *History of Sanskrit Literature* (London, 1928), p. 132 ff; *Rigveda,* X. 121, 2; X. 82, 3.

[5]III. 17,4.

[6]*Brihadāraṇyaka Upanishad,* IV. 4, 22; Radhakrishnan, *Indian Philosophy*, Vol. 1 (1923), p. 233.

epics may be due to the complex external ritualism and abstract speculations of the older Brahmanism, yet it is interesting to note that they did not so clearly break away from Brahmanism as Buddhism did. Almost all claim to be based upon the *Vedas*, though in fact there is not much in common between the Vedic literatures and their scriptures.[7] To a certain extent, there is truth in their profession. They have always drawn from the old store of Vedic literature, borrowing in part their formula and usages and even doctrines, and assimilating them for their own purposes. The cults peculiar to them are quite distinct from the cults of old Brahmanism, yet the latter is not entirely cast aside. It is true that they had their own scriptures, yet they dwell on the excellence of the former when it is in their interest to do so. In the *Bhagavadgītā*, Krishṇa declares expressly that he regards every religious act which is done in faith as addressed to God.[8]

The traditional, and to a certain extent mixed character of the majority of these religions may be accounted for by the fact that they were the results of the reconciliation between the older Brahmanic and the popular cults. Before we proceed, it is necessary therefore to discuss in brief the social and religious factors that led to and necessitated this synthesis.

The "record" of Brahmanism begins with the earlier *Vedas*, the earliest literary monument of the Indian people. They consist of hymns in honour of the divinities, namely, Indra, Rudra, Vishṇu, Varuṇa and other personified forces of nature. The religion transmitted to us in these hymns is an adoration of physiolatry developing into anthropomorphism, polytheism, pantheism, theism, and monotheism according to the profundity of vision of the worshipper. The deities are conceived as capable of causing harm and conferring benefit and in order to please them they are invoked in sacrifices and addressed as friends, benefactors and guardians.

The *Saṁhitās* represent varied religious thought. The plurality of gods has led many readers to think that the religion

[7]On the scriptures of the Bhāgavatas and Pañcharātras, Pāśupatas and Māheśvaras, see the *Bhagavadgītā*, the Nārāyaṇīya section of the *Mahābhārata;* H. T. Colebrooke, *Essays on the Religion and Philosophy of the Hindus,* pp. 261-69.

[8]*Gītā*, IX. 24, 25; VII. 20-23.

of the early Vedic people was entirely polytheistic. But on close investigation it appears that there was neither pure polytheism nor pure monotheism in the *Vedas*. The fact is that while polytheism continued, there arose speculations tending towards monotheism or unity of godhead. The mind of the Vedic people, as we find in the hymns, was highly impressionable and fresh. They extolled, unconsciously, any force of nature that proved beneficent to them. The deity which moved the devotion or admiration of the mind was the most supreme for the time being. This peculiar trait of the mind has been described by Max Müller as Henotheism or Kathenotheism—"a belief in single gods, each in turn standing out as the highest." That is, either a particular god is made to absorb all other gods who are declared to be manifestations of him, or else he is given attributes which in strict logic could only be given to a sole monotheistic deity. Sometimes a solution of the difficulties of multiplicity was the collective invocation of all gods as a sort of cooperative unit. Whether we call it monotheism or simply an extravagant praise of the powers of the deity in question, the tendency towards extolling a god as the greatest and the highest, gradually brought forth the conception of a supreme lord of beings and creation. Different names were given to him—"the lord of creatures" (Prajāpati),[9] the "all-maker", "Viśvakarman"[10] and the like. As these names show, the new figure was no longer ritualistic but abstract. This was an attempt at monotheism, but as stated before it did not result in the establishment of a full-fledged monotheistic religion all at once. Some centuries were to pass before monotheism gained a strong foothold in India. As we shall see, the later monotheistic religions owe their strength largely to other elements of more popular origin than these early suggestions.

Generally speaking, the religion of the *Rigveda* is the worship of a body of great and powerful gods. By the most simple logic it applies to the divine power the same principle which men apply to each other. It seeks to propitiate them by gifts and

[9] *Rigveda*, X.121, 2; Macdonell, *Vedic Mythology*, p. 118; Kaegi, *Rigveda*, pp. 88 and 89.

[10] *Yo naḥ pitā janitā yo vidhātā dhāmāni veda bhuvanāniviśvā| Yo devānāṁ nāmadhā eka eva ta śaṁpraśnaṁ bhuvanāyaṁtyanyā||* (*Rigveda*, X. 82,3.)

supplications. But when we pass from the *Rigveda* or from the *Saṁhitās* to the *Brāhmaṇas* we notice a distinct change in the spirit of worship. The *Brāhmaṇas* are ritual textbooks containing mainly practical directions regarding the performance of sacrifices. The priests were still powerful and they claimed to be seers though they made no new hymns. They engaged the attention of the people by elaborating on the technicalities of the sacrificial ceremony. These rituals, admixtures of magic and speculation,[11] were the tools by which the priestly class exercised control. The performance of sacrifice became a matter of expert knowledge and it is clear that from this time the priesthood constituted a distinct profession which was to some extent hereditary.[12] The old idea of working upon the goodwill of the gods disappeared, and in the theosophy of the *Brāhmaṇas* it is an accepted fact that the sacrifice has a magic power of its own which gave mastery even over the gods. In the philosophy of Pūrvamimāṁsā, which is the logical outcome of the *Brāhmaṇas,* the idea of gods is effectively disposed of. Briefly speaking, the Brāhmanic theology fastened itself upon the material foundation of an all-absorbing cult of sacrifice and the divine personalities were subordinated to it. Rituals then became more important than religion, and priests more important than gods.

As the formalism of the Brahmanical rituals could not satisfy the keen religious feelings of the people, a reaction set in. The *Brāhmaṇas* tried to broach the problem by widening the scope of the Vedic pantheon with Prajāpati as its unchallenged head, but that did not satisfy the intellectuals. Dissatisfaction gradually grew and was openly expressed by those who were outside the orthodox pale. An attempt was however made in the *Āraṇyakas* to bring about a compromise by incorporating new ideas and giving a philosophical interpretation to sacrifice.

The development of thought from the *Brāhmaṇas* to the *Āraṇyakas* signified by the transference of values from an interest in the actual sacrifice to its symbolic meaning and medita-

[11]Keith, *The Religion and Philosophy of the Vedas* (Lanman, Vol. 31), p. 260.

[12]J. Muir, *Journal of the Royal Asiatic Society*, London (New series), Vol. II, on the relations of the priests to other classes of Indian society in the Vedic age.

tions which were regarded as capable of yielding various earthly benefits. It is here that we find that amongst a certain section of the people the ritualistic ideas were giving way and philosophical speculations about the nature of truth became gradually substituted in their place. In the *Brihadāraṇyaka Upanishad*[13] we find, for example, that instead of horse sacrifice, the visible universe is to be conceived as a horse and meditated upon as such, the head of the sacrificial horse being the dawn, its eye the sun, its vital force the air, its open mouth the fire called Vaisvānāra, its ear the soul.

This indicates that religious speculations or meditation came to be regarded in course of time as more beneficial than complicated ceremonials. The growth of the idea that subjective speculation was capable of giving the highest good, lessened the importance of Vedic ritualism to a great extent and led to the establishment of the claims of philosophic meditation as the highest goal of life. The *Āraṇyakas* thus paved the way for the Upanishadic doctrines.

"The *Upanishads* are the earliest Brahmanical treatises, other than single hymns or brief passages, which deal professedly in the main with philosophical subjects." Though formally parts of the *Veda-Brāhmaṇas,* the religion they present is to some extent different from the practical, ritualistic side of the *Brāhmaṇas.* As a matter of fact, they are an intellectual revolt against the overdone Vedic ritualism. Their aim is not the attainment of earthly happiness and later bliss in the abode of Yama by offering sacrifices to the gods, but the release from mundane existence by the absorption of the individual soul through correct knowledge into the universal soul.

The *Upanishads* are, however, not systematic treatises. They are "tentative, fluid and one may say, unstable" as they present various currents of thoughts which are sometimes inconsistent with each other. There are over two hundred *Upanishads* in number and distributed over a long period. The earliest of them are about ten in number on which Śaṁkara commented. We cannot assign an exact date to them. Most of them are pre-

[13]*Ushā vā aśvasya medhyasya śiraḥ| Sūryyaśchakshuḥ| Vātaḥ prāṇaḥ vyāttamagnirvaiśvānarḥ, saṁvatsaraḥ ātmāśvasya medhyasya | (Brihadāraṇyaka Upanishad,* 1.1.*)*

Buddhistic; a few may date after Buddha. The accepted dates of these early ones are 1000 B.C. to 300 B.C. They fall into two main groups. The oldest ones are in prose and non-sectarian. They are the *Brihadāraṇyaka*, *Chhāndogya*, *Taittirīya*, *Aitareya*, *Kaushiṭakī*, and *Kena* (a part of it is a later addition).[14] The remaining ones are metrical and theistic in tone. These are *Īśa*, *Kaṭha*, *Muṇdka*, and *Śvetāśvatara*. The others belong to a much later period with which we are not directly concerned here.

The essential theme of the *Upanishads*, specially the older ones, is the conception of the Ātman and Brahman and their identity. "The universe is Brahman, but the Brahman is the Ātman." The etymology of the word Brahman is uncertain. According to some scholars, the Brahman is supposed to be "the will of man striving upwards to that which is sacred and divine." What, however, the word signifies is not certain. In the *Rigveda* it occurs several times in the sense of prayer or magic formula.[15] It is during the period of the *Brāhmaṇas* that the conception of Brahman came to have an established significance as the supreme principle which is the moving force behind the gods.[16] As an elaboration of the very same idea, we find the word Brahman in the *Upanishads* as signifying the holy principle which animates nature.

The etymology of Ātman is simpler. In the *Rigveda* it means breath or the vital essence.[17] Gradually it acquired the meaning of soul or self. In one of the later books of the *Śatapatha Brāhmaṇa*, this Ātman is invested with a high degree of abstraction and is said to pervade the universe.[18]

It may, however, be noted that the Brahman-Ātman doctrine as found in the *Upanishads* seems to have originated much earlier than is supposed, for some of the older passages in *Atharvaveda* show a full acquaintance with what is claimed especially as

[14]Deussen, *The Religion and Philosophy of India, The Philosophy of the Upanishads*, pp. 22 ff.

[15]*The Encyclopaedia of Religion and Ethics*, Vol. II, pp. 195, 197; Hume, *The Thirteen Principal Upanishads* (Eng. Trans.), p. 14.

[16]Eggeling's translation of the *Śatapatha Brāhmaṇa; Sacred Books of the East*, Vol. XLIV, pp. 27, 28.

[17]*Rigveda*, X. 16,3.

[18]*Śatapatha Brāhmaṇa*, X. vi. 3.

Upanishadic (viz. the doctrine of Brahman and Ātman), and that the *Atharvaveda* regards this philosophy as having come down from a remote antiquity: "The Brahman that was first born of old (*Purastāt*—in the east ?), Vena hath widened from a well shining edge (*sīmatas*, horizon)".[19] Further, in the *Atharvaveda* Skambha is the Ultimate Principle called indiscriminately Prajāpati, Purusha and Brahman. He includes all space and time, god and *Vedas* and the moral powers.[20] Perhaps it would be scientific to regard the *Rik*, *Yajus*, *Atharvan Brāhmaṇa*, *Āraṇyaka* and *Upanishad* types of religious ideas as more or less contemporary or traditional, being almost equally ancient and prevailing in different social circles or different regions of ancient India. There is no improbability in the existence of nature worship, henotheism, pantheism, ritualism and magic, devotionalism and personal theism, and scientific and philosophical theism in a complex, vast and ancient civilization like India. And it is not necessary to interpret all these varieties as derived one from the other in chronological sequence, either by way of degeneration or by way of development, reform, or revolution.

The Ātman and Brahman are commonly treated as synonymous in the *Upanishads*. Strictly speaking, Brahman represents the cosmic principle which pervades the universe, Ātman the psychical, manifested in the individual, and they have become united in the philosophy of the *Upanishads*. Thus goes the famous doctrine of Śāṇḍilya postulating their identity:

> This my Ātman in my inmost heart is smaller than a grain of rice, or a barley corn, or a mustard seed, or a millet grain.... This my Ātman in my inmost heart is greater than the earth, greater than the sky, greater than the heavens, greater than all spheres. In him are all actions, all wishes, all smells, all tastes ; he holds this all enclosed within himself ; he speaks not, he troubles about nothing: this my Ātman in my inmost heart is this Brahman. With him, when I depart out of this life shall I be united. For him to whom this knowledge has come, for him indeed exists no doubt. Thus speaks Śāṇḍilya, Yea, Śāṇdilya.[21]

---

[19] *Atharvaveda,* Whitney's translation, Lanman, Vol. 7, p.143.
[20] *Atharvaveda*, X. 7, 7; 13,17.
[21] *Chhāndogya Upanishad,* III. 14.

This identity of the human soul or self with the absolute is expressed in clear terms in the following lines of the *Chhāndogya* and *Brihadāraṇyaka :* "That art thou."[22] "I am Brahman ....It (the universal Brahman) is thyself."[23]

The main interest of the early *Upanishads* centres round Brahman which, as an absolute reality, has defied all positive definitions. Brahman is the "Infinite, Unchangeable, Eternal Absolute". It is Pure Being on which all that exists depends and from which it derives its reality. Yājñavalkya said, "He the Ātman is not this, nor that (*neti neti*). He is inconceivable for he cannot be conceived, unchangeable for he is not changed, untouched for nothing touches him".[24]

The early Upanishadic thinkers appear to have little interest in the worship of the Vedic gods, and shaken themselves from popular religion as completely as from ordinary society. The *Vedas* and the Vedic sacrifices were declared useless to them. They no longer desired those things which were demanded from the gods in return for sacrifices. Although it is perfectly plain that they stood apart in supreme contempt or indifference, from ordinary society and its practices and scriptures, they did not proceed to build a religious or sectarian organization or church as a counter-blast to sacrificial and ritualistic Vedism. As the idea of the impersonal Brahman is much too abstract and too speculative for average men to grasp, it hardly affected the religion of the ordinary people which centred round popular gods and ceremonies. On the other hand, there can also be no doubt that at many points the purely Upanishadic Brahman doctrine itself was profoundly modified by the popular religious tendencies, crystallizing later into sectarian doctrines which sought to conceive the unconditioned impersonal Brahman in more emotional and human terms.

The terms in which realization of Brahman is described in many of the Upanishadic passages of a theistic nature, indicate that Brahman was not only intellectually apprehended as a psychophysical principle but also directly realized cognitively

[22]*Ibid.*, IV. 8, 7, etc.

[23]*Brihadāraṇyaka Upanishad,* I. 4, 10, etc.

[24]*Sa esha neti netyātmā, agrihya na hi grihyate, aśīryo na hi śīryate asaṅgo nahi sajyate.* (*Brihadārañyaka Upanishad,* III. 9, 26.)

and emotionally (covering mind and matter) more or less as a personal being. The well known description of the individual lord *(Antaryāmī)* in the *Brihadāraṇyaka Upanishad* or of the Ātman as the upholder of the sun, moon, heaven, earth and the entire universe in the same text affords appropriate instances[25] in this regard. Like Krishṇa in the *Bhagavadgītā*, Indra describes himself to be the true object of knowledge and meditation in *Kaushiṭakī Upanishad.*[26] Although original idealism maintains itself, a similar attitude is noticeable also in the conception of Ātman Vaiśvānara as the Virāṭa Purusha or world soul in a famous passage of the *Chhāndogya.*[27] In all these passages the impersonal Brahman is spoken of no doubt, but it is spoken of in the most exalted, passionate terms ; if it is not full-fledged theism or devotionalism, it is the first step towards this, and betrays the influence of popular beliefs. Perhaps the best way of interpreting the interrelation between Vedism, popular beliefs, and Upanishadism is that the last is on the one hand a philosophic rationalization of the first and an emotional sublimation of the second, emphasizing the Jñāna path and the *Bhakti* path almost equally while subordinating the Karmapath to both.

The early *Upanishads* are marked by two distinct currents of thought, viz. (1) the theory of Ātman-Brahman, and opposition to ritualistic religion, and (2) the attempt at describing Brahman in theistic terms. They seem to be contradictory; this is due to the fact that the *Upanishads* are not codified treatises—they are simply a collection of the speculations of different thinkers. Briefly speaking, they contain no system but give the start towards various systems. Later Indian thought utilized these starts and developed them into various religio-philosophical schools, affecting profoundly the course of Brahmanism.

Among the organized philosophical systems that arose with the wave of Upanishadic teachings, three are very important, viz. those of the Jainas, the Sāṁkhyas and the Bauddhas. The

[25]*Vettha nu tvaṁ kāpya tamantaryāmiṇaṁ ya imaṁ cha lokaṁ sarvāṇi cha bhūtāni yo' ntarayāmayatīti (Brihadāraṇyaka Upanishad,* III, 7*). Etasya vā aksharasya praśasane Gārgī śūryāchandramasau vidhritau tishṭhataḥ (Ibid.,* III, 8,9).

[26]III, *9... Sa hovācha prāṇosmiprajñātmā/tam māmāyuramritamrityupāsva.*

[27]*Chhāndogya Upanishad*, V, 11; Deussen, *op. cit.*, p. 91.

Sāṁkhya, Buddhist and Jaina systems had one point in common with the Vedāntic doctrine (and other developments of Upanishadism)—the followers of all these four systems did not practise the worship of any god. Also, these three had one point in common which distinguished them from Vedāntism—only persons of the first three upper social classes could study the Vedānta, while the teachings and monastic orders of these three were open to all. The Sāṁkhya remained within Brahmanism while the Jainas and the Buddhists separated as they refused to acknowledge even nominally the authority of the *Vedas* and the caste privileges of the *Brāhmaṇas*.

When Buddhism and Jainism were agitating the eastern part of India, great changes took place at the core of Brahmanism. The Brahmanic rituals were too technical and the Upanishadic Brahman was too abstract to affect the religious ideas and practices of the masses which centred round popular deities and ceremonies. Even in the Rigvedic times, the ritual was an elaborate and expensive affair in which the rich alone could engage. It was, therefore, not only a hieratic but an aristocratic cult. The real religion of the masses was different. We find it best portrayed in the *Atharvaveda* which is a collection of hymns and magic charms intended to accompany a mass of simpler rites and ceremonies which were not connected with the hieratic cult of the *Rigveda*. Almost every conceivable human need and aspiration is represented by those popular performances. It is, however, wrong to hold that the popular and hieratic cult remained altogether separate from each other. The fusion of several cultures and assimilation of polygenous ideas were a potent factor since the early Vedic times and as a result of this a reaction between the hieratic and popular religions took place tending towards an amalgamation. That is why we find that the *Rigveda*, which is primarily an orthodox and hieratic composition, contains reference to popular beliefs and customs, and the *Atharvaveda*, which purports to depict the religion of the masses, contains higher philosophic speculations of the Upanishadic type and also knows the hieratic gods and deities of the aristocratic classes and the priesthood dependent on them. While one deals with Indian thought and religion,[28]

[28]General introduction by Whitney to his English translation of the *Atharvaveda*, Lanman, Vol. VII, p. *clv* ff.

one finds it difficult to separate the two elements—the orthodox and popular, which jointly contributed to their growth and development. The fact is that when specializations and technicalities were attempted the gulf between the two was widened, but at other times they tended to coalesce with each other. The doctrines of the *Brāhmaṇas* and the *Upanishads* were those of specializations. So the religions they evolved were not acceptable to the great mass of Indians, which weakened the basic structure of Brahmanism. As people acknowledging it were varied, it could survive by adjustments and assimilations only. And we shall see presently that orthodox Brahmanism had to stoop to introduce and assimilate the local and popular elements for its sustenance, though deemed heretical from its standpoint.

Buddhism and Jainism developed, as we know, into mass movements in the lifetime of Gautama Budddha and Mahāvīra. They threw their monastic orders open to all irrespective of caste and creed, while the Upanishadic or Vedāntic religion could be observed by the initiated only. Everything in Brahmanism was more or less impersonal, but the secret of the strength of the dissenting faiths, specially Buddhism, lies in the personal devotion shown to the founder. Though Buddhism repudiated the priest and priest-craft, and "recalled the mind of the worshipper to piety and good conduct from the barrenness of the rituals", it set up in the teacher or Śākyamuni, a being infinitely gracious, whom one could love, admire and trust,[29] even as one looked up to a personal deity. Its success was in a great measure due to the reverence Buddha inspired by the greatness of his personal character. Buddha came to be regarded as the ideal man, the perfection of humanity. His doctrines of universal charity, liberty, equality and fraternity were irresistibly attractive and drew adherents in great number. He became the real god of his faith. The personal element of Buddhism exercised a profound influence upon the fate and course of Brahmanism, inasmuch as it practically became a popular and theistic movement within a short time.

As Buddhism and Jainism were assailing the very core of Vedic religion, Brahmanism was faced with no less difficult a task of remodelling itself by recognizing and assimilating the

[29]Macnicol, *Indian Theism*, p. 72.

current popular cults and creeds.[30] The normal demand of the masses is for a personal god whom we can love and trust, a need which could not be well satisfied by the ritualistic or the philosophical varieties of Brahmanism. A merely spiritual and impersonal religion was not capable of taking hold of the mass mind and satisfying their religious craving, and it was necessary to provide them with a more acceptable cult. Brahmanism, to survive, had to expand, or shrink and die. The only way in which this change could be effected was by inventing personal, quasi-human and human divinities, and a system of mythology suited to the minds and requirements of the masses.

The earlier *Upanishads*, we have seen, are not free from quasi-personal touches, which is apparently by way of a concession to the popular mentality. But the real theistic movement starts with the younger *Upanishads* (the *Kaṭha*, *Īśa*, *Muṇḍaka*, *Śvetāśvatara* and a few others of the group) and the epics, the *Rāmāyaṇa* and the *Mahābhārata*. The marked features of these *Upanishads* are the doctrines of a personal god and along with it the idea of predestination and grace in which we have a more or less personal divinity in place of the Absolute. Theoretically they aim at the original doctrine of identity, but the individual Ātman is very often clearly distinguished from the Absolute Ātman, as is evident in the description of the supreme and the individual self as light and shadow in *Kaṭha* (1.3,1) and in the imagery in the *Muṇḍaka* (III, 1,1-3) of two birds dwelling in one tree, one eating the sweet fruit and the other merely gazing on the scene, thus fixing "in an almost deistic fashion the responsibility of the enjoyment of fruits of an action on the individual self."[31]

Further, the doctrine of grace which is the main theme of the *Bhagavadgītā*, seems to appear in *Kaṭha*, 1.2,23 which says:

> This self is not to be gained by word of mouth, nor by intellect, nor by the manifold scriptures. Only by the man whom

[30] *Hopkins, The Religions of India*, p. 349.

[31] *Samāne vrikshe purusho nimagno| niśayā śochati muhyamānaḥ| Jushṭam yadā paśyatyanyamiśa—| masya mahimānamiti vītaśokaḥ|| (Muṇḍaka*, III, 1.2.).
Yadā paśyah paśyate rukmavarṇam kartāramiśaṁ purusham Brahinayoṇim| Tadā Vidvān puṇyapāpe vidhūya nirañjanaḥ paramaṁ sāmyamupaiti|| (Ibid., III, 1-3.)

He chooses is He apprehended; to him the Ātman reveals His own form.[32]

The personal setting for the supreme godhead is clearly manifest in the *Śvetāśvatara* which equates Śiva with Brahman. It criticizes all the theories of creation and puts forth a fresh one:

> Rudra alone who stands before everything at the time of destruction and creates the universe at the time of its origin can be recognized as the Creator of all things that exist. He is the supreme godhead to whose power is due the whirling round of the universes. He is the supreme cause, the lord of the souls, of him there is neither the generator nor the protector, he is the self-subsisting mover of the unmoving manifold and causes the one primal seed to sprout the infinite.[33]

The *Śvetāśvatara* puts the popular mythological gods in place of the supreme Brahman and initiates the process of amalgamating the cults of the average people to whom Śiva was long a favourite figure, with higher speculations of the *Upanishads*. This shows that during the time when the *Śvetāśvatara* was composed (*c.*400 B.C. or earlier) the popular religions were coming to the forefront and began influencing the mind of the philosopher, or that these latter were recasting the popular cults in their own forms.

Thus the younger *Upanishads* did a great deal in bringing the Brahmanic religion in line with the popular which find their culmination in the epics the *Rāmāyaṇa* and the *Mahābhārata*, specially the latter, which is the most important source in regard to our enquiry into fresh additions to and adjustments in Brahmanism, giving it almost a new character designated by scholars

[32] *Nāyamātmā pravachanena labhyo / na medhayā na bahunā śrutena/ Yamevaisha vriṇute tena labhyaḥ tasyaisha ātmā vivriṇute tanūṁ svām//*
The doctrine of a personal god and with it predestination, appears to be taught also in *Kaushiṭakī Upanishad,* III, 9. "He is not exalted by good works nor degraded by evil works, but it is he who inspires to do good works the man whom he will lead on high out of these worlds and it is he who inspires to do evil works the man whom he will lead downwards." Deussen, *op. cit.*, p. 176.

[33] Ranade, *A Constructive Survey of Upanishadic Philosophy,* p. 100 ff.

as Neo-Brahmanism (otherwise known by the name of Hinduism). The *Rāmāyaṇa*, which depicts the life story of Rāma, is pre-Buddhistic inorigin. According to Jacobi and Macdonell, the original portion of this epic, which is a homogeneous text by Vālmīki, corresponds to Books II to VI, and Books I and VII are undoubtedly later additions. The kernel of the *Rāmāyana* was composed before 500 B. C. as Macdonell thinks, and its recent portions were added sometime after the second century B. C.[34] The *Mahābhārata* is an encyclopaedic work consisting of over 100,000 ślokas in its present form. It is a conglomerate of epic and didactic matter divided into eighteen books called *Parvan*, with a nineteenth, the *Harivaṁśa*, as a supplement. The epic nucleus has received and undergone tremendous additions. We find in Book I the statements that the poem at one time contained 24,000 ślokas before the episodes *(Upākhyānas)* were added, that it originally consisted of only 8,800 ślokas, and that it had three beginnings. These data render it probable that the epic has undergone three stages of development from the time it first assumed a definite shape. Its genuine portion is supposed to have come into being about the fifth century B.C. and it reached the present form by about 350 A.D. Farquhar observes that both the epics were recast under the influence of Brāhmin supremacy during the Śuṅga rule, when the didatic and sectarian elements were introduced in them.[35]

One of the important religious aspects of the epics is the exaltation of the gods Brahmā, Vishṇu and Śiva (practically the latter two) over others. The other gods including the chief Vedic deities, are acknowledged only formally. The deities have been adorned with a personal character with more or less fixed attributes and residences. Though possessed of godly supremacy they live like mortals with wives and children. The familiar characteristics and personalities of the deities made them attractive to the masses. As for the reasons why Brahmā, Vishṇu and Śiva became supreme it may be stated that Brahmā is the personalized form of the Upanishadic Brahman, and could not be easily forgotten. Vishṇu was treated as the personification of sacrifice since the Brāhmaṇa period and ultimately came to be

[34]Macdonell, *The History of Sanskrit Literature*, p. 308.
[35]Farquhar, *The Crown of Hinduism*, p. 359.

humanized as Rāma and Krishṇa, and Śiva with his dual character both as a malevolent and benevolent deity. The popular traits attributed to him have swayed the emotion of the Indian people since the earliest times. It may be mentioned here that Brahmā slipped out of the picture very soon and remained as a mere figurehead of the Indian triad Brahmā, Vishṇu, Śiva, in the role of the creator, preserver and destroyer respectively. The epic religion is to all intents and purposes divided between the worship of Śiva and Vishṇu who came to possess all the attributes of supreme godhead. As the *Mahābhārata* grew in bulk and content we find the tendency of society to divide into sectaries, each assigning to its own god the place of the supreme to the neglect of others, the leading two however being the Śaivas and Vaishaṇavas. The epic commentator recognizes in the epithet "*Pañchamāhakalpa*" a reference to the scriptures, *Āgamas*, of five diverse sects, Sauras, Śāktas, Gāṇesas, Śaivas and Vaishṇavas.[36]

The epic in reality recognizes the Sauras, Śaivas and Vaishṇavas, for the Gāṇesas[37] are unknown, and the mere allusion to "Shadow worship" (which the commentator explains as a left-hand rite) does not necessarily imply the existence of a body called Saktas.[38] But the Śaivas are known as having a religion called Pāśupata and the Sauras[39] and the Vaishaṇavas are referred to in the *Mahābhārata* vii, 82, 16, and xviii, 6,97 *(Ashṭādaśa Purāṇānāṁ Śravaṇād yat phalaṁ bhavet/tat phalaṁ samavāpnoti Vaishṇavo nātra saḥśayaṁ//)*. In Śantiparva (*Mahābhārata*, xii, 349, 63ff) Vaisampayana refers to the current systems of religion or philosophy, viz. Sāṁkhya, Yoga, Pañcharātra, Veda and Pāśupata and asserts that Nārāyaṇa is

[36]Hopkins, *The Great Epic of India,* p. 115.

[37]The earliest sculptural representations of Gaṇapati figures are found in a Mathura frieze of Kushāṇa period, *Journal of the Indian Society of Oriental Art*, 1937, p. 123

[38]Hopkins, *The Great Epic of India,* p. 115 f.

[39]A great part of the *Bhavishyapurāṇa* is specially consecrated to the sun. Traces of his worship are found on the coins of Kushāṇa kings who ruled over Nothern India in the early christian centuries. For Sūrya images of ancient Indian type see Sūrya on Bodh-Gayā Art (Śunga period), Sūrya on Bhāñjā sculpture, A.K. Coomaraswamy, *History of Indian and Indonesian Art*, figs. 24, 61, etc.

the chief object of devotion in all these diverse cults.[40] These passages show beyond doubt the all inclusive and dominating nature of Vaishṇava sectarianism.

Next to the Vaishaṇava, the strongest sectarian element in the epic is that of the Śaivas.[41] Throughout the epic, Śiva appears as a popular deity with a vigorous and dashing brilliance. He has been attributed 1008 names (which may be a copy of Vishṇu's). He is the Brahman of the *Upanishads*, the eternal, the supreme, the source of all gods, all beings (cf. *Śvetāśvatara*), as he is described in the didactic portion of the *Mahābhārata*.

The assignment of familiar and definite characters and attributes to the deities made the epic religion attractive and easily intelligible to the masses. But its overwhelming popularity and strength lie in providing mankind with human gods and with an easier way of salvation. It is clear that the editors of the epics felt that some popular heroes must be made the rallying centres to counteract the mighty influence of the heretical religions, and they performed this task by deifying Krishṇa-Vāsudeva and also Rāma, perhaps on the former's model. Both Krishṇa and Rāma are evidently human heroes in the early stages of the epics. Rāma is recognized as an incarnation of Vishṇu only in Book VII, which according to consensus of opinion is a later addition. Krishṇa, who was a local chieftain or the head of the Vrishṇi clan, appears as a supreme deity in the *Bhagavadgītā*. Indeed, he appears in human guise in the greater part of the *Mahābhārata*. In the *Gītā* he is still god and man, an incarnation of the deity in human form. In his divine character or as god, he has here all the attributes of a full-fledged personal monotheistic deity with love and friendliness towards his devotees and at the same time attributes of the Upanishadic Brahman. Krishṇa says to Arjuna:

[40]*Sāṁkhyaṁ yogaḥ pañcharātra vedāḥpāśupataṁ tathā/Jñānānyetāni rājarshe viddhi nānāmatāni vai//* v. 63.

Yathāgamaṁ yathā jñānaṁ nishṭhā Nārāyaṇaḥ prabhuḥ / na chainamevaṁ jñānanti tamobhūtā viśāmpate// v. 68.

[41]Neo-Brahmanism recognizes many gods but renders its best allegiance to Vishṇu and Śiva. Sometimes one, sometimes the other, is taken as an all-god in the epic. At times they are compared and then each sect reduces the god of the other to an inferior position. Again, they are united and regarded as one.

Who sees me everywhere and everything in me, I am not lost to him nor is he lost to me. Who so intent on unity devoutly worships me, who dwell in every being, in whatsoever state he may abide, that ascetic abides in me.[42]... That brilliance in the moon and fire, know thou, is mine.... Entering the earth I uphold all beings with my strength, and becoming Soma... I nourish all herbs.[43] ...The senseless think that I am the unmanifest that has came to manifestation, they do not know my higher being, immutable, supreme.[44]

The above illustrations, the like of which are numerous in the *Gītā*, show that Krishṇa (who was a popular god) has been characterized as one who is all-pervading and all-inclusive, the unmanifest and at the same time the supreme creator and lord of that universe. He is Vishṇu,[45] Vāsudeva,[46] Brahmaṇ, Ātman, Purushottama.[47] He combines in him the supreme Brahman of the *Upanishad*, a popular god Vāsudeva, and Vishṇu, the highest deity of Brahmanical mythology.

Krishṇa became the centre and pioneer of the theistic Bhakti movement which has exercised the profoundest influence on the religious history of India. He embodies the synthesis of the higher and popular spheres of thought—a synthesis for which neo-Brahmanism stands so prominently. The Upanishadic philosophy was too speculative to appeal to any but a small fraction of the population. The great mass of mankind demanded a personal and human god whom one could trust, love and admire, to whom one can appeal for help and succour in times of distress and difficulties.

This could not be satisfied by the contemplation of a nameless soul, even if it be the Soul of the Universe. A more acceptable outlet must be provided for the religious feelings and sentiment of the masses. We have reasons to believe that the demand was met through Krishṇa. The *Bhagavadgītā* sets an

[42]*Gītā*, vi, 30.31.
[43]*Ibid.*, xv, 12, 13.
[44]*Ibid.*, vii, 24.
[45]*Ibid.*, x, 21, xi, 24, 30.
[46]*Ibid.*, vii, 19, x, 31.
[47]*Ibid.*, viii, 1, x. 15.

incarnation or a living personality of god,[48] who appears on earth to extend his grace and love to his devotees, to save the righteous and punish the wicked, to remove the evils and establish righteousness.

> For whensoever right declines...and wrong uprises, then I create myself. To guard the good and destroy the wicked and to confirm the right I come into being in this age and that.[49]

God condescends to become man himself for the benefit of mankind. This is a new note in Indian religious thought, a great assurance to humanity, the beginning, in the practical sense, of the doctrine of Avatāras, a great feature of and a source of strength for the Vaishṇavism of later days. The god of the *Gītā* is the embodiment of love and mercy. Krishṇa says: "Taking refuge in me, though ever performing all acts by My grace, a man wins to the realm eternal and immutable.[50]... Fixing thy thought on me thou shalt surmount all difficulties."[51]

The religion of the *Gītā*, we have already seen, is a compromise between the speculation of the intellectual and the emotionalism of popular faith which best explains the synthetic character of Neo-Brahmanism. Krishṇa sets forth the notion of Bhakti or devotion without displacing the old intellectual theory of salvation by knowledge. The knowledge of Brahman is hard to attain.[52] The difficulties of the intellectual method are emphasized in the *Gītā*. Easier for mankind is a more emotional scheme of salvation. This is what the *Gītā* furnishes by its famous doctrine of Bhakti, "devotion or love of god". Though not entirely unknown to the *Upanishads*, it appears elaborately in the *Gītā* first. Though Krishṇa admits the validity of other means of salvation, he regards the way of devotion as favourite to him. After the mystic revelation of his true form to Arjuna, he declares that such a revelation can come to man through no means other than devoted love—"But by devotion undivided,

[48] *Ibid.*, iv, 7.8.
[49] *Ibid.*
[50] *Ibid.*, xviii, 56.
[51] *Machchittaḥ sarvadurgāṇi matprasādāttarishyati (Gītā*, xviii, 58).
[52] *Ibid.*, vii, 3.

Arjuna, in such a form can I be known and truly seen, and entered."[53] The mystic vison is granted by god as an act of grace. No amount of pious rites and performances can win it. It is granted only to the chosen of God, and we are told that Arjuna was the first of mankind:

> Grace have I shown to thee, O Arjuna, revealing to thee by mine own power this my form supreme which none save thee has ever seen. Not by the *Vedas*, not by sacrifice, not by scripture-reading, alms or rites can I be seen in such a form by any but thee in the world of man.[54]

The *Gītā*, in brief, can be called a layman's or householder's *Upanishad*. It promises salvation through the simple means of Bhakti to those who are unable to follow the way of knowledge and asceticism, the best required methods of gaining salvation in old thoughts. It has effected popular religious methods in the framework of higher thoughts, sucessfully.

It is scarcely possible to give any connected and comprehensive account of the popular beliefs and to describe their main features at length as we have no ancient records at our disposal in regard to them. The principal thing that can be said about them is that they are theistic and presumably tended towards monotheism[55] of a more or less qualified sort. That is due to the fact that the local or tribal deities were worshipped in India, each being regarded as the chief or perhaps the sole god of his people or tribe, though the existence of other gods was not denied. These local gods were of different types and origins. Sometimes they may have been old gods of aboriginal, non-

[53] *Ibid.*, xi, 54.

[54] *Ibid.*, xi, 47.

[55] Towards the end of the *Rigveda* we find an attempt to arrive at unity of godhead which gave rise to the conception of Prajāpati-Viśvakarman in the *Brāhmaṇās*. Prajāpati is the unchallenged head of the gods but pantheistically conceived. In the *Upanishads* also, Brahman and Ātman are conceived as identical and plurality is denied. It is difficult to say how far these monotheistic trends contributed to the growth of Neo-Brahmanic monotheism. Perhaps the best interpretation must be that Neo-Brahmanism synthesized the highbrow monotheism of the *Upanishads* with the tribal and local monotheism of popular groups.

Aryan tribes, and sometimes they seem to have been the local heroes deified after death (as for instance, Krishṇa-Vāsudeva).

The Neo-Brahmanic sectarian gods are complex products of the orthodox and popular elements. The Neo-Brahmanic Vishṇu and Śiva have their Vedic counterparts in the Vedic Vishṇu and Rudra-Śiva, no doubt, but their character underwent a change in form and functions due to the popular elements being added to them. The strength of Neo-Brahmanism lies in its capacity to absorb. We have ample evidence to show that most of the sectarian religions and their systems were non-Brahmanic if not anti-Brahmanic in their origin, and their unorthodox traits could not be fully covered even after their ultimate absorption into Brahmanism. The earliest documents of the Vishṇuites are the *Nārāyaṇīya* section of the *Mahābhārata*, the *Pañcharātra* and the *Bhagavadgītā*. In the *Nārāyaṇīya* section (*Mahābhārata*, XII, 335-351) we are told that there were seven Chitra-Sikhaṇḍi-Rishis who proclaimed the *Śāstra* on par with the four *Vedas* (*Mahābhārata*, XII, 335. 27 f) which (*Śāstra*) consisted of one lakh verses, and were meant for the populace (*Mahābhārata*, XII, 335, 39 etc). As it was to teach both *pravritti* and *nivritti*, it was made to conform to the *Vedas*. The very fact that the *Śāstra*, i.e. the Pañcharātra, was drawn up for the populace and was made consistent with the *Vedas* shows that the system was non-Vedic in origin. Further, we have direct statements in the *Mahābhārata* which regard the *Pañcharātra* and Pāśupata systems as differing from the *Vedas* (XII, 349, 1, 64).

There are certain passages in the *Gītā* which condemn the Vedic rituals[56] and others which commend them.[57] From this it may be inferred that the Bhagavatism of Krishṇa-Vāsudeva had a popular origin, though it was later reconciled with the Brahmanic system. There is evidence in the epic-Puranic literature of the anti-Vedism of Krishṇa-Vasudeva and his adherents and successors, and it is also known that anti-Vedism is reflected in various parts of the Vedic literature itself; in fact the anti-Vedic Buddhist and Jaina systems originated in the Vedic age. The reconciliation of diverse elements, popular

[56]*Gītā*, ii, 42, 43.
[57]*Ibid.*, iv, 31.

and orthodox, Vedic and anti-Vedic, is the excellence of Neo-Brahmanism (a sort of a "federal" religion).[58]

Like the Pañcharātra, the Pāśupata system also has been classed as a non-Vedic system in the *Mahābhārata*, as we have seen. The irreverent character of early Śiva worship is brought out in a dialogue between Daksha and Śiva in the *Mahābhārata*, in which the latter says that he formulated in ancient times the Pāśupata system which is opposed to duties laid down in respect of the four orders of men and four modes of life *(Varṇāśrama dharma)* and agrees with those duties in only a few particulars.[59]

The mixed character of all these sectarian religions show that they had a popular origin, but they became, in course of time, a part and parcel of Brahmanism in its new form called Neo-Brahmanic.

Neo-Brahmanism, which is the outcome of the hieratic and popular beliefs, is multiform in character. It arose out of many historical forces and consisted of different layers, superimposed one upon another in the course of ages. The most striking thing to notice is the steadfastness with which the forms and formulas of the old faith continue to survive in the epics and also in Buddhism. The *Upanishad* and the Buddhist and Jaina treatises do not ignore the existence of the Vedic deities, though they consider them inferior. In one epic passage we find, "Withered are the garlands of the gods and their glory is departed but they still receive the homage in the time of need."[60] In this homage is to be seen the survival of the worship of the *Veda*. In the epic, the Vedic gods are still invoked, though they play an insignificant part in the religious life of the people.

The earlier *Upanishads* gave scant recognition to sacrificial rites, while Buddhism and Jainism ignored them completely. But with the growth of the influence of the heretical religions,

[58]It is interesting to note that the political work of Krishṇa-Vāsudeva tended also towards federalism as between kingships and republics of various types, and as between diverse peoples of India.

[58]*Māhābhārata, Śāntiparva* (English translation by P. C. Roy), p. 510.

[60]*Mamlur mālyāni devānāṁ (Mahābhārata,* 1.26, 32, *Adiparva,* ed. by Sukthankar).

the later *Upanishads* were trying to bring back their pristine glory. The *Kaṭha Upanishad* (1.17) in a style quite opposed to the spirit of the Upanishadic teaching promises for fulfilment of certain ceremonials, "the overstepping of birth and death".[61] Again in the same text (III, 2), the Nachiketā fire is explained as a bridge which leads the sacrificers to the supreme eternal Brahman, to the fearless shore. The reaction reaches its climax in the *Maitrī Upanishad* which explains at the very outset (1.1) that the fire-laying for ancestors is in truth a sacrifice to the Brahman.[62] In the epic, despite the new faith, all depends on sacrifice as a matter of priestly and formal belief:

> Law comes from usage, in law are the *Vedas* established, by means of the *Vedas* arise sacrifices, by sacrifices are gods established; according to the rule of the *Vedas* and usage sacrifices being performed support the divinities, just as the rules of Brihaspati and Uśanas support men.[63]

This shows beyond doubt that the sacrifies had a lurking importance in the Neo-Brahmanic society. The Aśvamedha, Rājasūya and the like were the popular sacrifices of the time among the ruling classes as we find in the epic. Side by side with the growth of sectarian faiths, there were in our period, vigorous sacrificial activities. Pushyamitra Śuṅga performed two horse sacrifices; the Kāṇvas and the Śātavahanas and other princes also performed various sacrificial rites. The performance of the Aśvamedha by Pushyamitra has been regarded as the revival of Vedism by certain scholars, but viewed in the context of the religious development as a whole, it was nothing but a survival of Vedic sacrifices in Neo-Brahmanism.

[61] *Trināchiketastribhiretya saṁdhiṁtrikarmmakrittarati Janmamrityu/Brahmayajñaṁ devamīḍyam viditvā nichāyyemāṁ śāntimatyanamti//.*

[62] "That which for the ancients was (merely) a building up (of sacrificial fires) was verily, a sacrifice to Brahman. Therefore with the building of these sacrificial fires the sacrificer should meditate upon the soul (Ātman) etc." *The Thirteen Principal Upanishads* (English Translation) by Hume, p. 412.

[63] *Māhābhārata*, III. 149, 28, 29. *Āraṇyakaparva,* Part I, ed. by V. S. Sukthankar; *Vanaparva* (Eng. Tr.) by P. C. Roy, p. 450.

Pushyamitra may be regarded as a champion of Vedism but it is fallacious to call him a reviver of orthodox Brahmanism.

As time passed, the Vedic Aryans absorbed popular superstitions and beliefs as did Neo-Brahmanism to a remarkable degree. What is perhaps nearer the truth is that it showed more sympathy to popular beliefs and superstitions than did the older Brahmanism.

Among the various indigenous beliefs and practices that have entered into the Neo-Brahmanic faith are the worship of the Liṅga, the serpents, etc. Liṅga worship was a proto-historic practice in India (as the Mohenjodaro discoveries show) and it was affiliated to Brahmanism or Brahmanic Śaivism in epic times. Whatever might have been its original significance, Neo-Brahmanism (of the epic-Puranic tradition) has clothed it with sober and lofty ideas. In the epic-Puranic tradition, Liṅga is Purusha, while Yoṇi represents Prakriti (Devi), i.e. the male and female energies necessary for creation.[64]

The students of mythology know that certain ideas were associated by people of antiquity with the serpent (Nāga) and that it was a favourite symbol of particular deities throughout the world. Many indeed believe that the snake-worship was the earliest religion prevalent among all men in all parts of the globe, its general diffusion being partially accounted for by the fact that serpents are indigenous in almost every region where civilizations arose, whether riparian, or maritime or submontane. In India it came to be associated with Vaishṇavism, Śaivism and many other cults, apart from its existence as an independent cult. We have ample literary and archaeological materials to show that Nāga worship was prevalent on a large scale in India during our period.

Tree and plant worship is as old as snake worship. Trees and plants are objects of invocation in the *Rigveda*,[65] and Brahmanic law enjoins the faithful to give offerings *(bali)* to

[64]Just as the Liṅga is worshipped by the Śaivities, Śālagrāmaśilā is worshipped by the Vaishṇavites. What the Liṅga and Yoṇi are for Śiva and Pārvatī or Devi, the Śālagrāmaśilā and the Tulasī are for Vishṇu and Lakshmī.

[65]*Rigveda*, V, 41. 8.

the great gods, to the waters and to the trees.[66] They were also objects of veneration among the Buddhists and Jains, as we have pointed out in the body of our text.

Besides Neo-Brahmanic religious cults, the two other creeds that enjoyed wide popularity in our period are Buddhism and Jainism. Though offshoots of Brahmanism, they separated from the parent religion early and maintained an independent existence more or less throughout their course. Jainism as a thought or church movement is much older than Mahāvīra's time. Mahāvīra was the last great, though not the very last, reformer of this group and not the founder of the Jaina system. His two predecessors, Arishṭanemi and Pārśvanātha, were historical persons and their service towards the Jaina religion should be well known to the students of Jaina history and mythology. The period under review witnessed also the vigorous religious activities of the Buddhists, side by side with the other sectarian religious cults. An attempt has been made in the subsequent pages to describe in detail various cults and systems of India during the post-Mauryan period.

66 *The Sacred Laws of Apastamba, Sacred Books of the East,* Vol. 11, p. 107. *Manu*, III, 88.

2. Śaivism

Śaivism is one of the chief religious cults of our period as we have noted in the previous chapter. This creed, which centres round the worship of Rudra-Śiva, is of great antiquity. Śiva is a complex product and Śaivism is not a single cult, but a bundle of cults. Śiva has his many early elements. One is the Mohenjodaro male god, recognized by archaeologists as Śiva-Paśupati. Others are the various Rudras of the Vedic and post-Vedic literature combined with the local and village deities of somewhat similar nature and popular origin. With regard to the Mohenjodaro male god, Marshall says:

> The god who is three-faced is seated on a low Indian throne in a typical attitude of *yoga*...the lower limbs are bare and the phallus*(ūrddhvameḍhra)*...seemingly exposed, but it is possible that what appears to be a phallus is in reality the end of the waist band....Crowning his head is a pair of horns meeting in a tall head-dress. On either side of the god are four animals, an elephant and a tiger on his proper right, and a rhinoceros and a buffalo on his left. Beneath the throne are two deer, standing with heads regardant, and horns turned to the centre.[1]

The physical features and attributes of the deity connect him evidently with Śiva as represented in the epic-Puraṇic tradition. The deity (i.e. the Mohenjodaro male god) is three-faced and representations of Śiva with three faces are not unknown and

[1]Marshall, *Mohenjodaro and the Indus Civilisation,* Vol. 1, p. 52, pl. xii, No. 17. Sir A. Stein found the humped bull and other emblems of Śiva at various sites of the Chalcolithic period in Gedrosia, *Journal, Royal Anthropological Institute,* 1934, pp. 184-85, 90 ff.

uncommon.[2] The deity has been depicted in a yogī's posture. Śiva is the best of the yogīs, and as such he is known under the appellations Yogendra, Yogeśvara, Mahātapāḥ, and Mahāyogī,[3] etc. Besides being a yogin, Śiva is also known as the lord or protector of the animals, "pastor of the flock or herd" *(paśupati)*, a title which has been attributed to Rudra-Śiva in Vedic and subsequent literature very often.[4] All this shows that there is a good deal of pre-Aryan or non-Aryan element in the character of Rudra-Śiva.

Some of the other threads which wove the composite figure of Rudra-Śiva are to be found in Vedic and post-Vedic literature. In the *Rigveda* itself, Rudra has been represented as a complex figure and described by incompatible qualities, as both fierce and benevolent. He wields the lightning and thunderbolt,[5] and is armed with a bow and arrows.[6] His worshippers implore him not to injure them, their men, and cattle with his wrath; his malevolence may be diverted towards others.[7] On the one hand his anger, ill-will, and destructive shafts are deprecated, on the other, he is described as benevolent, easily invoked, beneficient, and gracious and auspicious (Śiva).[8] He is the protector of the creatures and lord of this vast world.[9] He possesses healing remedies and is once described as the greatest of the physicians.[10]

In the *Rigveda* Rudra is closely associated with the Maruts whose father he is and who are known as Rudras or Rudrīyas. This relationship brings him into affinity with Indra and Agni, for the Maruts are described in certain Vedic passages as wor-

[2]Gopinath Rao, *Elements of Hindu Iconography,* Vol. II, Part II, p. 382 ff; *Archaeological Sutvey Reports, 1926-27*, p. 282.

[3]Monier Williams, *Religious Thought and Life in Ancient India,* p. 83.

[4]This is a favourite idea with many religious systems, which have been embellished with various spiritual interpretations; as a parallel, one is at once reminded of Gopāla Krishṇa or Vrajeśvara Krishṇa, of Jesus the pastor, or Pan the shepherd, or Orpheus the charmer of animals. The Vedic Pūshan too is a pāśupati (Macdonell and Keith, *Vedic Index,* p. 35).

[5]*Rigveda,* II. 3, 3.

[6]*Ibid.,* II. 10, 14; 42, 11.

[7]*Ibid.,* II. 33, 11.

[8]*Ibid.,* I. 114, 9; II. 33, 5; II. 33, 7; X. 92, 9.

[9]*Rigveda,* I. 129, 3; I. 114, 9; II. 33, 9.

[10]*Rigveda,* I. 43, 4; I. 114, 5; II. 33, 2, 4, 7, 12, 13; V. 42, 11; VI, 74, 3; VII, 35, 6; 46, 3; VIII. 29, 5.

shippers of Agni and in others as followers of Indra whose associates they are. "They are furious like wild beasts, but playful like children or calves." They are the real storm gods as the sons and associates of Rudra and Indra, both representing the powerful aspects of storm, rain, thunder and lighting, etc. The affinities between Indra and Rudra can be traced not only through the Maruts, but also through elephant symbolism, fertility characteristics and sex symbolism. Besides his having affinities with Indra, Rudra is also regarded as a form of Agni. The term Rudra has been applied unequivocally to Agni in a hymn which has been exclusively dedicated to that divinity.[11] All this would show that in the *Rigveda* itself Rudra was conceived under various forms and described as such.

Affinities between Agni and Rudra are remarkable. There took place a complete blending of the two in the *Śatarudrīya* as Professor Weber points out.[12] The epithets of Rudra-Siva in the *Śatarudrīya* hymn fall into two distinct categories. The epithets Giriśa, Giriśaya, Giriśanta, Giritra (meaning dweller in the mountain) and Kapardin,[13] Vyuptakeśa, Ugra, Bhīma, Bhishaj and Śiva, Sambhū, Śiva and Saṁkara take us to the storms and Nīlagrīva, Sitikaṇṭha, Hiraṇyagarbha, Vilohita, Bhava, Sarva and Paśupati to fire or Agni. Again, the *Śatapatha Brāhmaṇa* treats Rudra in various forms as the names of Agni : "Agni is a god. These are his names—Sarva as the eastern people call him, Bhava as the Bāhikas, Paśūnāṁpati, Rudra and Agni."[14] A late part of the *Vājasaneyī Saṁhitā* enumerates as forms of one god Agni, Aśani, Paśupati, Bhava, Sarva, Mahādeva, Ugradeva,[15] and several others. In the epic-Puranic tradition, Skanda or Kārttikeya is regarded sometimes as the son of Rudra-Śiva, and sometimes as that of Agni;

[11]See Professor Wilson's Introduction to the first and second volumes of his English translation of the *Rigveda*; Barth, *The Religions of India*, pp. 12 ff; *Rigveda*, VIII. 65, 2; VIII. 7, 24, ii, 1. 6.

[12]*Indische Studien*, II, 19-22.

[13]Kapardin is an epithet of Rudra in the *Rigveda* also. (*Rigveda*, I, 114,1). It is also a title of Pūshan, *Rigveda*, VI. 55, 2.

[14]*Agnir vai sa devastasyaitāni nāmāni Sarva iti yathā prāchyā āchakshate, Bhava iti yathā Bāhīkāḥ paśūnāṁpati Rudrogniriti (Śatapatha Brāhmaṇa,* I. 7. 3. 8*)*.

[15]*Vājasaneyī-Saṁhitā*, XXXIX, 8.

this is due to the close affinities existing between these two gods since early Vedic times.

Further, in *Vājasaneyī-Saṁhitā*, Rudra is attributed the names Tryambaka and Śiva,[16] two very important epithets of Rudra-Śiva in post-Vedic times. Further, he is called here Krittivāsa.[17] Ambikā, who is called Śiva's wife in post-Vedic literature, is mentioned here for the first time as Rudra's sister.[18]

The *Śatarudrīya* hymn of the *Vājasaneyī-Saṁhitā* (xvi, 1 ff) throws abundant light on the character of Rudra-Śiva. Rudra appears here with all the characteristics of a deity of a purely popular origin in vital relation to all aspects of an advanced, settled, as well as a rough and troubled life. He is invoked as a patron of craftsman, cartwrights, carpenters, smiths, potters, hunters, waterman and foresters. He is the leader of armies, lord of the regions and the beasts. He is the god of the brave, of footsoldiers, of those who fight in chariots and who earn their living by the bow and sword. He is called as one lying on the mountains. He is blue necked, and of a red countenance. His cry "echoes in the thick of the battle and his voice resounds in the war drum".[19] He is the patron of thieves[20] and free-booters. He is also the lord of the Vrātyas.[21] But he dwells in the forests, and is the lord of the open field and protector of cattle which roam there. He is invoked under the names of

16 iii, 58, 63; the word Tryambaka seems to have been an epithet of Rudra in the *Rigveda*, vii, 59, 12 *(Tryambakaṁ yajāmahe sugandhiṁ pushṭivardhanam,* etc.). "Śiva" is applied to Rudra in the *Rigveda* euphemistically as noted above.

17 *Vājasaneyī-Saṁhitā,* iii, 61.

18 Macdonell, *Vedic Mythology,* p. 74.

19 The drum seems to apear in the hands of Śiva on the coins of the Kushāṇa kings (Whitehead, *Catalogue of Coins of the Punjab Museum*, Vol. 1, pp. 187, 192, 203, etc.).

20 In the *Mrichchhakaṭikam,* some burglars invoke Skanda, son of Śiva, as their patron deity. These characteristics of the god have been transferred to his consort Kālī (she is looked upon as the patron and guardian of thieves and robbers).

21 Bk. xx of the *Atharvaveda* is devoted to the glorification of the Vrātya. Vrātya, here, is the name of a band of wandering religious mendicants and their chief god is Ekavrātya. The various manifestations of this god are Mahādeva, Īśāna, Bhava, Sarva, Rudra, and so forth. It seems that the Vrātyas were among the earliest devotees of Śiva.

Bhava and Sarva. When his wrath is appeased, he becomes Śiva, Śaṁkara and Śaṁbhū.

The *Śatarudrīya* credits Rudra with activity in almost every aspect of nature[22] (in the mountains, the woods and other places), and associates him with hunters, foresters, thieves, brigands, etc. who are beyond the pale of higher society. This association speaks of large non-Aryan, aboriginal, unorthodox, ungenteel elements in Rudra-Śiva. As Rudra has been portrayed here, there appears an amalgamation with him of a forest or a mountain deity or some kindred god such as the vegetation spirit.

Rudra-Śiva is thus a remarkable conception. It is a reconciliation of irreconciliables. He is malevolent as well as benevolent at one and the same time. He has the power to destroy, and preserve or protect. The *Śatarūdrīya* associates him with all classes of people conceivable on earth. One can easily understand the popularity of spiritual worship and theistic devotion round Vishṇu-cum-Krishṇa as the divinity here is one of light and love, who appears as a friend and saviour. But it is amazing in no small degree how the Indian mind could transform the strange character of Rudra-Śiva into an object of love and devotion and how out of the dry core of Śaivism could spring the gracious and majestic figure of Śiva who swayed the emotions of the people through the length and breadth of the land.

Now we may come to the *Atharavaveda* and other Vedic sources regarding our study of Rudra-Śiva. In the *Atharavaveda* also (as in the *Rigveda*) a reference is made to the therapeutic character of Rudra, and to the destructive arrows and lightning of Bhava and Sarva.[23] Rudra is identified with Agni[24] and also with Savitri.[25] But it is interesting to note that Bhava and Sarva have been treated as deities distinct from Rudra.[26]

[22]Quite in keeping with this (i. e. Rudra's association with every aspect of nature) offerings are given in the rituals to Rudra in manifold places and on varied occasions (Keith, *Religion and Philosophy of the Veda,* Harvard Oriental Series, Lanman, Vol. 31, p. 145).

[23]*Atharvaveda,* ii. 27, 6; vi. 93, 1; x. 1, 23; xi. 2, 1, 12.

[24]*Ibid.*, vii. 87, 1.

[25]*Ibid.,* xiii. 4, 4.

[26]Bhava and Sarva, and again Bhava and Rudra have been spoken of in the dual in the *Atharvaveda,* x. 1, 23; xi. 2, 1; xi. 2, 14, 16; xi. 6, 9 xii. 4, 17.

Sarva is represented as an archer, and Bhava as king.[27] They and Rudra are said to have poison and consumption at there command.[28] The gods made Bhava the archer, the protector of the Vrātyas in the intermediate space of the eastern region, Sarva of the southern region, Paśupati of the western region, Ugra of the northern region, Rudra of the lower region, and Īśāna of the intermediate region.[29]

The *Śatapatha* and the *Kaushiṭakī Brāhmaṇas* add one more name, Aśani, to the above seven.[30] In the *Athārvaveda* the seven names figure almost as seven distinct deities, but in the *Brāhmaṇas*, these seven and Aśani are the names of one and the same god, Rudra. Sarva, Ugra and Aśani represent the destructive side, whereas Bhava, Paśupati, Mahādeva and Īśāna are the benign aspects of Rudra. The darker side of Rudra was however, never forgotten. The *Grihyasūtras* mention a sacrifice called *Śūlagava* in which a bull is sacrificed to appease Rudra.[31]

In the *Brāhmaṇas*, Rudra appears as one of the foremost members of the Vedic pantheon. Even the gods are afraid lest they should be killed by him. In the *Aitareya Brāhmaṇa* we hear of the incest of Prajāpati and the determination of the gods to punish him, "which led to the decision to create from their most dreaded forms the figure of Bhūtapati, who pierced Prajāpati and for his act received the name of Paśupati."[32] This shows that the period of the Brāhmaṇas was one when the old polytheism was in a state of decline and Śaivism was gaining ground. "It is impossible not to feel in the *Brāhmaṇas* that the figure of Rudra has a very different reality from that possessed by the more normal members of the pantheon and that he as the lord of creatures was successfully contending with Prajāpati as creator."

Rudra's glory was further enhanced in the *Śvetāśvatara* and

[27] *Ibid.*, iv. 93, 2.

[28] *Ibid.*, vi. 93; xi, 2, 26.

[29] *Ibid.*, xv. 5, 1-7.

[30] *Śatapatha Brāhmaṇa*, vi. 1. 3. 7; *Kaushiṭakī Brāhmaṇa*, vi. 1. 9; *Sānkhāyana Brāhmaṇa*, vi, 1, 9; see also *Veda-Brāhmaṇa* by Keith, pp. 378-79.

[31] *Āśvalāyana Grihyasūtra*, iv. 9.

[32] *Aitareya Brāhmaṇa*, iii. 34.

Atharvaśiras Upanishads. The former, which is a theistic treatise,[33] equates Rudra-Śiva with the supreme Brahman[34] and declares, after criticising the various theories of creation, that "Rudra is one who rules the world by his powers, who stands before everything at the time of destruction, and creates the universe at the time of its origin, can be regarded as the creator of all things that exist. He is the supreme godhead, the lord of all souls. of him there is neither the generator nor protector. He is the 'self-subsisting mover of the unmoving manifold'."[35] The *Atharvaśiras Upanishad* also speaks of Rudra's superiority in more or less similar terms. It states: "The gods went to heaven. They asked Rudra, 'Who are thou ?' He said, 'I was before all things, and I shall be. No other transcends me'."[36]

The cult of Rudra-Śiva or Śaivism as it is known in historical times, is found in an expanded form (or the form in which we know it even now) in the epics, the *Rāmāyaṇa* and the *Mahābhārata*, specially the latter which is the chief source with regard to the study of Neo-Brahmanic religions. Neo-Brahmanism, as we have discussed earlier, is a synthesis of Vedic and popular ideas, its mains features being the monotheistic worship of personal gods, within various sectaries. Though Vedic and popular were admitted, the chief divinities of the epics are Vishṇu and Śiva.

In the *Rāmāyaṇa*, Śiva appears as a popular god not only of nothern India, but also of the south. Here also (as in older texts) he has been offered various epithets, old and new. He is called Mahādeva, a great god with three eyes,[37] Śambhu,[38] Tryambaka,[39] and Bhūtnātha.[40] He took the world destroying

[33]*Śvetāśvatara Upanishad* has been characterized by Deussen as a "monument of theism"; *The Religion and Philosophy of India (Upanishads)*, p. 288 f.

[34]While speaking of the highest self or the Highest Brahman, the *Śvetāśvatara* applies such names to him as Hara (1. 10), Rudra (iii. 2), Śiva (iii. 14), and Maheśvara (iv. 10).

[35]Ranade, *A Constructive Survey of Upanishadic Philosophy*, p. 100.

[36]*Atharvaśiras Upanishad*—see the beginning.

[37]*Rāmāyaṇa*, VI, 120. 3.

[38]*Ibid.*, IV, 43, 59.

[39]*Ibid.*, II, 43, 6.

[40]*Ibid.*, VI, 59, 9.

poison, and destroyed Daksha's sacrifice.[41] It should be noted that the *Rāmāyaṇa*, which as a whole is a Vishṇuite poem, gives Vishṇu a position superior to that of Śiva. To illustrate Vishṇu's superiority it narrates a fight between these two gods in which Vishṇu came out victorious and was regarded by the gods as superior to Mahādeva.[42]

The *Rāmāyaṇa*, however, throws invaluable light on the extent of Śiva worship. It shows that Śiva was a favourite diety with the southern people includingt hose of Ceylon. Indrajit, we know, was favoured by Mahādeva, with a boon to kill the *Vanaras*. In a passage of Sundarakāṇda (Bk. V, Gorresio's edition as noted by Muir) Vibhīshaṇa is represented as being received with favour by Mahādeva, after he has deserted his brother.[43]

Now we may come to the great epic, *Māhābharata*. It was a work of a long period, having undergone several stages of development. In the early portions of this epic, Śiva does not occupy any superior position. He seeks advice from Brahmā; the latter calls him *Putraka* or son, sets him a task and tells him not to kill.[44] He drank poison at the instance of Brahmā and came to be known as Nīlakaṇtha.[45] Mahādeva is regarded as a title of Vishṇu.[46] The importance and popularity of the Śiva cult were spreading with the growth of the epic. In its later portions, there are innumerable references to Śiva's exploits and achievements, and he is ranked equal to Vishṇu-cum-Krishṇa and sometimes superior to them. It is not necessary here to refer to all such passages. We shall rest content with some relevant facts only.

In the *Droṇaparva*, Krishṇa and Arjuna are represented as going to Mahādeva with a view to securing the Pāśupata weapon to slay Jayadratha. They recited a hymn in honour of him in the course of which he (i. e. Śiva) was designated as the soul of all things *(Viśvātmane Viśvasrijie Viśvamāvritya tishṭhate)*. He became pleased and conferred upon Arjuna his bow and arrow

41 *Ibid.*, i, 66, 9.
42 *Ibid.*, 1, 175.
43 Muir, *Original Sanskrit Texts*, Vol. iv, p. 355.
44 *Mahābhārata*, i, 211, 4; vii, 52, 45; 54, 13.
45 *Ibid.*, i, 18, 42.
46 *Ibid.*, iii, 14, 147, etc.

(the Pāśupata weapon)[47] with the power of fulfilling his engagement to kill Jayadratha. In various passages in the *Anuśāsanaparva*, Mahādeva is extolled as an "all god" with the attributes of the supreme Brahman. Asked by Yudhisṭhira to declare the names of the deity, Bhīshma expressed his inability as Mahādeva is all-pervading but nowhere to be seen.[48] He is the creator and the lord of Brahmā, Vishṇu, and Indra, whom the gods from Brahmā to piśāchas worship. He transcends material nature and is meditated upon by the rishis versed in contemplation. He is indestructible and supreme Brahman. He is both existent and non-existent.[49] In the same *Parva,* Krishṇa is represented as going to the Himalayas to propitiate Śiva to have a soṇ for Jāmbavatī. Upamanyu, devotee of Śiva, acquainted Krishṇa with Śiva's exploits and said that Mahādeva was the only god whose phallus (a symbol) was worshipped by all, including the gods.[50] Again, in the same *Parva,* we find that Krishṇa recited the *Śatarudrīya* to Yudhisṭhira and said that Sankara had created all things stationary and moving, and that there was nothing superior to Mahādeva.

The above discussion shows that Śiva-worship was widespread throughout the length and breadth of India from remote antiquity. It may be noted that in his character of both Rudra and Śiva, this god has enjoyed a cultus which probably goes further back than that of Vishṇu. From the Mohenjodaro civilization and after, the history of Rudra-Śiva has continued without any break or interruption. Of the two deities Vishṇu and Rudra-Śiva, the latter was the first to receive a special personal adoration and a cultus, though in subsequent times the worship of the former became far more generally extended. It is true that the worship of Vishṇu is mentioned in the *Rigveda,* but mostly as a special aspect of that of the sun. On the other hand Rudra appears quite early in the *Rigveda* with a well-recognized and well-marked personality of his own.

[47] Arjuna received a Pāśupata weapon once earlier in the *Vaṇaparva* to kill the formidable enemies.

[48] P. C. Roy's English Translation of the *Anuśāsana Parva,* Section xiv, p. 49 ff., *Mahābhārata,* xiii, 14, 3. ff.

[49] *Ibid.*

[50] P. C. Roy, *op. cit.*, p. 73, ff.

The wide popularity of Śiva worship in historical times is testified to by varied literary and archaeological sources. Megasthenes, who lived in India towards the close of the fourth century B.C., tells us quite a lot about the Indian representatives of Heracles (identified with Krishṇa-Vāsudeva) and Dionysus (identified with Śiva). Regarding the worship of the latter (i.e. Diynosus or Śiva), he says that it was specially popular in the hill regions where grew the vines.[51] Kautilya, a contemporary of Chandragupta Maurya and Megasthenes, refers in his *Arthaśāstra*[52] to the apartments of various gods, including Śiva, which should be made in the centre of the town. An image of Siva is mentioned also in *Āpastamba Grihyasūtra.*[53] It is interesting to note that Śaivic emblems like the bull and Nandipada occur very frequently on punch-marked coins,[54] the earliest coinage of India (much of it going to as early as sixth-fifth century B. C.). All this would show that the Śiva cult was widely prevalent in the fifth and fourth centuries B.C.[55]

The *Mahābhāshya* of Patañjali (second century B.C.) provides important data regarding Śiva worship during the post-Mauryan period. Commenting on the Pāṇini *sūtra*, v.3.99 (*Jīvikārthe chāpanye*) Patañjali says:

apaṇya ityuchyate tatredam na sidhyati| Śivaḥ Skandah, Visākhaiti|| Kiṁkāraṇam Mauryairhiraṇyārthibhirerchāḥ prakalpitāḥ|| Bhavettāsu na syāt|| Yāstvetāḥ samprati pūjārthāstāsu bhavishyati.[56]

This passage is highly important inasmuch as it shows that the images of Śiva, Skanda and Viśākha were made in his time for the purpose of worship. Further, we are told here that the

[51]McCrindle, *Ancient India as Described by Megasthenes and Arrian*, pp. 34,35. Megasthenes compares the hunting expedition of the king (Chandragupta) with the procession of Dionysus *(ibid.*, p. 71*)*.

[52]*Arthaśāstra,* ed. by R. Shama Śastri, p. 55 ff.

[53] *Apastamba Grihyasūtra* Vii, 20,3.

[54]Smith, *Catalogue of the Indian Museum Coins,* Vol. 1, pp.140-41.

[55]Jayaswal described in the *Journal of the Indian Society of Oriental Art*, Vol. II, p.1, a Hara-Parvātī gold plaque and ascribed it to the Maurya period. But opinions differ as to the date of this plaque.

[56]Kielhorn, *Vyākraṇa Mahābhāshya,* Vol. II, p. 429,

Mauryas sold the images with a view to earning money (cf the sale of Indra icons in Vedic days). Patañjali refers to a Śiva-bhāgavata[57] (devotees of Śiva, *bhāgavatoayamiti bnāgavataḥ, Śivasya bhāgavataḥ iti Śivabhāgavataḥ*) in his commentary on the Paṇinian *sūtra*, V. 2.76. He mentions in the *Mahābhāshya* different names of Rudra-Śiva, viz. Rudra, Śiva, Giriśa, Mahādeva, Tryambaka, Bhava and Sarva,[58] etc., and used the word "Śaiva"[59] the name under which the sectarian Śiva worshippers are generally known. All this shows that Śaivism was a popular cult in Patañjali's time.

Besides Patañjali's *Mahābhāshya* we have at our disposal plenty of archaeological materials regarding the wide diffusion of Śiva worship in India in this period. The frequent occurrence in the epigraphs of post-Mauryan India (*c*.200 B.C.—300 A.D.) of personal names such as Mahādeva, Rudra, Rudraghosha Rudradāsa, Śivadeva, Śivaghosha, Śivanandi, Śivasena, Śivaskanda Gupta, Śivaskandavarmā, Śivayaśā[60] and similar others, prove beyond doubt that Śiva was worshipped as a popular deity throughout the length and breadth of India during the period under review. This is amply corroborated by a large number of coins, sculptures and seals of the period, containing Śiva's symbols and images. Before we refer to the anthropomorphic representations of Śiva, we may notice some of the well-known symbols associated with his cult.

The bull is traditionally associated with Śiva as his Vāhana. "Vrisha-Vāhana" is one of his very common epithets in epic-Puranic literature. In the *Mahābhārata*, Śiva is described as the snake-wearer, and the club-bearer with many forms, who bears a trident in his hands and who has a bull[61] as his ensign. The bull is a very common device on the coins of the indigenous and foreign rulers of our period. One very interesting instance of this device is the humped bull appearing on a unique gold coin of an uncertain Indo-Scythian king with the legends Taures and

[57]*Ibid.*, pp. 387-88.

[58]*Ibid.*, p. 91. The names Bhava, Sarva, Rudra and Mriḍa are found also in the aphorism of Pāṇini, iv, 1.49.

[59]Kielhorn, *op.cit.*, p.282.

[60]*Epigraphia Indica*, Vol. X, Appendix, and Index of personal names occuring in Brāhmī inscriptions (Lüders' list).

[61]*Mohābhārata*, III, 167, 47 f; 173, 42 f.

Ushabhe (vrishabha) in the Greek and Kharoshṭhī scripts.[62] The different varieties of this device are found in the coins of Diomedes, Apollodotos, Philoxenos, Maues, Azes, Azilises and several others. This device occurs also on the indigenous coins of Mūladeva, Viśākhadeva, Śivadatta, Vijayamitra of Ayodhya, Brihaspatimitra II, Aśvaghosha, Agnimitra, Jeṭṭhamita of Kausambi, and also on those of Mālava, Arjunāyana, Andhra and some other kings of our period.[63]

Apart from the bull, the coins bear two other very common Śaivic emblems, the trident and the Nandipada. A trident between two pillars is used on the reverse of the coins of the pañchāla king Rudragupta.[64] The close association of the name Rudragupta with the Śaivic emblem trident would tend to show that he had strong leanings towards Śaivism. On his other coins the object appears to be a star or a kind of double trident with prongs below as well as above.[65] According to Cunningham, there is a trident on the base of a Buddhist railing on the reverse of a coin of the Pañchāla king Dhruvamitra. In this connection, he observes that Dhruva is the name of the north pole star but it is the name of Śiva also, and this trident, he opines, belongs to Śiva.[66] While writing on this device Allan remarks that the object on Dhruvamitra's coin is not a trident as Cunningham thinks but a battle axe and on no. 55, pl, *xxviii*, *A Catalogue of Indian Coins, Ancient India,* the bend of the shaft is well marked.[67] J. N. Banerjea holds that even if the symbol is a battle-axe, it can very well be taken to be a Śaivic symbol.[68] It may be noted that the trident with axe appears on the reverse of the coins of the Audumbara King Dharaghosha.[69] That the com-

[62]Gardner, *British Museum Cata ogue of Coins of the Scythic Kings of Bactria and India,* pl. xxix, 15.

[63]Smith, *op. cit.*, pp. 17, 18, 30. 39, 45, 48, 50, 148; Rapson, *Catalogue of Coins, Andhras, Western Kshatrapas, Traikuṭakas and Bodhi Dynasty,* pp, 55, 56, 57, 58, 85, 187, etc.; and Allan, *Catalogue of Indian Coins, Ancient India,* pp. 130-38, 120 ff, 154, 155 ff.

[64]Allan, *op. cit.*, pl. xxvii. 2.

[65]*Ibid.*, p. cxix.

[66]Cunningham, *Coins of Ancient India,* p. 81, p. VI, fig. 3.

[67]Allan, *op. cit.*, pl. cxviii.

[68]J.N. Banerjea, *The Development of Hindu Iconography,* Vol. I, p. 129.

[69]Allan, *op. cit.*, p. 124.

bined trident and battle-axe symbol has a Śaivic association is evident from its apearance on the obverse of the Kushan king Vima Kadphises coins, where the king, a Māheśvara by faith, puts offerings in honour of his diety on the sacrificial fire.[70] The very same symbol (combined trident and battle-axe) is also seen on the obverse of Jayadaman's coins.[71] On the obverse of some anonymous coins attributed toKunindas there is the figure of Śiva holding a trident with axe and shaft in the right hand.[72] Besides, it may be noted here that the trident with axe is the usual reverse type[73] of the Audumbara kings, viz. Śivadāsa, Rudradāsa, Mahādeva, Dharaghosha and Rudravarmā. The trident behind a bull is found on the obverse of the coins of Dhanadeva, Agnimitra and Jeṭṭhamita of Kausambi (Allan, *op. cit.*, pp. 153, 154). As the bull, the trident, and battle-axe symbols are numerous, only the important specimens have been referred to. Now we may turn to another very important Śaivic emblem, namely Nandipada. This symbol has been represented very widely on the coins of Northern India, and occasionally on South Indian coins too.

Nandipada occurs with tree, serpents and a few of other symbols on the reverse sides of Ayodhyā coins of that one of Mūladeva, Vāyudeva, and Viśākhadeva.[74] It is to be noted that one of the obverse symbols appearing on most of these coins is the bull. These symbols taken together constitute distinct Śaivic associations and this group of Ayodhyā kings had perhaps strong leanings towards Śaivism.

An elaborate Nandipada has been inserted in the face of the reverse symbols of the Almora coins attributed to Śivadatta, Śivapālita and Haridatta,[75] the obverse types including a bull before a tree and sometimes a snake-like object, suggesting Nāga-Śaiva associations. The reverse of Brahmamitra's coins (Kanauj) has a Nandipada on a pillar within a railing on the left.[76] The

[70]J. N. Banerjea, *op. cit.*, p. 129; Whitehead, *op. cit.*, p. xvii, 37.
[71]Rapson, *op. cit.*, p. 76.
[72]Allan, *op. cit.*, p. 167.
[73]*Ibid.*, pp. 122-26.
[74]*Ibid.*, pp. 130-32.
[75]*Ibid.*, pp. ixxi and 120.
[76]*Ibid.*, pp. xciii and 147.

reverse type of Kausambi coins include very often a Nandipada and the obverse of them has the bull.[77] It is to be noted that Nandipada is sometimes placed on the obverse of Kausambi coins with a bull by its side. The Nandipada symbol has been placed in some cases on a hill-like object and it may be noted that a similar symbol with a curved object, most probably a snake, appears also as the reverse type of the Kuninda coins.[78] A Nandipada with a snake below is seen among other symbols, on the reverse of the coins of the Audumbara ruler, Amoghabhūti.[79]

Nandipada occurs also on the reverse of Yaudheya[80] and Malava coins[81] with the bull usually on the obverse. It is a common symbol on the obverse of some coins of Gautamīputra Viḷivāyakura.[82] It figures on the obverse of certain uninscribed coins of the period, while the reverse is occupied by a Nāga symbol.[83]

From the wide distribution of these noted Śaivic emblems we may well conceive the extent of the popularity of Śiva worship during the period under review. To the devotees of Śiva, they are as deserving of veneration as his image or phallus.

One of the important aspects of the Śiva cult enjoying wide prevalence in our period is the worship of the Liṅga or phallus (the symbol of creation). Phallicism is one of the ancient forms of worship in India and the ancient world.[84] The association of phallus worship with the cult of Śiva (who is often regarded as a god of generation[85] in spite of the destructive function assig-

[77]*Ibid.*; pp. 148, 150, 151, 152, 153.

[78]*Ibid.*, pp. 162-3, ff.

[79]Smith, *op. cit*, p. 167.

[80]*Ibid.*, pp. 180-81.

[81]*Ibid.*, pp. 171, 174.

[82]Rapson, *op. cit.*, p. 15.

[83]*Ibid.*, p. 53. The trident, bull or Nandipada cannot be taken as symbols of a particular sect exclusively. They have been used by other sects as also by the Śaivites. But we feel justified in regarding the trident, bull or Nandipada symbols referred to above as Śaivic emblems on account of their particular group combinations, the trident and bull, or a Nandipada and a bull or a Nandipada and a snake.

[84]Sir John Marshall, *op. cit.*, p. 58.

[85]*Ibid.*, p. 58 ff.; and Staniland Wake, *Serpent Worship and Other Essays*, p. 8 ff.

ned to him in the Hindu Trinity) played an important role in the religious life of the Neo-Brahmanic people. It is a matter of common knowledge that though Śiva was worshipped in various forms, his phallic form is most widely worshipped. The phallic rite in India is pre-Aryan in origin though it was foreign to the early Vedic people.

The Mohenjodaro male god depicted in a yogic posture with animals around him (and described as the pre-Aryan prototype of historic Śiva) has been represented with an *Ūrddhvameḍhra.*[86] Moreover, among the minor antiquities discovered in Mohenjodaro and Harappa, there are a large number of aniconic stones, representing phallic symbols.[87] From this it is evident that phallus worship in India is as old as Mohenjodaro. Further evidence for the existence of this form of worship in protohistoric times is provided by the discovery of two sṭones, one a phallus and the other a Yoṇi at the chalcolithic sites of Mughal Ghundai and Periano Ihundai[88] respectively.

The *Rigveda,* which deals with the orthodox and hieratic religion of the Aryans, contain incidental references to phallus worship as a non-Aryan religious belief. In the *Rigveda* (vii, 21 5,) Indra is implored not to allow the Śiśnadevas to approach the sacrifice.[89] The Rigvedic verse (x, 99.3) describes the god as having slain the Śiśnadeva and having conquered by his craft, the riches of the city with a hundred gates. The word Śiśnadeva has been variously interpreted by scholars. In the opinion of some modern European and Indian scholars, the word refers to those who worship the phallus as their deity (*Śiśnaṁ devāḥ yeshām te*). In following Yāska, Sāyaṇa takes the word to refer to those people who sport with śiśna (membrum virile), i. e. the unchaste men (*śiśnena dīvyanti krīḍamata iti śiśnadevāḥ, abra-*

[86]Marshall *(op. cit.,* p. 52*)* was in doubt as to the representation of the phallus and he remarked, "It is possible that what appears to be a phallus is in reality the end of the waistband." But on close examination the phallus can be seen clearly.

[87]*Ibid.,* p. 59 ff, pl. xiv, Nos. 2 and 4; Madhosarup Vats, *Excavations at Harappa,* Vol. 1, pp. 369-71.

[88]Marshall, *op. cit.,* Vol. 1, p. 59, pl. xiii, Nos. 1, 7, 9.

[89]*Na Yātava Iṁdra Jūjuvurno na | Vaṁdanā Śavishṭha vedyābhiḥ | Sa śardhadaryo vishuṇasya Jaṁptor mā | Śiśnadeva api gurṛītam naḥ,* (*Rigveda, vii,* 21. 5.)

hmacharya itayrihaḥ). According to Durgāchārya, the commentator of the *Nirukta*, Śiśnadevāḥ are those who "dally carnally with prostitutes forsaking Vedic sacrifices". The Śiśnadevas are mentioned along with the Yātava in the *Rigveda* (vii, 21. 5). Further, in explaining the word śiśna in the Rigvedic passage x, 27, 19, Sāyaṇa takes it to refer to the Rākahasas (*rākshasādi vrimdāṇi*). It is quite possible that the śiśna of the passage x, 27.19 and the śiśnadevas of the passage x, 99.3 of the *Rigveda* denote the same people. In all probability they were a class of people who were beyond the pale of the Vedic society and the followers of phallic rites. That the Liṅga was not originally a Brahmanical object of worship is evident also from the fact that several places considered sacred as the peculiar residence of Jyoti Liṅgas are generally in the south and north-east of India at a great distance from the original settlements of the Brahmanical faith. In Marhatta country where Śaivities greatly prevail, the Brāhmanas do not officiate in the Liṅga temples. There is a caste separate for that known as Gurava, a distinct order of men being originally of Śūdra stock.

With the growth of Neo-Brahmanism the non-Aryan phallic rite came to be associated with the Aryan belief[90] as an essential element of historic Śaivism. In the *Anuśāsāna Parva* we are told that Krishṇa proceeded to the Himālayas to propitiate Śiva to have a son for Jāmbavatī through his (Śiva's) grace. On his way Krishṇa met Upamanyu, an ardent devotee of Śiva, who aquainted him with the glories and attributes of the god (Śiva). To test his devotion Mahādeva appeared before Upamanyu in the guise of Indra and offered to grant him a boon of his choice. The devoted Upamanyu refused to accept a favour from any god other than Mahādeva and dwelt at length on the various attributes of Śiva and the reasons as to why he was

[90]There is an obscure indication in the *Liṅga Purāṇa* itself that the worship of Liṅga was introduced into the Brahmanical faith at a later period. It is the famous passage in the 17th Adhyāya where the fiery Liṅga is introduced as settling the dispute between Brahmā and Vishṇu for superiority (*Liṅga Purāṇa,* edited by Jivananda Vidyasagar). Brahm āand Vishṇu seem to have occupied the field between them till Śiva came to set aside the claims of both.

regarded as the supreme creator. The following lines from Upamanyu's speech are very significant in this connection :

> Is Īśa (Mahādeva) the cause of causes for any other reasons ? We have not heard that the Liṅga of any other person is worshipped by the gods.... He whose Liṅga Brahmā, Vishṇu, and thou (Indra), with the deities, continually worship is therefore the most eminent. Since children bear neither the mark of the lotus (Brahmā's), nor of the discus (Vishṇu's) nor of the thunderbolt (Indra's), but are marked with the male and the female organs, therefore offspring are derived from Maheśvara. All women produced from the nature of Devī as their cause are marked with *the female organ* and all males are manifestly marked with the Liṅga of Hara.[91]

From this passage it is clear that Liṅga worship was widely prevalent in Aryan society in the epic times.

References to Liṅga worship occur abundantly in Puranic literature as well. In the *Liṅga Purāṇa* an account is given of the fiery Liṅga of Mahādeva which sprang up before Brahmā and Vishṇu while they were fighting for supremacy. Both of them (i. e. Brahmā and Vishṇu) were put to shame, as after travelling for a thousand years in each direction neither could approach its termination. The sacred monosyllable "Om" visible on the Liṅga enlightened Brahmā and Vishṇu and they acknowledged and eulogised the superior might and glory of Śiva.[92] Further, in the same text, the Liṅga is called the Pradhāna (nature) and Parameśvara is called Liṅgin[93] (the sustainer of the

[91] *Mahābhārata*, xiii, 14, 129 ff (Bombay Edition, Leaf No. 20). The *Anuśāsana Parva* contains many more interesting references to the Liṅga worship some of which may be noted here : "When his (Mahādeva's) Liṅga remains constantly in a state of chasity, and people reverence it, this is agreeable to the great god. The constant worshipper of *Liṅga* who shall worship the image *(vigraha)* or the *Liṅga* of the great (god), enjoys great prosperity. It is the *Liṅga* raised up which the rishis, gods, gandharvas and Apsaras worship." Muir, *op. cit.*, p. 144.

[92] *Liṅga Purāṇa* (Edited by Jivananda Vidyasagar), Chapters xvii and xviii.

[93] *Pradhānam Liṅgamākhyātam Liṅgīcha Parameśvarah (Liṅga Purāṅa,* xvii, 5 ,edited by Jivananda Vidyasagar).

Liṅga), the pedestal of the Liṅga is Mahādevi (Umā) and the Liṅga is the visible Maheśvara.[94] The epic-Puranic tradition reveals that phallic worship came to be clothed with a mystic and philosophical meaning and recognized as an inseparable part of the Śaivic cult in the Neo-Brahmanic society.

R. G. Bhandarkar held that Liṅga worship had not come into use at the time of Patañjali and it was unknown even in the time of Vima Kadphises.[95] In support of his theory he remarked:

> Patañjali, in his commentary on the Pāṇinian sūtra V. 3. 99, refers to the image of Śiva and not his Liṅga as an object of adoration. On the coins of Vima Kadphises who was a devout worshipper of Śiva, there is the anthropomorphic representation of Śiva either with the trident or the bull, but the phallus is conspicuous by its absence.[96]

D. R. Bhandharkar also held more or less similar views. Further, in his lectures on "Ancient Indian Numismatics," he assigned the Gudimallam Liṅga to the early fourth century A.D. and observed that it was in the beginning of the Gupta period that Liṅga worship was being foisted on the Śiva-cult.[97]

The above theories cannot be accepted in the light of what has recently come to our knowledge. Even if the historical value of the *Anuśāsana Parva* as an evidence of the existence of the Liṅga worship in the period prior to the Christian era is questioned, there is an abundance of archaeological material to prove that Liṅga worship associated with the Śiva cult was widely prevalent in orthodox society from the second or probably the third century B. C.

Regarding the date of the Gudimallam Liṅga which bears a handsome Śiva figure, scholars hold different opinions. But the close similarity between the Śiva figure and the Sāñchi Yaksha

[94]*Liṅga vedī Mahādevī Lingaṁ Śākshād Maheśvaraḥ. (Ibid.*, chapter xviii).

[95]Sir R. G. Bhandarkar, *Vaishnavism, Saivism and Minor Religious Systems,* p. 115.

[96]*Ibid.*

[97]D. R. Bhandarkar, *Lectures on Ancient Indian Numismatics,* pp. 19-20. Dr. Bhandarkar's theory regarding the date of the Gudimallam Liṅga is open to controversy.

is obvious.[98] Hence the Gudimallam Śiva can be dated to the second or first century B. C.

The Gudimallam Liṅga is one of the best sculptural specimens of the class. It shows not only that Liṅga worship was associated with the Neo-Brahmanic Śiva cult as early as the second-first century B. C.,[99] but also that Śaivism was a well-recognized cult in south India before the Christian era.[100] It may be mentioned in passing that the Sātavāhanas were among the earliest benefactors of Śiva worship in south India. The Talagunda inscription[101] of the time of Kadamba Śāntivarman, refers to an ancient Śiva temple as being worshipped by Śātakarṇi who was probably Śrīśātakarni (first century B. C.) of the Śātvāhana dynasty. That Śaivism was a popular cult in south India during the Śātavāhana times is proved also by the occurence of such names as Bhūtapala, Mahā-devanaka, Śivadatta, Śivapālita and Bhavagopa[102] in the south Indian inscriptions belonging to Śatavāhṇa rulers and there contemporaries.

Reverting to the subject of Liṅga worship, we may refer now to another very important representation of the Liṅga belonging to the post-Mauryan period. This Liṅga was found at Bhita (Uttar Pradesh). R. D. Banerjee describes it as follows:

> The top of the Liṅga is shaped as the bust of a male holding a vase in the left hand while the right hand is raised in the Abhayamudrā posture. Below the bust where the waist of the figure should have been, are four human heads, one at each corner...and the phallus is marked by deeply drawn lines.[103]

[98]Gudimallam is a village 6 miles to the north east of Renigunta Railway junction. See A. K. Coomaraswamy, *History of Indian and Indonesian Art* (1927), p. 27

[99]Grüwedel's *Buddhist Art in India*, Translated by Gibson and Burgess, p. 5.

[100]Gopinath Rao, *Elements of Hindu Iconography*, Vol. ii, part i, p 65 ff; Coomaraswamy, op. cit., p. 39.

[101]The Tālagunda Inscription of the time of Śāntivarma, (*c.* 455-70); Būhler, *Indian Antiquary*, xxv, p. 27 ff; *Epigraphia Indica*, Vol. VIII, p. 31 ff; *Epigraphia Carnatica*, viii, p. 200 ff; D. C. Sircar, *Select Inscriptions*, p. 450 ff.

[102]D. R. Bhandarkar, *Indian Antiquary*, June 1919, p. 78.

[103]*Archaeological Survey of India, Annual Reports*, 1909-1910, pp.147-48.

R. D. Banerjee took the four faces on the corners as four female busts (evidently on the consideration of the mode of their hair dressing and large rings worn in the lobes of the ears); but on close examination they appear beyond doubt to be the representations of four male figures. Hence this sculpture can perhaps be regarded as one of the Mukaliṅga having five faces "corresponding to the Īśāna, Tatpurusha, Aghora, Vāmadeva, and Sadyojāta aspects of Śiva."[104]

The above sculpture contains an inscription which has been read and translated by R. D. Banerjee thus:

> *Kajahuṭiputānaṁl [iṁ] go paṭithāpita Vāsethiputena Nāgasiriṇā piyatā [ṁ] d [e] vatā.* 'The Liṅga of the son of Kajahuṭi, was dedicated by Nāga Siri, the son of Vāseṭhi. May the deity be pleased.'[105]

This inscription, as Banerjee holds, can be assigned to the first century B. C. on palaeographical grounds.[106]

Dr. Fürher, who discovered this sculpture, took it to be a column or capital.[107] D. R. Bhandarkar has questioned the correctness of R. D. Banerjee's reading and interpretation of the inscription.[108] In following Bloch, he says that the word read as "Liṅga" by Banerjee is in fact "Lago" whatever it may mean, and he states further that the sculpture itself cannot be taken evidently to be one of the Liṅga. Regarding the script of the inscriptions he holds that they cannot be earlier than the time of Vāsudeva, the Kushāṇa king.

The above mentioned theories of D. R. Bhandarkar do not seem to be plausible. The sculpture, we have seen before, is perhaps a Liṅga as Banerjee held. The scripts of the inscription tally very closely with those of northern India about the first century B. C. In view of this, we feel justified in taking the Bhita Liṅga as a valuable piece of evidence with regard to

[104]Gopinath Rao, *Elements of Hindu Iconography*, Vol. ii, Part i, p. 64.

[105]*Archaeological Survey of India, Annual Reports*, 1909-1910, p. 148.

[106]*Ibid.*, p. 147.

[107]*Ibid.*

[108]D. R. Bhandarkar, *Charmichael Lectures on Ancient Indian Numismatics*, 1919, pp. 20, 21.

Liṅga worship in the first century B. C. Several Śiva Liṅgas with the figures of Śiva, belonging to the Kushāṇa period have been found at Mathura.[109]

Besides their sculptural representations the Liṅgas occur as coin devices in the centuries before the Christian era. Allan describes an uninscribed cast coin (third and second century B. C.)[110] as follows:

> Building (?) on the left, tree in centre, on right, female figure to left; Rev. tree in railing on left, Liṅga on square pedestal on right.[111]

The symbols taken together would indicate Śaivic associations. The building may stand for a Śiva sanctuary, the female figure a devotee, a tree in railing a sthaḷa-vriksha, and Liṅga the cult object.

J. N. Banerjea is of the opinion that the representation of Liṅga may be seen on two sugare copper coins (third-second century B. C.) which may perhaps be attributed to Taxila.[112] The coins to which he refers are coin Nos. 154 and 154a, noted on p. 233 of the *Catalogue of Coins, Ancient India* by Allan. The pedestal on which the Liṅga stands has been summarily represented. Allan recognizes a Liṅga on a pedestal between two different trees in railing on Ujjayini coins[113] (third-second century B. C.). It may be noted here that there is probably a Liṅga on a square pedestal in the centre of a punch-marked coin also.[114]

About the existence of Liṅga worship and its intimate association with the Śiva cult we have an incidental reference in Vākāṭake copper plates which deal with the rise of the Bhāraśivas. The copper plates say that the Rājavaṁśa of Bhāraśivas owes

[109]V. S. Agrawala, *Handbook to the Sculptures of the Curzon Museum of Archacology*, p. 42; *Journal of the Indian Society of Oriental Art*, Vol. iv, 1937, pl. xxii, fig. 1.

[110]Allan, *op. cit.*, p. LXXVII.

[111]*Ibid.*, p. 85, pl. XI, coin No. 2.

[112] J. N. Banerjee, *op. cit.*, p. 126.

[113]Allan, *op. cit.*, p. 243, No. 19, pl. xxxvi, No. 15.

[114]*Ibid.*, pl. V., No. 21.

its origin to the satisfaction of Śiva inasmuch as they carried on their shoulders "the load of his symbol"[115] (i. e. Liṅga). The rise of the Bhāraśivas has been placed by scholars somewhere in the beginning of the third century A. D.[116]

In view of the above discussion we may hold that (*i*) phallus worship is pre-Aryan in origin; (*ii*) it has had inseparable connections with the Śiva cult from the time of Mohenjodaro; (*iii*) it was not prevalent among the early Vedic people but in the post-Vedic period it formed an important religious element in Aryan society, being connected with the Neo-Brahmanic Śiva cult as early as the third-second century B.C.; and (*iv*) it is not possible to subscribe to D. R. Bhandarkar's theory that it was foisted upon the Śiva cult in the beginning of the Gupta period and not earlier.

The most conspicuous aspect of Śiva worship during the period under review was the of Śiva worship in human form. But his anthropomorphic representations on coins, seals and sculptures are numerous. While discussing the growth of Śaivism and phallic worship we referred to some of them. The others may be studied now.

The human from of Śiva as a coin device seems to appear for the first time on a number of Ujjayini coins (third-second century B.C.). On some of them he is shown as a single standing figure with a vase in the right hand, and a staff in the left and a bull looking up at him.[117] On others he is represented as a three-headed figure with more or less similar attributes.[118] Cunningham described this latter figure as Śiva-Mahākāla.[119]

[115]Fleet, *Corpus Inscriptionum Indicarum,* Vol. iii, pp. 236, 245. It may be noted here that the Liṇgayats of South India actually wear the Linga in a silver or metallic casket suspended round their necks with a cord like necklace.

[116]Of about the same period or the early Gupta period we have an interesting specimen of Ekamukha Śiva Liṅga from Khoh *(Archaeological Survey of India, Annual Reports)*, 1904-5; pl. xxvi, figs. a-d). The lower part is roughly chiselled; above it there is a plain cylinder which contains on one side the bust of Śiva.

[117]Allan, *op. cit.*, p. 249. Water-vessel and staff are among the attributes of Siva also on Kushāṇa coins, Smith, *op. cit.*, pp. 7, 75, 78, etc.

[118]*Ibid*, p. 245.

[119]*Ibid*, p. 97 ff, pl. X, figs. I-6.

On the obverse of a silver coin of the Audumbara prince Dharaghosha, there appears a figure with the Kharoshṭhī legend which reads as Viśvāmitra. The legend of Kharoshṭhī states, "*Mahādevasa raña Dharaghoshasa Odubarisa.*" On the reverse are a trident with axe (or a combined battle axe) on the right and a tree within an enclosure on the left. Opinions differ regarding the identification of the figure in question. Cunningham interprets it as Śiva, while Allan describes it as that of Visvāmitra. The latter suggestion is more plausible in view of the fact that the legend Viśvāmitra is engraved around the body of the figure. The Śaivic leanings of some of the Audumbara cheifs can, however, be guessed from the presence of symbols like the trident and battle axe.

Further, some of the Kuninda coins (second century A.D.) have on their obverse, a standing figure of Śiva,[120] with his right hand holding a battle-axe and the left hand placed on the hip. The legend in Brāhmī characters of the second century A.D. is "*Bhagavata Chatreśvara Mahātmanaḥ*", or "the worshipful one, the noble-souled lord of Chhatra." From the device and the legend it appears that Śiva was the tutelary deity of the Kunindas.

Śaivism seems to have been patronised and also adopted by several foreign rulers and chiefs during our period. On the billon coins of Gondophares there is a standing figure of Śiva[121] with his left leg slightly forward, head a little towards the left, a long trident in his right hand and a palm branch in the left resting on his hip. Faint traces of jaṭā may be discovered on his head. The legend on the coins described Gondophares as *Mahārāja rājarāja tratara devavratas Guduphara.*[122] The title "*Devavrata*" is interesting. It is possible that the word "*Deva*" here has been applied in its special sense meaning the god Śiva, and not in its general or usual sense meaning simply God.[123]

[120]Cf. Allan, *op. cit.*, p. 167.

[121]Whitehead, *op. cit.*, 151, pl. xv.

[122]*Ibid.*, p. 151, pl. xv, coin No 42.

[123]One of the important causes of semantic changes in languages is the specialization of the general term and generalisation of the special term. Cf. the early and later meanings of the word "deer" in English and "Mriga" in Sanskrit.

It is well known that one of the important appellations of Śiva is Mahādeva (the great god). In the *Aitareya Brāhmaṇa* (ii, 34, 7), it is prescribed that a formula must be altered from the form in which it occurs in the *Rigveda* in order to avoid the direct mention of the name "Rudra" of the god.[124] In another passage of the same text, it is interesting to note he is never named, but is referred to as "the god here", and the same avoidance of the direct use of the name is also to be seen elsewhere.[125] Thus it is evident that the word "Deva" while retaining its general sense, came to acquire a particular significance, i.e., "the god Śiva". Hence the title "Devavrata" given to Gondophares may be construed as "Gondophares devoted to god Śiva" which is supported by the presence of the figure of the divinity.

The figure of Śiva seems to appear on certain coins of Maues, one of the earliest Indo-Parthian rulers of India. Gardner describes the types as follow : "Male figure l..., Chalmys flying behind, holds club and trident."[126] The attributes are quite similar to those of the Śiva figure on the Sirkap seal.[127] Hence it can be presumed that the figure on the coins of Maues is one of Śiva.

Śiva appears in various forms and with various attributes on Kushāṇa coins. Vima Kadphises issued an extensive gold and copper coinage of beautiful workmanship. The obverse of these coins shows his life-like representation with a tall cap, a long open overcoat and long boots, and the reverse, without exception, is devoted to the worship of Śiva. On the obverse of the coins, his name occurs in Greek letters, while the legend on the reverse calls him *Mahārājasa rajadirajasa, Sarvaloga īśvarasa Mahīśvarasa Vima Kaṭhphisasa tratarasa*[128] (coins of the great king, king of kings, lord of the world, the Mahiśvara). The word Mahīśvara or Maheśvara is the name of Śiva. Its occurrence on Vima's coins shows that he was a follower of the Śaivic faith (Mahīśvara or Maheśvara can here be taken as an equivalent to Māheśvara, i. e. a devotee of Maheśvara).

124 *Aitareya Brāhmaṇa* (*Bibliotheca Indica series*), III, 34, 7.
125 *Ibid.*, III, 33; 3rd Pañchika, pp. 149-59.
126 Gardner, *op. cit.*, p. 71, pl. xviii, 3.
127 Konow, *Corpus Inscriptionum Indicarum*, Vol. II, p. 102.
128 Smith, *op. cit.*, pp. 68 and 69.

On the coins of Vima, Śiva occurs as a two-handed figure, leaning against a bull.[129] In the right hand he usually carries a long trident and a battle-axe, and in the left a gourd, water-vessel or tiger-skin wrapping round the fore-arm.[130] The skin upper garment is a feature of the Viśvāmiṭrā figure on Dharaghosha's coin and of Herakles on those of Demetrius.

The reverse sides of the coins of Kaniska and Huvishka present a strange and extensive gallery of deities with Greek, Iranian and Indian names.[131] Among the Indian deities Śiva and his associates occur more frequently than others.

On the coins of Kanishka and Huvishka, Śiva appears as both two-handed and four-handed, having various attributes. When two-handed he generally holds a trident in the right hand and a gourd in the left. When he is depicted four-handed, various sets of attributes occur: *vajra* (or small drum), water vessel, trident, antelope, elephant goad, horse, goat, club and wheel, etc., arranged in different combinations.

On a unique Kushāna coin preserved in the British Museum, Śiva (Oesha in the coin legend) is represented together with his consort Umā.[132] Certain coins of Huvishka in the Lahore Museum collection also contain representations of Umā. Besides the image of Umā, the figures of Mahāsena, Skanda-Kumāra, Viśākha[134] (the son of Śiva) occur on the coins of Huvishka which show beyond doubt that the entire Śivā pantheon was held in high esteem in the period under consideration.

Vāsudev, the son and successor of Huvishka seems to have been a patron and follower of the Śiva cult. The reverse side of the coins bear very frequently the figure of the two-armed Śiva[135] with a noose in the right hand, a long trident in the left, and a bull standing by the side. One of the coins of Vāsudeva

[129]Whitehead, *op. cit.*, pp. 183 and 184.

[130]*Ibid.*

[131]*Ibid.*, p. 18 ff., 187 ff.

[132] *Ibid.*, pp. 186 ff.; Smith, *op. cit.*, p. 69 ff.

[133]Rapson, *Journal of the Royal Asiatic Society*, London, 1897, p. 324.

[134]Gardner, *op. cit.*, pp. 138, 149, and 150. Patañjali also mentions the images of Skanda and Viśākha being worshipped in his commentary on *Pāṇini śutra* V. 3, 99. The figure of Skanda-Kārtikeya occurs also on Yaudheya coins (Allan, *op. cit.*, p. cxlix, *ci*).

[135]Whitehead, *op. cit.*, p. 209 ff.

in the British Museum collection shows the diety as five headed.[136] The latter Kushāṇa and Kushāṇo-Sasanian rulers also, like Kanishko, Vasu and Vasudeva, adopted the figures of Śiva and the bull as the reverse device of their coins.

From the above survey of Kushāṇa coins it is evident that Śaivism was a highly flourishing cult in India during the early centuries of the Christian era. Numismatic evidence is corroborated by certain archaeological finds in Mathura, (*i*) by the Śiva-Pārvatī in Dampatibhāva (Kushāna period);[137] (*ii*) by the statuette of the Arddhanārīśvara form of Śiva in his Ūrddhvareta, aspect and standing against the bull Nandi (Kushāṇa period).[138] This confirms the iconographic injunctions regarding the Arddhanārīśvara images (cf. Liṅgārddham Ūrddhvagam Kuryāt, *Matsyapurāṇā*, Ch. 260, Vangavasi Edition). (*iii*) The two-armed Śiva Arddhanārīśvara mūrti with the right half bearing the male and the left half female features, viz. breasts, extended hip, long dhoti and bracelet. Śiva is shown as Ūrddhavareta.[139]

The worship of Śiva in his Arddhanārīśvara aspect seems to have been very popular in our time, as the above sculptures show. Further, this is corroborated also by a passage quoted from Bardsanes by Stobaeus. The passage in question gives the account of an Indian visiting Syria in the time of Antonius of Emesa (218-222 A. D.), and contains a striking reference to an image of the Arddhanārīśvara.[140] Śiva, as depicted in the epic-Puranic tradition, is the impersonation of the eternal productive power, perpetually re-intigrating after disintegration (whence his name Bhūtabhāvana). The Ardhanārīśvara aspect of Śiva symbolizes both the duality and unity of the generative act and the production of the universe from the union of two principles (*Prakriti* and *Purusha*, *Māyā* and *Ātmā*) according to the Sāṁkhya and Vedānta systems of philosophy.

Another interesting Śaivic antiquity to consider in this connection is the Trimūrti image[141] in the Peshawar Museum. The

[136] Whitehead, *op. cit.*, p. 211.

[137] V. S. Agrawala, *Hand-Book to the Sculptures of Curzon Museum of Archaeology, Muttra*, p. 44.

[138] *Ibid.*, No. 800. Apart from the above, the Mathura Museum contains several more images pertaining to Śiva-pantheon of this period.

[139] *Journal of the Indian Society of Oriental Art*, 1937, pl. *xiv*, fig. 2.

[140] Coomaraswamy, *op. cit.*, p. 54.

[141] *Archaeological Survey of India, Annual Report*, 1913-14, pp. 126 ff.

image in question was found in a small village mound called Akhaura Dehri of Charsadda, the ancient Pushkalāvatī. The central figure in the sculpture is Śiva leaning against his vehicle, the bull, the head to the proper right is that of Vishṇu and the corresponding one on the other side is that of Brahmā distinguished by his grisly beard. The sculpture has been assigned to the reign of the Kushāṇa king, Vāsudeva, who appears from his coins to be a devotee of Śiva. As the central figure is that of Śiva, it is probable the person who dedicated the image was a Śiva worshipper.

The Trimūrti[142] in its Brahmanic conception is the manifestation of the supreme spirit in three forms, Brahmā, Vishṇu and Śiva. According to the original theory of Brahmanism no one of these three ought to take precedence over the other. They are equal and their functions are sometimes interchangeable, so that each may represent the supreme lord (Parameśvara) and each may take the place of the other. In Kālidāsa's *Kumārasambhava* and *Raghuvaṁśa* we have the following hymns on Trimūrti.

Namastrimūrtaye tubhyaṁ Prāksrishṭeḥ kevalātmane/
Guṇatraya Vibhāgāya Paśchādbhedamupeyushe//[143]
Namo viśvasrije pūrvaṁ viśvaṁ tadanubibhrate//
Atha viśvasya saṁhartre tubhyaṁ tredhāsthitātmane//.[144]

The original idea of equality of these deities sometimes gave way to sectarian zeal and each sect assigned the central and supreme place to its own deity in preference to others.

In the early portions of the epics Brahmā is assigned the highest place. But Vishṇu and Śiva come into prominence gradually. Though Brahmā has retained his nominal superiority throughout, the epics are devoted mostly to the praise of Vishṇu and Śiva. As sectarian rivalries were very keen and strong between the followers of those deities, attempts were made to reconcile

143The older Brahmanical triad is that of Agni, Vāyu or Varuṇa and Surya. The Buddhist triad is represented by Mañjusrī, Avalokiteśvara and Vajrapāṇi.

143*Kumārasambhava,* II, 4.

144*Raghuvaṁśa,* X, 16.

their claims by declaring the essential oneness of the two. While addressing a hymn to Mahādeva (in the *Vanaparva*) Arjuna says: "Adoration be to Śiva in the form of Vishṇu and Vishṇu in the form of Śiva, the destroyer of Dakhsha's sacrifice, to Hari-Rudra..."[145] The *Śāntiparva* narrates a furious fight between Rudra and Nārāyaṇa. Brahmā came and dissuaded Rudra from fighting and asked him to propitiate Nārāyaṇa. Being praised by Rudra, Nārāyaṇa said to him "He who knows thee knows me, he who follows thee loves me, there is no distinction between us, do not entertain any other idea."[146] This idea of Hari-Hara finally developed into the Trimūrti conception as we find it in the *Harivaṁśa.* The *Harivaṁśa* narrates a fight between Aniruddha, the son of Prdyumna, and Bāṇa, the Asura king. Krishṇa took the side of Aniruddha and Śiva that of Bāṇa. Brahmā came to the aid of the earth and created peace between these two gods by declaring them one with himself.[147] The following speech of Mārkaṇḍeya which dwells in this connection on the oneness of Brahmā, Vishṇu and Śiva is worth quoting. Mārkaṇḍeya says:

> I perceive no difference between Śiva who exists in the form of Vishṇu and Vishṇu in the form of Śiva.... He who is Vishṇu is Rudra; he who is Rudra is Pitāmaha (Brahmā), the substance (Mūrti) is one, the gods are three: Rudra, Vishṇu, Pitāmaha.... I shall laud the gods Hari, and Hara associated with Brahmā, and these two are the supreme deities, the originators and destroyers of the world.[148]

The main theme of the above passage is the reconciliation of the rival claims of Vishṇu (or Krishṇa) and Śiva by declaring them as one and the same as Pitāmaha Brahmā, the highest mysteries of the world. The conception of Trimūrti thus envisaged became instrumental in reconciling the sectarian difference of the

[145] *Śivāya Vishṇu-rūpāya, Vishṇava Śiva-rūpine ¦ Dakshayajña-Vināya Hari-Rudraya vai namaḥ ||* Quoted by Muir, *op. cit.*, p. 195.

[146] *Yastvāṁ vetti sa māṁ vetti, yastvāmanu sa māmanu | Nāvayor antaraṁ Kinchid ma te bhūt buddhiranyathā ||* (Quoted by Muir, *op. cit.*, pp. 202-03).

[147] Muir, *op. cit.*, p. 236.

[148] *Ibid.*, pp. 236-38.

Neo-Brahmnic religions responsible for the creation of the liberal monotheistic view point is characteristic of Indian religious thought.

The Trimūrti image of the Peshawar Museum shows that the conception of Trimūrti was well known as early as the second century A.D. and that the Gandhāra region, though predominantly a centre of Buddhist religion and art, was not free from Brahmanical influences.

It may be stated that Śaivism was popular with the Śaka Satraps as with some of the Kushāṇa princes. The names Rudradāman, Rudra Siṁha, Rudrasena, and Śivasena Kshatrapa, etc. (in the seal inscriptions of Taxila)[149] show that most of the Satrap chiefs were thoroughly Indianized and devoted to Śaivism. This is corroborated by the frequent occurrence of Śaivic emblems, like the bull and Nandipada, etc. on the coins of the well known Satrap kings as noted before, and also on their seals, one being of Mahādevī Prabhudāmā, sister of Rudrasena, and daughter of Mahākashatrapa, Rudra Siṁha, found at Basarh.[150] Further, the sealings found at Bhita show the popularity of Śaivism in the area during the Kushāṇa and Gupta times.

As is evident from the Gudimallam Liṅga, Śaivism was popular in South India as early as the second-first century B.C. Though not much authentic evidence on the early history of Śaivism in South India is available, it is sure that the cult subsequently continued to flourish in this region. One of the inscriptions of Nagārjunakonda refers to the construction of a temple of Śiva under the name of Pushpabhadrasvāmī during the sixteenth year of the reign of the Īkshvāku king Ehuvala Chāntamula *(Indian Archaeology*, 1957-58, p. 54).

A few words may be said about the Śiva sectaries or those who were exclusively devoted to the worship of Śiva, and their practices. In most parts of the *Mahābhārata* (the chief source of our knowledge regarding Neo-Brahmanic religions) Śiva is seen being worshipped by all sections of the people including the Pāṇḍavas, Yādavas and others, but we have only meagre information about the sectarian aspect of his worship. Though it is difficult to say precisely as to how and when

[149]Konow, *Corpus Inscriptionum Indicarum,* Vol. II, p. 102.
[150]*Archaeological Survey of India,* New Imperial Series, Vol. II, p. 24.

Śiva was first converted into a sectarian deity, there is no doubt that the development of Śiva-sectarianism began much before the Christian era. Patañjali, it is well known, refers to a Śiva-Bhāgavata while commenting on and illustrating the Pāṇini *sūtra*, V. 2. 76, *ayaḥśūla daṇḍājinābhyām ṭhakṭhañau*. This particular devotee, we are told by Patañjali, is to be called an *āyaḥśūlika* inasmuch as he carried an iron lance and he sought to attain his object by violent means, "the fulfilment of which should be sought for by mild ways, i.e., *kiṁ yo yaḥśūlenānvichchati sa āyaḥśūlikaḥ kiṁ chātaḥ Śiva-Bhāgavate prāpnoti....Yo mridunopāyenānveshṭavyān arthān rabhasenanvichchati sa uchyata āyaḥśūlikaḥ*" (Kielhorn, *Vyākaraṇa Mahābhāshya*, Vol. II, p. 387-88). Three important facts emerge from the above passage : (*i*) that there was in Patañjali's time (*c*. 200 B. C.) a Śaiva sect under the name of Śiva-Bhāgavatā; (*ii*) that the members of this sect carried an iron lance as their characteristic emblem, and (*iii*) that they resorted to various practices to attain their spiritual goals.

The other Śiva sectaries that deserve a special mention here are the Pāśupatas and the Māheśvaras. The *Mahābhārata* refers, as we know, to the Pāśupata doctrine as a contemporary religious system with the Sāṁkhya, Yoga, Vedāraṇyaka (or Veda) and Pañcharātra.[151] As stated there, Kapila formulated the Sāṁkhya, Hiraṇyagarbha the Yoga, Apāṁtarātmā was the teacher of the Veda, Śiva-Śrīkaṇṭha declared the Pāśupata and Vishṇu the Pañcharātra.

About the Pāśupata system which is the subject of our present enquiry, we derive more specific information from the Purāṇas. In the *Vāyupurāṇa*, Chapter 23, and *Lingapurāṇa*, Chapter 24, Śiva is represented as having told Brahmadeva:

> During the 28th repetition of the Yugas when Vāsudeva would be born as the son of Vāsudeva at the time of Krishṇa Dvaipāyana, I whose essence is yoga, will, by the magic power of yoga assume the form of a Brahmachāri and entering an unowned corpse thrown out into a cemetry, will live under the name of Lakulin. At the time Kāyarohaṇa [according to *Vāyu*] and Kāyāvatāra [according to *Liṅga*] will become famous as a sacred place. And there will be born my sons

[151] *Mahābhārata*, XII, 349, 63 ff.

[disciples] the ascetics, Kuśika, Garga, Mitra and Kaurushya; these Pāśupatas, their bodies besmeared with ashes, having attained the Māheśvara Yoga, will depart to the world of Rudra, whence it is difficult to return.[152]

From the above it is quite clear that the Pāśupata doctrine, though it is said to have been formulated by Śiva himself in the *Mahābhārata*, originated with Lakulīśa, a human teacher, who was later on regarded as an incarnation of Śiva.

The Pauranic tradition regarding Lakulīśa has been preserved in a number of epigraphic records. The Chintrapraśasti of the time of Śāraṅgadeva (thirteenth century A.D.) says that the god Śiva descended on earth in the form of Bhaṭṭāraka Śrī-Lakulīśa and dwelt at Karohana. There appeared his four disciples, Kuśika, Gargyha, Kaurusha and Maitreya who performed the special Pāśupata vows.[153] The Ekalingaji temple inscription[154] also refers to the incarnation of Śiva as Lakulīśa (a man with a club). Verse 13 of the same introduces his four disciples, i. e. Kuśika and the others who performed the Pāśupata vows. This inscription belongs to 971-972 A. D. A still earlier epigraphic reference to Lakulīśa is to be found, as D.R. Bhandarkar informs us, in an inscription from Hemavati in Mysore.[155] This record, which is dated 942 or 943 A.D., says that Lakulīśa, fearing that his name and doctrine might be forgotten, descended upon the earth born as the great saint Chilluka. This actually implies praise of the local saint Chilluka in a hyperbolical style, and not a second incarnation of Lakulīśa.

All the above epigraphic records belong to the mediaeval period and they do not help us in ascertaining the date of Lakulīśa. While writing on this subject in the *Journal of the Bombay Branch of the Royal Asiatic Society* (Vol. XXII 1905), Bhandarkar made some important observations regarding Lakulīśa's date which may be summed up as follows.

[152] *Vāyupurāṇa and Liṅgapurāṇa,* edited by Panchanana Tarkaratna, Calcutta. Sir R. G. Bhandarkar, *Vaishnavism, Saivism and Minor Religioūs Systems* (Collected Works of Sir R. G. Bhandarkar, Vol. IV, Poona, 1929), pp. 1929 ff.

[153] *Epiraphia Indica,* Vol. I, p. 281 ff, vv. 14-17.

[154] *Journal of the Bombay Branch of the Royal Asiatic Society,* Vol. XXII, p. 151 ff.

[155] *Journal, Bombay Branch of the Royal Asiatic Society,* Vol. 1, pp. 151-53.

Lakulīśa and his disciples are mentioned in the *Vāyupurāṇa* which, in its account of the great dynasties of India, mentions at the end the Guptas reigning over Saketa, Magadha, and along the Ganges as far as Prayaga. Applying to the early and imperial Gupta dynasty, this can only refer to the territories of Chandragupta I (*c.* 320-335 A. D.) before the expansion of the Gupta kingdom by Samudragupta. This shows that the *Vāyu* was completed shortly after the reign of Chandragupta I. Hence, the incarnation of Śiva as Lakulīśa, mentioned as an object of faith in the *Vāyupurāṇa* in the early fourth century A. D. must already have been known, probably not later than the first century A. D.

About 25 years after he published the above theory regarding Lakulīśa, Bhandarkar edited the Mathura Pillar Inscription of Chandragupta II, Gupta Era 61, in the *Epigraphia Indica,* XXI, and in the light of its contents[156] fixed Lakulīśa's date between 105-130 A. D. The epigraph in question credits Uditācharya, a Māheśvara teacher, with the establishment in the teachers' shrine, of two Liṅgas, "Upamiteśvara" and "Kapileśvara" named after his deceased preceptor and preceptor's preceptor, Upamita and Kapila respectively. Uditāchārya as described in the epigraph is tenth in descent from Kuśika (and hence, eleventh from Lakulīśa). His own teacher was Upamita. The latter again was a pupil of Kapila, and Kapila, a pupil of Parāśara. "If we now allot," observes Bhandarkar, "twenty five years to each generation, we have to assign Lakulī to A. D. 105-130. This agrees pretty closely with the view I expressed twenty five years ago (*J. B. B.R.A.S.*, Vol. XXII, p. 151 ff), that Lakulī has to be placed as early as the first century A. D. My conclusion was then based merely on the mention in the *Vāyupurāṇa*, of Lakulī as the first incarnation of Śiva. Evidence of this type will always remain of a somewhat conjectural nature. Epigraphic evidence, on the other hand, is more accurate. We may, therefore, take it now as

[156]I. L. 5...*[bha]ga [vat-ku] śikād dasamena bhagava*—
L. 6. *t-parāśarāch-chatur [the] [na] [bhagavata-ka] pila Vimala-śi*
L. 7. *Sṅya-śishyeṇa bhagavad [-upamita] Vimala-śishyeṇa*
L. 8. *āryya-odi [tā] chāryyeṇa [ṇa] [sva] pu [ṇyā] pyāyena-nimittaṁ*
L. 9. *Gurūṇāṁcha krityā [rtham-upamiteśva] ra-kapileśvarau*
L.10. *guruv-āyatane guru...pratishṭhāpito* (*Epigraphia Indica,* Vol. xxi, pp. 8-9).

well nigh proved that Lakulī flourished in the first quarter of the second century A. D., about half a century later than the time so long ascribed to him."[157]

The date 105-130 A. D. assigned to Lakulī by Bhandarkar on the basis of his interpretation of the Mathura Pillar Inscription Gupta Era, 61, does not seem to be a satisfactory one for various reasons. The *Mahābhārata (Śānti Parva)*, we have seen, regards the Pāsupata, Sāṁkhya and Pañcharātra, etc., as contemporary religions. The Puranic tradition asserts that the founder of the Pāśupata system was Lakulīśa, who was an incarnation of Śiva and a contemporary of Krishṇa-Vāsudeva and Krishṇa-Dvaipāyana. Even if it is presumed that the Lakulīśa and the Pāśupata systems cannot be given such an early date, yet they cannot be as late as 105-130 A. D. That the Pāśupata system is older than the Christian era is evident from the points of close similarity between the Śiva-Bhāgavatas and the Pāśupatas in respect of their doctrinal practices. The very characteristic reference in Patañjali's *Mahābhāshya* to the adoption of violent means by the Śiva-Bhāgavata reminds us distinctly, as J. N. Banerjea, points out,[158] of the fourth Vidhi or means to which the Pāśupatas resorted to reach their desired goal, i. e. Duḥkhānta (termination of ills or final liberation). The fourth Vidhi of the Pāśupatas, as Madhvāchārya tells us, includes certain extreme practices, like loud laughter, song, dance, muttering of *aum* and pious ejaculations.[159] "This led R. G. Bhandarkar to describe the Pāśupata school or schools with two of its offshoots, the Kapāla and Kālamukha, as atimārgika schools, that are away from the common path or go astray, and are spoken of by Śambhudeva as revealed by Rudra."[160] These discussions show beyond doubt that the Śiva-Bhāgavatas and the Pāśupatas were allied sects, some of the practices common to both were known to Patañjali and that they flourished earlier than his time, i. e. 200 B. C.

[157]*Epigraphia Indica*, Vol. XXI, p. 7.

[158]Presidential Address by Dr. J. N. Banerjea at the Indian Historical Congress, 9th session (1946), Patna.

[159]*Sarvadarsa Saṁgraha of Mādhavāchārya*, English translation by E. B. Cowell and A. E. Gough, pp. 103 ff.

[160]Sir R. G. Bhandarkar, *op. cit.*, p. 126.

Further, the Pāśupatas, who were also known as Māheśvaras, were an important sectarian organization in the middle of the first century A. D. Vima Kadphises, a celebrated Kushāṇa ruler of this time was an adherent of this sect as in evident from one of his appellations "Mahiśvra" on the reverse sides of his coins. The generally accepted date of Kanishka is 78 A. D. Hence Vima, who was his predecessor, must have belonged to the period between 50-77 A. D. Thus, the rise of the Lakulīśa and the Pāśupata sects must also be placed earlier than the first century A. D. If we accept Bhandarkar's date of Lakuli, it is difficult to explain the presence of a Māheśvara or Pāśupata sect in Vima's time.

Lastly, the words *Kuśikāddasamena*, etc. in the Mathura Pillar Inscription, Gupta Era 61, should be taken in the sense of a spiritual descent and not in that of a generation. The spiritual succession does not follow chronologically the generation. The allotment of 25 years to each spiritual generation is nothing but a conjecture and cannot lead us to any definite conclusion. The arguments put above tend to show that Lakulīśa and his doctrines are older than the time assigned to them by Bhandarkar.

3. Bhāgavatism

The Bhāgavata or the Krishṇa-Vāsudeva cult is the basis of the *Bhagavadgītā* (in the present from) and has proved to be the chief source of inspiration of modern Vaishṇavism. Bhāgavatism is an old cult, certainly older than Pāṇini who mentions *bhakti* with reference to Vāsudeva (its founder and cult-god) in his *Sūtra*, iv, iii, 98. It is now a recognized fact that Krishṇa-Vāsudeva was a historical person who belonged to the Yādava Vrishṇi or Sāttvata tribe[1] of the Kshatriyas, originally inhabiting Mathura, and who was the same as Krishṇa-Devakīputra mentioned as a disciple of Ghora Āṅgirasa in the *Chhāndogya Upanishad* (III, xvii, 6). It must, however, be made clear that we know very little about the religion orginally propounded by Vāsudeva. All that can be said about its early character from the epic-Puranic traditions is that it grew outside the pale of orthodox Brahmanism, and that it was strongly monotheistic, the object of worship being Bhagavat, the adorable one. It taught *bhakti* or single-minded devotion to the supreme one as the best means of salvation. It was at first confined to Krishṇa's kinsmen, the Yādavas. Gradually, he was deified and indentified with Bhagavat or the supreme lord, and his cult spread to different parts of India. Its success was overwhelming inasmuch as its cult-god (Krishṇa-Vāsudeva) ultimately came to be recognized as the same as Vishṇu and Nārāyana of the Brahmanic theology[2] as is evident from the *Mahābhārata* and the *Purāṇas*.

Bhāgavatism, we are aware, exercized a profound influence upon the domain of India religious thought. When Brahmanism

[1]Dr. H. C. Raychaudhuri, *The Early History of the Vaishṇava Sect* (Calcutta, 1936), Lectures i and ii.

[2]I. Garbe, *Journal of the Royal Asiatic Society*, London, 1905, pp. 385-6; *Indian Antiquary* (1908), pp. 251 ff.

was confronted with the dissenting movements of Gautama Buddha and Mahāvīra, and when it was found that the abstract and impersonal Absolute was more than the mind of the average people could grasp, Bhāgavatism offered a personal god in Krishṇa-Vāsudeva, a god of love and grace and provided an easier means of salvation, salvation through *Bhakti*. Krishṇaism permeates the whole of the *Mahābhārata*. It is true that the belief in the saving grace of god is found in the metrical *Upanishads* like the *Kaṭha*,[3] *Śvetāśvatara*[4] and *Muṇḍaka*,[5] but in the epics it is asserted that the god whose grace saves is Krishṇa alone. Salvation, not through knowledge, even of god, not through grace of god, but through grace of the man-god, Krishṇa, is the saving way.[6]

We have made in the following pages an attempt to give the history of the Bhāgavata cult during the post-Mauryan period. For the study of the subject we have, fortunately, ample archaeological material at our disposal, besides the literary traditions.

One of the earliest and most important historical documents of the period relating to the Bhāgavata cult is the Garuḍa pillar inscription of Heliodoros at Besnagar. It records that the Garuḍa pillar (i. e. the column surmounted by Garuḍa) was erected in honour of Devadeva Vāsudeva, i. e. Vāsudeva, the god of gods, by Heliodoros, the son of Diya (Dion). The donor is described as Bhāgavata or the worshipper of Bhagavat (i.e. Vāsudeva) and a resident of Takshaśilā. He had come to Besnagar as an envoy from the great king Aṁtalikata (Antialkidas) to the court of Kāśīputra Bhāgabhadra (two was a Śuṅga king), then in the fourteenth year of his reign.[7] Antialikidas has been placed on numismatic grounds between 175-135 B. C. Hence the date of the

[3]1.2. 30.
[4]iii, 20; vi, 21.
[5]iii, 2-3.
[6]Hopkins, *The Great Epic of India*, p. 188.
[7]*[de] vadevasa Vā [sude] vasa Garuḍadhvaje ayam/kārite i [a] Heliodoreṇa Bhāga-/vatena Diyasa putrena Takhkhasilākeṇa/ Yona-dūtena [a] gatena Mahārājasa./Aṁtalikitasa upa [ṁ] ta sakāsam raña./[Ko] sīpu [tra] sa [Bhā]ga bhadrasa trātarasa./Vasena cha [tu] daseṁna rājena vadhamānasa.// Archaeological Survey of India, Annual Reports*, 1908-9, p. 126; *Journal of the Bombay Baanch of the Royal Asiatic Society*, Vol. XXIII, p. 104.

inscription could be somewhere near the middle of the second century B. C.[8]

From the inscription it is clear that the Bhāgavatas were the followers of Vāsudeva and that the deification of Vāsudeva (as the god of gods) was an established fact in the second century B. C. Regarding the antiquity of Bhāgavatas we derive some valuable information from Pāṇini's grammar. Pāṇini, in his *sūtra* iv, iii, 95, says that an affix comes after a word in the first case in construction in the sense of "this is his object of *bhakti*". As for example, one can say: *Srughnobhaktirasya Sraughnaḥ*. Further in the *sūtra* iv, iii, 98 *(Vāsudevārjunābhyaṁ vun)* he says that the affix *vun* is added to the words *Vāsudeva* and *Arjuna* in the above sense. The words formed according to the *sūtra* would be Vāsudevaka and Arjunaka (not Ārjunaka because of the prohibition of *cha* and *an*). Vāsudevaka would denote a person to whom Vāsudeva was an object of *bhakti*. Similarly, Arjunaka would refer to him to whom Arjuna was an object of *bhakti*. Without going into controversies regarding Pānini's date, we can accept for him a central date in *c*. 500 B. C. and hold that Vāsudeva was regarded as divinity at least a century before Pānini's time, i.e. *c*. 600 B. C. Umesh Chandra Bhattacharya[9] is of the view that *bhakti* in the *sūtras* iv, iii, 95 ff can hardly denote religious *bhakti* as, according to the *sūtra achittādadeśakālāṭṭhak*, it has been applied even to cakes *(āpūika*, etc.*)*. According to him *bhakti* here stands for "fondness" simply. Jayaswal holds that Pāṇini used the term in the sense of "political or constitutional allegiance." In support of his arguments he observes, "Take for instance the *bhakti* owed to the holders of the Janapadas in iv, iii, 100. The holders of the Janapadas were certainly not worshipped. Take again the preceding *sūtra* (iv, iii, 97) where *bhakti* to the Mahāraja is mentioned. Nobody would contend that the Mahāraja either as a man or a country was worshipped. Again, the scholars have taken note of Vāsudeva, while Arjuna, who is placed along with Vāsudeva in the same *sūtra*, has been ignored. There is no evidence that Arjuna was deified. *Bhakti* to these two Kshatriyas is the political *bhakti*."[10]

[8]*Journal of the Royal Asiatic Society*, London, 1909-10, p. 1088.
[9]*Indian Historical Quarterly* (1925), pp. 483-9.
[10]Jayaswal, *Hindu Polity*, pp. 121-2.

We admit that *bhakti* referred to in the *sūtras* iv, iii, 95 ff has been used in a wide sense. But whatever may be the interpretation of this term with reference to Arjuna and Mahārāja etc., we have no doubt that *bhakti* applied to Vāsudeva in the *sutra* iv, iii, 98, cannot be taken in any sense other than that of religious adoration as shown below. In other words, Vāsudeva here is implied as a divinity and not in the sense of Vasudevādapatyam as under the *sutra Rishyandhakavrishṇikurubhyaścha*, iv, i. 114. If Vāsudeva was regarded as a human being, then being a Kshatriya he could have been included under the *sutra*, iv, iii, 99, *Gotrakshatriyākhyebhyo bahulam vuñ* which also comes under the *adhikāra* of *bhakti*. Patañjali, while commenting on the *sūtra* iv, iii, 98, righty raises the question as to why *vun* is used for Vāsudeva though the affix *vuñ* comes diversely after the words denoting Gotra and Kshatrya. He suggested that the *sūtra* iv, iii, 98 has been devised to show the *Pūrvanipāta* of Vāsudeva (i. e. to show that Vāsudeva being more revered should be placed before Arjuṇa in a compound though the latter begins with a vowel and has also fewer vowels than Vāsudeva) or Vāsudeva here is not the designation of a Kshatriya but a designation of Tatrabhagavat or Tatrabhavat.[11] Kielhorn says that Tatrabhagavat is found only in the Benares edition of the *Mahābhāshya* and it is a wrong reading. The actual word which Patañjali used is Tatrabhavat as found in a dozen other manuscripts.[12]

According to Kielhorn, the tatrabhavat by which saṁjñaishā is followed "does not in the least suggest that the personage denoted by the proper name is a divine being; the word indeed conveys an honorific sense, but it would be equally applicable to a human being."[13] Though tatrabhavat is applicable both to a divine being and a human being, yet from the trend of his argument it appears that he is inclined to consider Vāsudeva as a human being rather than a divine one.

[11]*Kimarthaṁ Vāsudevaśabdādvunvidhīyate na Gotrakshatriyākhyebhyo bahulam vuñ* (iv, 3. 99)/ *Ityeva siddham nahyasti viśesho Vāsudevaśabdabvuno vā vuño vā/ Tadevarūpam sa eva svaraḥ. Idam tarhi prayojanaṁ Vāsudevaśabdasya pūrvanipātaṁ vakshyāmīti. Athavā naisha Kshatṛiyākhyā/ saṁjñaishā tatrabhavataḥ.* Kielhorn, *Patañjali Mahābhāshya* (Vol.II, p.314).

[12]*Journal of the Royal Asiatic Society,* London, 1908, p. 503.

[13]*Ibid.*

The above theory of Kielhorn has been controverted by Keith and Bhandarkar in whose opinion tatrabhavat as used by Patañjali in his commentary on the *sūtra* iv, iii, 98, has been used to signify Vāsudeva as a divinity and not as a human being.[14] Further, Kielhorn himself has pointed out that the precise pharse *saṁjaishā tatrabhavatāḥ* which occurs with regard to Vāsudeva occurs also with regard to *Ka* (in the sense of Prajāpati and not Saravanāma) in the *Mahābhāshya (Journal of the Royal Asiatic Society*, London, 1908, p. 503*)*. So his own views, i. e. the example of *Ka* as a tatrabhavat, go to prove that tatrabhavat refers to a divine being and not an ordinary mortal. Thus Kaiyaṭa (though a later authority, *c.* 1300 A. D.), who describes Vāsudeva of the *sūtra*, iv, iii, 98, on the basis of Patañjali's commentary as *Nityaḥ paramātmadevatāviśesha iha Vāsudevo grihyate* is precisely accurate in equating *Paramātmadevatā* with *tatrabhavat* when he finds Prajāpati also thus described.

Now we may refer in brief to the opinions of other grammarians on the point. The authors of Kāśikā (Jayāditya and Vāmna) lay down:

> *Vāsudevārjunaśabdābhyaṁ vun pratyayo bhavati, so'sya bhaktirityetasmin vishaye chānorapavāda, Vāsudevo-bhaktirasya, Vāsudevakaḥ, Arjunakaḥ nanu Vāsudevaśabdadgotra-Kshatriyakhyebhyaiti vuñastyeva.... Kimarthaṁ Vāsudevagrahaṇam saṁjñaishā devatā viśeshasya, na kshatriyashya, alpāchtaramajā dyadantamiti, vā Arjunaśabdasya pūrvanipātamakurvan jñāpayatyabhyarhitaṁ pūrvaṁ nipatatiti.*

From this it is clear that Vāsudeva, if treated as a human being, could have come under the *sūtra* iv,3,99*(gotrakshatriyākhyebhyo bahulaṁ vuñ*, as *vuñ*) makes no difference in the form or vowel of the word Vāsudeva. So the very fact that he has been included under *sūtra* iv, 3. 98 shows that he was regarded as a divinity in Pāñini's time. Again is to be noted that Vāsudeva precedes Arjuna in the *sutra* though according to grammatical rules, *alpāchtaramajādyadantam*, Arjuna should have come first. This also implies that Vāsudeva was more revered than Arjuna and consequently come to be placed first. Further, that Vāsu-

[14] *Ibid.*, pp. 847-48; 1910, p. 168-70.

deva was more revered than Arjuna just on the ground of his divinity and not any other reason (i. e. age or other considerations) has been fully brought out in Jinendra Buddhi's Nyāsa *(abhyarhitatvaṁtu Vāsudevaśabdasya devatā-viseshatvād)*.

Bhaṭṭoji Dikshit, summing up the arguments of previous grammarians, says that from all points of grammatical considerations *vun* or *vuñ* makes no difference in the case of Vāsudeva. He further observes that the maxim of *abhyarhitatva* is not strictly mentioned as we find such compounds as *Svayuvamaghonām*. He says that *abhyarhitatva* has been introduced by way of discussion. The real reason why Vāsudeva has been included in the *sūtra* iv, iii, 98, and placed before Arjuna is that Vāsudeva has been taken for a divinity and not as a human being. If he were taken as the latter, he could have been included in the next *sūtra* iv, iii, 99 *(Gotrakshatriyākhyebhyobahulam)*. He places his reliance on Patañjali's suggestion: "*Saṁjñaishā bhagavataḥ iti*" and explains the word Vāsudeva as:

sarvatrāsau samastaṁcha vasatyatreti vai yataḥ |
tato' sau Vāsudeveti vidvadbhiḥ parigīyate ||
iti smriteḥ paramātma iha Vāsudevaḥ |
sarvatrāsau vasati sarvamatra vasatīti vā vyutpatyā Vāsudevaḥ ||
bahulakāduṇ Vasuśchāsau devaścheti vigrahaḥ |
tathā neyaṁ gotrākhyā nāpi kshatriyākhyeti yukta eva vunvidhiḥ ||

It is thus clear that the authors of the Kāśikā, and Kaiyaṭa, and Bhaṭṭoji Dikshit regarded Vāsudeva of the *sūtra* iv, iii, 98, as a divinity and leave no doubt as as to the correctness of their interpretation, though they are much later in time. They have fully established the point that Pāṇini used and could have used the Vāsudeva of the *sūtra* iv, iii, 98, only in the sense of a divine being.

Regarding Arjuṇa one notices that from the very beginning he was regarded as an incarnation of Nara who is often mentioned in the *Mahābhārata* along with Nārāyaṇa as a double divinity.[15] In Book I of the epic it is said that Nārāyaṇa accompanied by Nāra took the nectar from the Dānavas and consequently there was an encounter between the gods and Dānavas for it. Nārāyaṇa came to the battlefield, with Nara possessed of a heavenly bow. Nara defeated the Asuras and he was entrusted with the nectar for its preservation. (In Book III Nara and Nārāyaṇa are represented as two divine sages in whose Āśrama at Badari the sons of Pāñḍu lived for some time). Vāsudeva has been identified with Nārāyaṇa and Arjuna is regarded as an incarnation of Nara in the epic.[16] The association of Arjuna with Vāsudeva in the *sūtra* iv, iii, 98, may have a bearing on this fact, but we are not sure. To explain the significance of the *sūtra* it is not necessary either to attribute divinity to Arjuna as to Vāsudeva, though the former is regarded in the *Mahābhārata* as an incarnation of Nara and a constant associate of Nārāyaṇa. The grammarians, such as the authors of the Kāśika and others, consider Arjuna as a Kshatriya and offer very cogent reasons to account for his inclusion in the *sūtra* iv, iii, 98. They say that as a Kshatriya, Arjuna ought to have come under the *sūtra* iv, iii, 99 *(gotrakshatriyākhyebhobahulaṁvuñ)* but it has not been so because the addition of *vuñ* would have given rise to an undesirable form such as Ārjunaka (as *vuñ* is bound to cause *vriddhi* of the first vowel of the word Arjuna). Thus the Nyāsa on Kāśikā lays down—*Nanu Arjunasabda Kshatriyākhyaḥ | Tasmāduttarasūtrapräeṇasypta vuño'pavāda yuktaḥā.*

[15]Obeisance is paid to Nara along with Nārāyaṇa in the opening stanzas of the *Mahābhārata*. The conception of the dual divinities is very old and can be traced back to the *Rigveda* in a developed form, as for instance, Dyāvāprithvī, Dyāvākshamā, Dyāvābhūmī. Besides these, Mitra and Varuṇa share 28 hymns as dual deities, Indra and Varuṇa 9, and Soma shares one hymn each with Pūshan, Rudra and Agni.

[16]In the *Vaṇaparva* (12, 46 and 47) Janārdana says to Arjuna, "O invincible one, thou art Nara and I am Hari-Nārāyaṇa, and we the sages (rishis) Nara-Nārāyaṇa have come to the world at the proper time; thou art no different from me, oh Pārtha, and I am not different from thee; it is not possible to know any different from us." In the *Udyoga Parva* (49,19) it is said: "The two heroes Vāsudeva and Arjuna who are great warriors are the old gods Nara and Nārāyaṇa, this is the tradition."

The cult of Arjuna seems to have been arrested in its growth due to the phenomenal rise to importance of Krishṇa-Vāsudeva who become identified with Vishṇu and Nārāyaṇa of the Brahmanical theology. The icono-

In summing up we may say, (i) if the word Vāsudeva is treated as a Kshatriya, there is no difficulty in including him in iv, 3,99, as Vāsudeva being already an *ādyodātta* word, the addition of *vuñ* would have made no difference in regard to its form or vowels. His inclusion in iv, 3, 98, shows that he was regarded by Pāṇini as a divinity as Patañjali supposes and other grammarians fully assert. (ii) Arjuna, though he is a Kshatriya as the Kāśika holds, cannot come under the *sūtra* iv, 3, 99, as the addition of *vuñ* would have given rise to the form Ārjunaka which is undesirable. (iii) Whether we regard Arjuna as a divine being or not, the Vāsudeva of the *sūtra* iv, 3, 98 can on no ground be regarded as one other than a divine being. In other words, while explaining the *sūtra* iv, 3, 98 it is not necessary to regard Arjuna also as a divinity (as in the case of Vāsudeva) though from other sources we know that Arjuna too was looked upon as a divine being. (iv) In view of the above we cannot agree with interpretations given of the *sūtra* iv, 3, 98 by Jayaswal and Umesh Chandra Bhattacharya and we hold that *bhakti* relating to Vāsudeva of *sūtra*, iv, 3, 98 implies religious adoration and not natural fondness or constitutional allegiance.

Bhāgavatism seems to have originated in Mathura. Its propounder Krishṇa Vāsudeva was a scion of the Sāttvata or Vrishṇi family of Mathura. That Krishṇa-Vāsudeva was a member of the Vrishṇi family had been declared by Krishṇa himself in the *Bhagavadgītā* which is one of the oldest sources of the Bhāgavata religion : *Vrishṇīnaṁ Vāsudevo' smi.* The *Ghaṭajātaka*[17] also mentions him and the members of his family as belonging to a royal family of Mathura. The *Mahābhārata* knows of two contemporary Vāsudevas, the false one and the true one. The former was the king of the Puṇdras,[18]

graphic representation of Nara-Nārāyaṇa is found in one of the side niches of the Daśāvtara temple (Gupta period) at Deoghar, Jhansi, Madhya Pradesh. See Presidential Address of Dr. J. N. Banerjea at the Indian History Congress, Patna, 1946.

[17]The *Jātakas* (Cowell's edition), p. 56 ff.

[18]The name of Pauṇḍra Vāsudeva is mentioned in the *Sabhā-parava* by Krishṇa, as an ally of Jarāsandha:

Jarāsandham gatasteva purā yo na mayā hataḥ| Purushottamavijñāto yo, sau Chedishu durmatiḥ || Ātmānaṁ pratijānāti lokesmin Purushottamam| ādatte satataṁ mohād yaḥ sa chihnam cha māmakaṁ || Vaṅga-Puṅḍra Kirā-

while the true Vāsudeva who first taught the Bhāgavata cult was Krishṇa-Vāsudeva, the famous prince of the Yādava, Vrishṇi or the Sāttvata family of Mathura. The Greek writers Megasthenes and Arrian state that Herakles was held in special honour by the "Sourasenoi", an Indian tribe who possessed two large cities, namely, Methora and Cleisobora.[19] As Sir R. G. Bhandarkar correctly points out, the "Sourasenoi" were the same as the Sāttvatas and "Herakles" was the Greek hero-god closest to the Indian hero-god Krishṇa-Vāsudeva. In the opinion of Lassen, M'Crindle Hopkins, and several others, Methora and Cleisobora clearly stand for Mathura and Krishṇapura[20] respectively.

We hear very little about the Bhāgvatas in the third century B. C. though we have ample archaeological evidence regarding the condition of this sect in the second century B. C. H. C. Ray Chaudhuri points out that the Bhāgavatas are "almost wholly ignored"in the ancient Buddhist records, literary and epigraphic, of Magadha and the neighbouring provinces. The *Aṅguttara Nikāya* mentions various sects incuding the Ājīvikas, the Nigaṇthas, the Muṇḍa-sāvakas, the Jaṭilakas, the Paribbājakas, the Aviruddhakas, the Gotamakas, the Devadhammikas and several others but never the Vāsudevakas and Arjunakas. The Seventh Pillar Edict of Aśoka refers to the Ājīvikas, the Niganthas and the Samaṇas, etc. but not the Bhāgavatas. "There is a solitary reference to Vāsudevavāṭikā and Baladevavāṭikā (signifying the worship of Vāsudeva and Baladeva), in a passage found in the *Chulla Niddesa* and *Mahā-Niddesa*.[21]

In view of the above, Dr Ray Chaudhuri holds that the ommission of the Vāsudevakas in almost all the ancient Buddhist records of Eastern India is due probably to the fact that "they were as yet a local sect confined to the Yamuna valley included

---

tesu rājabala-samanvitaḥ | Puṅḍrako Vāsudevo yo'sau loke bhiviśrutaḥ||.

Purushottama is a well known epithet of Vāsudeva. The above passage shows that in Bengal and the eastern provinces there was a powerful personage who adopted the titles of Vāsudeva and behaved like him,

[19]M, Crindle, *Ancient India as Described by Megasthenes and Arrian*, p. 206; Sir R. G. Bhandarkar, *Collected Works*, Vol. IV, *Vaishnavism, Saivism and Minor Religious Sects*, p. 17.

[20]Krishaṇapura is equivalent to Vrindāvana, Vraja, etc. in the suburb of Mathura.

[21]Ray Chaudhuri, *op. cit.*, pp. 94-95.

among the Devadhammikas or some other sects and little known in Magadha and its neighbourhood."[22]

It is a fact that the Bhāgavatas or Vāsudevakas find little mention in the Buddhist and also other literary records of eastern India in the third century B. C. or near about, but it is not safe to suggest on that negative evidence that the Bhāgavatas were as yet more or less a local sect confined to the Yamuna valley, little known in Magadha and eastern India. Further, the statement of Megasthenes that "Herakles" was held in special honour by the "Sourasenoi" cannot be taken to mean that the Bhāgavata activities were confined only to the limits of the Yamuna valley during his time. For throughout the ages, Krishṇa has been specially honoured in Mathura while Krishṇa and Balarāma worship and the type of Bhāgavatism or Vaishṇavism associated with them have been widely prevalent throughout India since early times. It seems from epic and Puranic accounts of Krishṇa's career, that his religious leadership and his brand of Vaishṇavism came to be accepted in Magadha, Puṇḍra and Pragjyotisha, with his career of political conquests in those regions. Puṇḍraka Vāsudeva claimed to be the real incarnation of Vāsudeva and assumed his insignia. At Nārada's protest he invaded Dvārakā and was killed by Krishṇa. Śisupāla opposed Krishṇa's claims as put by Bhīshma at the Rājasūya sacrifice of Yudhishṭhira. Here again Krishṇa established his divinity by killing the unbeliever. These and many other stories reveal that Vāsudevism spread and was widely known in different parts of India in Krishṇa's lifetime in spite of strong opposition by some sections of the people. Hence, it may be suggested that the omission of the Vāsudevakas in the *Aṅguttara Nikāya* or in the Aśokan inscriptions (in which, however, they might have been included under the term *Sarvapashaṇḍas*) cannot be taken to prove that they were a local cult in Mathura only, up till the time of Megasthenes and also in the third century B. C. and that they were either little known or not at all known in eastern India in the early days of their history.

Whatever might have been the state of Bhāgavatism in the third century B. C. we have authentic materials to show that it

[22] *Ibid.*

was gaining in popularity throughout India in the post-Mauryan period. During this time the centre of Bhāgavatism is usually taken to have shifted from Mathura to Central India which has yielded a number of valuable Bhāgavata records. But this may not be a real shifting, for in Krishṇa's time the Vrishṇi and other Yādavas atached to Vaishnavism occupied the whole region from the Yamuna valley to Surashtra which included Central India, Malwa, Rajputana, Gujarat, and Kathiwar while Mathura was abandoned by the Yādavas in Krishṇa's lifetime.

The bulk of the Bhāgavata inscriptions and monuments belonging to our period come from Central India (Vidisa or Malwa region), specially from Besnagar. The most important Bhāgavata record of Besnagar, we know, is the inscribed Garuḍa column erected, as noted before, in honour of Vāsudeva by Heliodoros, a Greek ambassador to the court of the Śuṅga king, Kāśīputra Bhāgabhadra. This shows that Bhāgavatism was extensively popular during this period inasmuch as foreigners too were attracted by it. D. R. Bhandarkar has drawn our attention to a fragment of another Garuḍa column preserved in the Besnagar Museum.[23] It contains a broken Brāhmī inscription[24] which records that the column was erected for the Bhagavat by one Gautamīputra who was a follower of Bhāgavatism during the twelfth regnal year of Mahārāja Bhāgavata. Mahārāja Bhāgavata, according to Bhandarkar is the Śunga king[25] of the same name mentioned in the *Purāṇas.* If so, he was perhaps the last but one in the list of the Śuṅga family and belonged to *c.* 100 B. C.

Besides these two Garuḍa columns, Bhandarkar noticed remains of another Vaishnavite archaeological evidence at Besnagar. These consist of a capital of a column, and a *makara*[26] which might have originally surmounted the capitals. These were found lying a few yards of the Garuḍa column of Heliodoros. Taken

[23] *Archaeological Survey of India, Annual Report,* 1913-14, Part II, pp. 189-90.

[24] *(i) Gotamīputena, (ii) bhāgavate na, (iii)................................. (iv) [Bhagava] to prāsādota (v) masa Garuḍadhvaje (kārito), (vi) [dva] dasa - vasabhi-site, (vii) .... Bhāgvate Mahārāje, Archaeological Survey of India, Annual Report, 1913-14,* Part II, p. 190.

[25] *Archaeological Survey Reports, 1913-14,* Part II, p. 190; *Memoirs, Archaeological Survey of India, No. 5,* pp. 161-63.

[26] *Ibid.,* pp. 189-90.

together, the capital of the column and the *makara* would constitute what is known as *Makaradhvaja.* In the epic and *Purāṇa* literature, Pradyumna, son and deified spiritual successor of Krishṇa has been attributed the *makara* symbol. He is one of the four Vyūhas of the Pañcharātra or Bhāgavata cult. On the basis of these facts, it is reasonable to suppose that there stood at Besnagar a shrine of Pradyumna.

Another important centre of the Bhāgavata activities during this period was the Udaipur state, Rajputana, as is evident from the text of the Ghosundi and Hathibada inscription of the second century B. C. It records the erection of an enclosing wall round the stone object of worship called Nārāyaṇa Vāṭikā (compound) *(Pūjā-śilā-prākāro-Nārāyaṇa vāṭikā)* for the divinities Saṁkarshaṇa and Vāsudeva[27] *(bhagava[d]bhyāṁ Saṁkarshaṇa Vāsudevābhyām)* by one Sarvatāta[28] who was a devotee of Bhagavat and had performed an Aśvamedha sacrifice. The Pūjā-silā, as J. C. Ghosh points out, refers to Śālagrāmaśīlā, a sacred stone typical of Vishṇu as the Liṅga is of Mahādeva.[29] Among the varieties of Śālarāma in the *Purāṇas* one variety is called Saṁkarshaṇa and another Vāsudeva.[30] Thus it appears that the Pūjāsilās here refers to Śālagrāmasilās representing Saṁkarshaṇa and Vāsudeva. The wall which was constructed round their place of worship was in the compound called Nārāyaṇa Vāṭikā. The original site of this shrine was in Hathibada, half a mile east of the village Nagari in Udaipur state. As more than one copy of the text of the inscription is found, it appears the inscription was incised on several stones of the enclosure and as D.R. Bhandarkar points out, the inscribed stone of the Ghosundi well was in fact a part of the Nārāyaṇa Vāṭikā of Hathibada. That Hathibada was an important site of the Vaishṇava religion is evident also from another short inscription on a stone wall of the Hathibada enclosure. This inscription is in the script of the seventh century A. D. and reads as *Śrivishṇu-pādābhyām.*[31]

27 *Epigraphia Indica,* Vol. XVI, p. 27; *Lūders List No. 6, Epigraphia Indica,* XVII, p. 189 ff.

28 Sarvatāta has been regarded by D. R. Bhandarkar as a Kāṇva king, *Epigraphia Indica,* XXII, pp. 204-5.

29 *Indian Historical Quarterly,* IX, p. 796.

30 *Ibid.*

31 *Memoirs, Archaeological Survey of India, No. 4,* p. 129.

The Ghosundi-Hathibada inscription which records the erection of a stone enclosure for the worship of Saṁkarshaṇa and Vāsudeva within the Nārāyaṇa compound shows beyond doubt that the Bhāgavatas accepted the identification of their cult-god Vāsudeva with Nārāyaṇa by the second century B. C.

The Bhāgavata cult seems to have extended to north-west India also at a very early period; we have seen that it was the religion of the (Yona-Gandhāra) ambassador Heliodoros of the second century B. C. His adoption of the Bhāgavata religion shows that it was in vogue in the Punjab and the North West Frontier from some time before, because a religious cult or doctrine must necessarily be well-established on the native soil before it can attract the notice of foreign settlers. This seems to be corroborated by the statement of Q.Curtius that an image of "Herakles" was carried in front of the army of Porus as he advanced against Alexander.[32] It is very consistent that Porus, as a Paurava prince, descended from the epic family of Arjuna, the incarnation of Nara and counterpart of Nārāyaṇa-Krishṇa, should have carried before his war-chariots the image of Krishṇa-Vāsudeva, the hero of Kurukshetra.

As it appears from Zenob's story of the Indians in Armenia, the Bhāgavata cult travelled beyond the borders of India as early as the second century B. C. Two Indian chiefs, Zenob tells us, called Gisane (Kisane) and Demeter (Temeter) fled westward with their clan and found shelter with Valarashak, or Valarsaces, the first Arsacide monarch of Armenia (*c.* 149-127 B. C.). Fifteen years later, the king of Armenia put Gisane and Demeter to death, but their sons and descendants continued to live there. They erected two temples to their gods Gisane and Demeter. St. Gregory (304 A. D.) invaded their temples and razed them to the ground. The Indians offered a stiff resistance, but were overpowered.[33]

Demeter and Gisane are names common to men and gods. Kennedy thinks that Demeter must be some compound of Mitra, perhaps Devamitra,[34] but about Demeter we have no details.

[32] J. N. Banerjea, *The Development of Hindu Iconography* (1st edition), Vol. 1, p. 98; Coomaraswamy, *History of Indian and Indonesian Art*, p. 42.
[33] *Journal, Asiatic Society*, London, 1904, pp. 310-11 ff.
[34] *Ibid.*, p. 312.

Kisane, as Zenob informs us, was represented with long hair. His worshippers also wore it long. Lassen suggested long ago that Kisane might be Krishṇa.[35]

During the post-Mauryan period, Mathura became a cosmopolitan centre of diverse contemporary religions—Buddhism, Jainism, Brahmanism, Śaivism and Bhāgavatism. The Indo-Scythic rulers of Mathura patronised all the Indian regions more or less with an equal interest.

Mathura has yielded several objects throwing light on the history of Bhāgavatism during the Śuṅga-Kāṇva and Kushāṇa periods. Noteworthy among them is a well-preserved standing image of two-armed Balarāma with a canopy of serpent-heads above the head and snake coils carved on the back and sides of the body. He has as usual, a club *(mushala)* in the right hand and a plough*(phala)*in the left. The figure belongs to the second century B. C. Balarāma, as is well known, is the elder brother of Krishṇa-Vāsudeva, and one of the four Vyūhas (emanations) of the Bhāgavata cult.

The Bhāgavata records of Mathura in our period are the Mora Well inscription and the New Mathura inscriptions, both of the time of Soḍāsa, the son of Rājuvula. The Mora Well inscription of the time of Mahākshatrapa Soḍāsa[36] (the first century B. C.) refers to the enshrinement of the images of five heroes *(Pañcha Vīras)* of the Vrishṇis in a stone temple by a lady called Toshā. On the authority of the Jaina texts, the *Antagaḍa Dasāo*, and *Harivaṁśapurāṇa*,etc. Vogel identified them with Balarāma, Akrūra, Anādhrishṭi, Sāraṇa and Viduratha.[37] The Jaina texts use, it should be noted, always the term Baladeva-pamokha-paṁch-Mahāvīrā, thus mentioning specifically only one (i.e. Baladeva) of the five Vrishṇi heroes. J.N. Banerjea shows more convincingly that the five Vrishṇi heroes as known to the *Purāṇas* are Saṁkarshaṇa, Vāsudeva, Pradyumna, Sāmba, and Aniruddha,[38] four of whom, excepting Sāmba, constitute

[35]*Ibid.* According to Kennedy, both Demeter and Gisane were probably forms of solar deities.

[36]*Epigraphia Indica,* Vol. XXIV, p. 194 ff.

[37]*Ibid.*

[38]*Journal of the Indian Society of Oriental Art,* Vol. X, pp. 65-68, *Vāyupurāṇa*, Ch. 47 (opening verses), Vangavasi Edition.

the four Vyūhas of the Pañcharātra cult. The opening verses of Chapter 79, *Vāyupurāṇa*, read as follows :

Manushya-prakritīn devān kīrtyāmānān nibodhata//
Saṁkar-shaṇo Vāsudevaḥ Pradyumnaḥ Śāmba eva cha//
Anirudhseha pañchaite vamśavīrāḥ prakrītitāḥ//

The New Mathura Inscription[39] records the erection by one Vasu, of a quadrangle enclosed by four buildings, a gateway and a square terrace at the shrine of Bhagavat Vāsudeva, during the reign of the Mahākshatrapa Soḍāsa. The epigraph reads as follows :

L. 6 *Vasunā bhagava [to Vāsude]*
L. 7 *vasya mahāsthāna [chatuḥśā]*
L. 8 *laṁ toraṇaṁ ve [dikāprati]*
L. 9 *shṭhāpito prīto bha [vatu Vāsu]*
L. 10 *deva-svāmisya [mahākshatra]*
L. 11 *pasya Soḍāsasya*
L. 12 *saṁvarteyatām*

From the above it apears that Soḍāsa was a patron, if not a follower of Bhāgavatism.

The Bhāgavata inscriptions of Mathura during our period are very few in number as compared with the enormous contemporary Buddhist and Jaina records. H.C. Ray Chaudhuri suggests that this paucity of the Bhāgvata inscriptions at Mathura is probably due to the fact that Bhāgavatism did not find much favour with the Śaka and Kushāṇa rulers of Mathura (first century B. C. to third century A.D.) who were mostly Buddhists or Śiva worshippers with a few exceptions, and probably not well disposed towards the religion of Vāsudeva.[40] In this connection it may be suggested that there is no direct evidence to show that the Indo-Scythic rulers of Mathura were anti-Bhāgavata in their attitude. Whatever might have been the personal

[39]Edited by R. P. Chanda, *Memoirs of the Archaeological Survey of India, No. 5*, p. 170.

[40]Ray Chaudhuri, *op. cit.*, pp. 164-65.

creed of the Śaka and Kushāṇa rulers, from the coins and inscriptions of their time it appears that they were eclectic in their religious attitude.

The paucity of Bhāgvata records in Mathura during the Indo-Scythic rule seems to be merely accidental and cannot be taken in any way to imply an anti-Bhāgavata attitude of the Indo-Scythic rulers. Though the Bhāgavata records at Mathura of Indo-Scythic times are very few, we have a reasonably good number of Bhāgavata sculptures of Mathura assignable to *c.* 150 B. C. to 250 A. D. which would show that Bhāgavatism was in a flourishing condition there during the period under consideration. One of the most interesting Bhāgavata sculptures of Mathura belonging to our period is the Mathura Museum relief No. 1344 which represents Vāsudeva carrying his new-born babe Krishṇa to Gokula across the river Yamuna.[41] The river is shown by means of waves with aquatic animals such as fish, tortoise and alligators, etc. This relief has been assigned on stylistic grounds to the Kushāṇa period. It is one of the earliest sculptural representations relating to the life of Krishṇa-Vāsudeva with whom originated the Bhāgavata cult. Besides this, the Mathura Museum contains a few more interesting Vaishṇava antiquities of the Kushāṇa period, *viz.* *(i)* the figure of Vishṇu with one hand in Abhayamudrā and the other having an *amrita-ghaṭa* with two additional hands holding a *makara* and *chakra;*[42] *(ii)* four armed Vishṇu image with the typical drapery of the Kushaṇa period;[43] *(iii)* eight armed Vishṇu figure probably in his Virāṭa form;[44] and *(iv)* a Brahmanical relief containing among other Neo-Brahmanic deities a four-armed Vishṇu,[45] etc. The Balarāma image of Mathura belonging to the Śuṅga-Kāṇva period has already been mentioned above.

From the study of the sculptures referred to above, it is quite evident that Bhāgavata traditions continued in Mathura uninter-

[41]*Hand-Book to the Sculptures in the Curzon Museum of Archaeology, Muthura* by V. S. Agrawala, p. 29; *Archaeological Survey of India, Annual Report, 1925-26*; p. 184f, pl. Lxvii, Fig. c.

[42]V. S. Agrawala, *op.cit.*, p. 44.

[43]*Ibid.*

[44]*Ibid.*

[45]*Ibid.*

rupted even in the Indo-Scythic period and there is hardly any reason to believe that Bhāgavatism ceased to be a popular or influential religion in Mathura during the Indo-Scythic rule.

Being not far off from Mathura, the original home of Vaishṇavism, the Panchala region, it is natural, might have been affected by the movement quite early. Vāsudeva Vishṇu seems to apear on one of the coins of Vishṇumitra of Panchala (second century B. C).[46] On the basis of this it may reasonably be inferred that the family of Vishṇumitra had leanings towards Vaishṇavism. Bhita (an ancient site near Allahabad) provides a number of interesting seals supplying evidence of the prevalence of Vaishṇavism during the early centuries of the Christian era. As is well known, the conch and the wheel, two important Vaishṇava symbols, occur on a number of the Bhita seals, discovered in the course of excavations there in 1911-1912. One of the seals containing a symbol like the wheel, bears in northern script of the third-fourth century A. D. the legend: *Namo-Bhagavate Vāsu*[*devāya*]. It is needless to say that the author of the seal was a staunch follower of Vaishṇavism (*Annual Report*, Archaeological Survey of India, 1911-12).

Bihar, like the other parts of northern India, seems to have been influenced by the Bhāgavata or Vaishṇava cult quite early in its history. The defeat of Jarāsandha at the hands of Bhīma helped by Krishṇa perhaps indicates a major step towards the introduction of Vāsudevism in Bihar. The *Arthaśāstra* of Kauṭilya and the *Mahābhāshya* of Patañjali, both of them closely associated with Bihar, refer to the prevalence of Vishṇu and Krishṇa worship. In fact, the *Mahābhāshya* of Patañjali constitutes a valuable piece of evidence as to the different aspects of the Bhāgavata cult, as hinted above.

Again, the seals discovered at Basarh (Mazaffarpur district, Bihar) would show that Vaishṇavism was in a flourishing condition in Bihar during the third-fourth century A. D. A large number of these seals bear the Vaishṇavite symbols like the *śaṅkha* (conch) and *chakra* (wheel). Further, the names occurring on them include Hari, Harigupta, Varāha, Varāhadatta, Keśava, Keśavadatta, Krishṇadatta, Vāsudeva and several others,

[46]Cunningham, *Coins of Ancient India*, p. 84, pl. VII, Fig. 21. Allan, *Catalogue of Indian Coins (Ancient India)*, Introduction, p. CXIX.

indicating the Vaishṇavite affiliations of the authors of the seals in question. One seal contains the legend: *Śrī Vishṇuyaśasvāmi Nārāyaṇa (Annual Report*, Archaeological Survey of India, 1903-1904).

An interesting Vaishṇavite antiquity of the Kushāṇa period from Bihar is the Ekānaṁśā triad found in Devangarh, District Gaya. The triad consists of Balarāma, Ekānaṁśā and Vāsudeva, shown separately. On stylistic considerations they can be ascribed to the second century A. D. These sculptures are made of buff sandstone. All the three figures are standing and two-armed Balarāma is distinguished by the presence of a snake-hood behind his head. His right hand is raised in the *abhaya* pose, the left hand rests on the waist holding a *Siṁha-lāṅgala* (plough with lion-faced share). He wears a head dress (turban) with a lateral knot on the left side. He wears a *dhoti* tied with knots on the two sides of the waist with one fold falling down between the legs. He is provided with a necklace and earrings.

Ekānaṁaśā has her right hand in the *abhaya* pose, and the left hand rests on her waist, holding an unidentified object. She is provided with ornaments and wears a *dhoti* with one fold falling down between her legs and her other fold passing through her right hand falling down sideways.

Vāsudeva is four-armed. The back right and left hands hold a *gadā* and *chakra* respectively. The front right hand is raised in the *abhaya* pose, the left rests on the waist and holds a *śaṅkha*.

The Ekānaṁśā triads ascribable to the Kushāṇa period were found also in Mathura. All these reliefs carved on the slab are very mutilated (P. L. Gupta, *Journal, Bihar Research Society*, Vol. 7).

South and western India were also affected by the Bhāgavata movement during the period under review. It still exercises a very important religious influence with the people there. We do not know as to when exactly the Bhakti cult first penetrated into this region. We have, however, an important inscription belonging to the our period which shows that the Bhāgavata religion came to the West and the south at least two centuries before the Christian era. The epigraph in question is the Nanaghat Cave inscription of Naganika of the second half of the first century B. C.[47] which opens with an invocation to a number of deities among whom occur the names of Vāsudeva and Saṁkarshaṇa: *No Dhaṁmasa namo Īdasa Saṁkaṁsaṇa-Vāsudevānāṁ chaṁda-Sūrāṇām.*

The Nasik inscription[48] (A. D. 140-49) also contains the name of Balarāma and Krishṇa in the following passage: *Ekadhanurasa ekasūrasa ekabahmṇaasa Rama-Keśavājuna-Bhīmasena tula parākramasa.* The names of Rāma and Keśava mentioned in the above passage are clearly the names of Balarāma and Krishṇa[49] respectively. The epithet "Bhagvat" which is usually used before the names of Saṁkarshaṇa and Vāsudeva is conspicuous by its absence in this record. Here Saṁkarashaṇa and Vāsudeva have not been called Bhagavat but treated as great heroes. But we should remember that the Nasik inscription, as we know, is not a Bhāgavata record, and what has been stated in it is in keeping with the Buddhist tradition which considered Vāsudeva a historical prince and a member of the royal family of Mathura. It may be stated here that the China inscription of Śriyajña Śātakarṇi opens, in the opinion of N. G. Majumdar, with an invocation to Vasudeva.[50] From the epigraphic evidence it is clear that Bhāgavatism was widely known in South India in our period.

Regarding the antiquity of Bhāgavatism or Vaishṇavism in South India we have some valuable information in ancient South Indian literature. Some of the extant Sangam works which are not later than the first century B. C. reveal that among the religions prevalent in South India in the first century A. D., Vaishṇavism was one of the most prominent. *Tolkāppayam,* which is generally regarded as supplying the basic grammar for the works of the Sangam period in Tamil literature, and consequently the earliest Tamil work in existence, has a section devoted to Agattinai, or the grammar of subjective life with

[47]Lüders, *List of Brahmi Inscriptions,* 1123; Būhler, *Archaeological Survey of Western India,* Vol. IV, p. 180 ff, No 18.

[48]Lüders, *List of Brahmi Inscriptions,* No. 1112.

[49]The compound "Rāmakeśava" occurs also in a passage of Patañjali's *Mahābhāshya;* Kielhorn, *Vyākaraṇa Mahābhāshya,* Vol. I, p. 436.

[50]Ray Chaudhuri, *op. cit.,* p. 163.

special reference to love and happiness in the Tamil country; and we are told that one of the regional varieties of the Tamil country is Mullainilam or pastoral land of which the guardian deity is Vishṇu."[51]

The Shilappathikaram and other ancient Tamil poems refer to the dedication of temples in the early centuries of the Christian era to Krishṇa and his brother at Madura, Kaviripattinam and other cities.[52] Further, according to a description in the Silappadikaram the celebrated Tamil classic of the second century A. D., seven or nine cow-herdesses engage in a dance each joining her hands to that of another. This dance is originally said to have been danced by Krishṇa himself in the presence of Yashoda and subequently brought into popular practice by the members of the cow-herd folk as a form of prayer to Krishṇa to avert impending calamities.

In *Puram*, Krishṇa and Balarāma are described as Mayon and Valiyon. Mayon was dark and Valiyon white. Mayon bears the discus and kite (Garuḍa) flag while Valiyon has the plough and palmyra as his symbols. The dwarf incarnation of Vishṇu and the discomfiture of Bali are mentioned in the *Manimekhalai* (xix: 51-52) and *Tirukhal* (61.10).[53]

The popularity of Vaishṇavism in South India during the period under review is also attested by the discovery of the remains during the course of excavations at Nāgārjunakoṇḍa, of the brick temple of Ashṭabhujasvămin and a limestone slab with a large slit (for the insertion of the base of a wooden image) with an inscription further confirming this. The inscription refers to the consecration of Ashṭabhujasvāmin (eight-armed Vishṇu) made of Audumbara wood, a material described in all Āgama-literature as the most suitable for making images.[54]

[51] "Kulasckhara Alvar and His Date," *Indian Historical Quarterly*, p. 644, 1931.

[52] Kanakasabhai, *The Tamils Eighteen Hundred Years Ago*, pp. 13, 26; V. R. Ramchandra Dikshitar, *Indian Culture*, Vol. 4. (1937), p. 269.

[53] K. R. Srinivasan, "Some Aspects of Religion as Revealed by Early Monuments and literature of the South," *Journal of the Madras Univ.*, Vol., XXXII, p. 144.

[54] *Ibid.*, p. 141.

As noted before, the orthodox view regarding the origin of the Vāsudeva-cult (which is also known as Bhāgavata or Sāttvata or Pañcharātra or Ekāntika religion[55]) is that it was founded by the Kshatriya preacher Krishṇa-Vāsudeva, who was later identified with Bhagavat, the name under which the Bhāgavatas worshipped the Supreme Being. This view has been opposed by Keith and few others. Referring to Patañjali's *bhāshya* on the Pāṇinian *sūtra* iii,i, 26, Keith writes, "The *Mahābhāshya*[56] tells us that in the Kaṁśavadha the Granthikas divided themselves into two parties, one, the followers of Kaṁśa, the other, the followers of Krishṇa, and that the former were Kālamukha and the latter Raktamukha.[57] Weber was puzzled to find that Krishṇa's friends were red in colour, but the whole thing explains itself when we regard the contest as one of the many old nature rituals where two parties join in a mimic strife, the one trying to rescue, the other to capture the sun. The supporters of Krishṇa as indentified with the sun-Vishṇu naturally wear the red colour of the luminary as an act of sympathetic magic." He further observes, "The mention of the colour of two parties is most significant; the red man slays the black man; the spirit of spring and summer prevails over the spirit of the dark winter."[58] Dr. Macnicol says:

> There are...gods of spring and vegetation deities, whose mythology and the facts in nature to which it corresponds, suggest death and resurrection. Of this class were Dionysus and Demeter in Greece, Attis in Phrygia, and probably also Krishṇa in India.[59]

With reference to the *bhāshya* of Patañjali on the Pāṇinian *sūtra* iii, 1. 26, R. P. Chanda[60] has shown on the authority of

[55] *Mahābhārata*, xii, 337.1, 335. 19; 335, 24, 348 (Bombay Edition).

[56] *Journal of the Royal Asiatic Society*, London, 1901, p. 172 ff.

[57] *Kechit Kamsabhaktā bhavanti, kechit—Vāsudevabhaktāḥ Varṇānyatvam khalu-api pushyanti. Kechit-raktamukhā bhavanti kechit Kālamukhāḥ*, Kielhorn, *Vvākaraṇa Mahābhāshya*, Vol. II, p. 36.

[58] *Journal of the Royal Asiatic Society*, London, 1911, p. 1008.

[59] Macnicol, *Indian Theism*, p. 32.

[60] R. P. Chanda, *Indo-Aryan Races*, p. 95:

Indian commentators like Helaraja and Haradatta that "it was not the Granthikas or narrators who divided themselves into the two parties, but the audience, some of whom sided with Kaṁśa and others with Krishṇa, the partisans of the former pale with grief and the partisans of the latter beaming red with joy on the triumph of their hero." Even if we assume that the granthikas divide themselves into two parties, one for Kaṁsa, painted dark and the other for Krishṇa, painted red, the passage can be interpreted more reasonably than has been done by Keith, in a common sense way. Since Krishṇa was already deified and it was Krishṇa and his followers who gained a victory, the red colour suited their make-up best; while since Kaṁśa was acknowledged a dark oppressor, his was the defeated party, the black; it is to be noted that Krishṇa too has very often been associated with dark colour, equally with the red, yellow, green and blue colours. Hence, the interpretation of the passage in Patañjali's *Mahābhāshya* as given by Keith on the basis of colour-scheme is difficult to accept.

The *Mahābhārata*, it may be stated, has given more than one etymological meaning of the word "Vāsudeva". Though it is commonly regarded by it as a patronymic of Krishṇa, other derivations and meanings are not unknown:

Vasanāt sarvabhūtānāṁ vasutvāddevayoṇitaḥ |
Vasudevastato vedyo brihatvād Vishṇuruchyate ||
Chādayāmi jagadviśvam bhūtvā Sūrya ivāṁśubhiḥ |
Sarvabhūtādivāsaścha Vāsudevastato hyaham||[61]

In the two above passages the name "Vāsudeva" has been explained figuratively and qualitatively. A. Govindacharyasvami holds that as the name "Vāsudeva" means one who permeates all, it cannot be said that the Bhāgavata Dharma originated with a human being.[62] The argument of the above scholar ignores the fact that all ancient Indian (and also later Indian) personal names have a very good philosophical, religious or poetical significance and when the bearer of such a name comes to be the subject of honour, devotion, canonization or even

[61] *Mahābhārata,* V. 70, 3, XII, 341, 41 (Bombay Edition).
[62] *Journal of the Royal Asiatic Society*, London, 1911, p. 936.

deification, the other meaning comes to be attached to the historical person. Several interpretations of the name Vāsudeva are quite natural in view of the fact that not only have we two Vāsudevas (the Puṇḍraka and Vrishṇi), but also two brothers, Saṁkarashaṇa and Krishṇa, both Vāsudevas, and Vāsudeva, the form of Vishṇu as popularized by Krishṇa and his contemporaries, Balarāma, Arjuna and the Pāṇḍavas, Akrūra, Uddhava, etc., and his successors Pradyumna and Aniruddha and probably also his predecessor (Satvant).

The epic and Puranic traditions are unanimous with regard to the Kshatriya origin of Krishṇa-Vāsudeva. The Buddhist and Jaina sources corroborate this fully. The Buḍdhist Ghatajātaka describes Krishṇa-Vāsudeva as a scion of the royal family of Mathura as we have seen. The Jain *Uttarādhyayanasūtra*[63] also points to the same. Ray Chaudhuri points out that the name Sāttvata Dharma as applied to Bhāgavata Dharma shows that it originated with the Sāttvata prince Vāsudeva;[64] rather, we should say that the Sāttvatas from Satvant onward (who was a younger contemporary of Rāma Dāśarathi), the predecessors of Krishṇa were all Vaishṇavites, believing in Vishṇu worship characterized by love, devotion and service to a monotheistic divinity and that Krishṇa Vāsudeva developed this theism into a special cult later on known as Vāsudeva or Bhāgavata or *Pañcharātha*, but also called Sāttvata which was particularly associated with Mathura and the Yādavas, and adjacent regions and branch clans. In the inscriptions of this period Saṁkarshaṇa and Vāsudeva have been mentioned together. Saṁkarshaṇa has been traditionally described as a brother of Krishṇa as the latter is called Saṁkarshṇānuja. The association of Vāsudeva with Saṁkarshaṇa proves beyond doubt that the Bhāgavata religion had its founder in the Yādava prince Krishṇa-Vāsudeva and was not a pre-existing full-fledged one, independent of Krishṇa Vāsudeva. The Mora Well inscription refers to the enshrinement of five Vrishṇi heroes[65] who should be identified, as J. N. Banerjea has shown,

[63]Lecture XXII *(Sacred Books of the East,* Vol xiv*)*, p. 112.

[64]Ray Chaudhuri, *op. cit.*, p. 35.

[65]*Mahākshatrapasa Rājuvulasa putrasa svāmi....Bhagavatām Vrishṇīnaṁ pañchavīrānām pratimaḥ śāiladevagri....ya [s] To [Shā] yāḥ śailam śrīmadgriham ...archādeśam śilam pañch, jvalataiva paramava pushā*, Vogel, *Epigraphia Indica*, Vol. xxiv, p. 194 ff.

with Vāsudeva, Saṁkarshaṇa, Pradyumna, Sāmba and Aniruddha.[66] The *Vāyupurāṇa* explicitly states that they were originally human beings later on raised to the position of divinities.[67] Further, in the *Chhāndogya Upanishad* Krishṇa has been described as a disciple of Ghora Āṅgirasa and as Devakīputa, i. e., a son of Devakī.[68] The above facts are sufficient to show that the Bhāgavata Dharma has been propounded by Krishṇa-Vāsudeva, the prince of Mathura.

The Garuḍa column of Besnagar and the Bhāgavata inscription of Hathibada and Ghosundi show that the Bhāgvatas accepted the indentification of Vāsudeva-Krishṇa with Nārāyaṇa-Vishṇu by the second century B. C. Now the question arises as to when exactly and how the amalgamation of Nārayāṇa-Vishṇu and Krishṇa Vāsudeva took place, as these deities were originally different from each other.

Vishṇu is a Rigvedic god, and like most of them probably a nature god. He seems to have been a personification of the sun, and became important chiefly because of the three strides with which he is supposed to have strode over the universe.[69] His greatness is inconceivable, and his highest place is the abode of the departed spirits where "he dwells inscrutable."

From the times of the later *Saṁhitās* and *Brāhmaṇas*, Vishnu increases in importance. In the *Satapatha Brāhmaṇa* he comes to be recognised as the personification of sacrifice.[70] The fourteenth Kāṇḍa of the same Brāhmaṇa states that he came out triumphant in the contest among the gods and he was declared most eminent of them.[71] The *Aitareya Brāhmaṇa* also

[66]*Journal of the Indian Society of Oriental Art*, Vol. X, pp. 65-68.

[67]*Ibid.*

[68]*Chāndogya Upanishad,* iii, xvii, 6.

[69]*Idaṁ Vishṇur vichakrame trdehā nidadhe padaṁ (Rigveda,* 1. 22. 17). According to Sākapuṇi the three steps of Vishṇu are the triple manifestations of the god, in the form of fire on earth, of lightning in the atmosphere, of the solar light in the sky : *"Tredhā-bhāvāya prithivyāṁ antarikshe, divi' iti Sākapuṇiḥ|(Nirukta.* xii, 19). Aruṇavābha interprets the passage differently. He understands the three steps of Vishṇu, not of fire, lightning, and solar light, but of the different positions of the sun at its rising, culmination, and its setting; *Samārohaṇe Vishṇu-pade, Gayāśirasu iti*, Aruṇāvabhaḥ *(Nirukṭa.* xii, 19).

[70]*Satapatha Brāhmaṇa,* 1. 2. 5. 3.

[71]*Ibid.*, XIV, 1. 1. 1 ff.

assigns Vishṇu the highest place among the gods.[72] Though Vishṇu came to the forefront in Brahmanical literature, some hold that his position as such did not acquire stability, for in the *Aitareya Brāhmaṇa* he is called Devānāṁ Dvārapaḥ.[73] The oldest *Upanishads* have, of course, nothing to say about Vishṇu, but in the theistic *Upanishads* like *Kaṭha*, a philosophical significance is attached to his *paramapada* as the end of the path, the final goal of existence.[74]

Vishṇu rose to the highest distinction in the epics. In fact the whole of the *Mahābhārata* is permeated by Vishṇu. The blessed lord is the all which is the base and crown of its speculation. In the *Mahābhārata*, five current religio-philosophical systems are mentioned, viz. the Sāṁkhya, Yoga, Pañcharātra, Vedāranyaka (Vedāḥ) and Pāśupata. In all these systems, Vishṇu is declared to be the *nishṭhā* or the chief object of worship.[75] In the epic (*Mahābhārata*), Vishṇu is identified with many gods. He is Parameshṭhin, Svayambhū, Kāla, Dharma, Prajāpati, Varuṇa, Tvashṭri, Viśvakarmā, Agni, Vasu, Śiva, Vāchaspati, and the Jyotir-Āditya, etc.

> As an all-god, Dyaus is his head, earth is his feet, water his sweat, and the stars are his hairpits.[76] He looks after the gods and he is the Saviour. He is the ruler of all and creator of all and one who is eternal (bhagavānityaḥ).[77]

The epic describes several incarnations of Vishṇu. Krishṇa-Vāsudeva is one of them. It is as Krishṇa-Vāsudeva and Nārāyaṇa that Vishṇu commands supreme respect in the epic. It must be stated that Vishṇuism[78] as a sectarian doctrine is not found as an isolated and definite form as Narayaṇism, or

[72]*Agnir vai devānām avamo/Vishṇuḥ paramastadanantreṇa sarvā anyā devatāḥ.*

[73]Max Müller, *Ancient Sanskrit Literature*, p. 390.

[74]*Kaṭha-Upanishad,* 1. 3. 9.

[75]*Mahābhārata*, xii, 350, vv. 63, 67; English Translation of the *Mahābhārata* (*Sānti Parva*) by P. C. Roy, p. 859.

[76]Hopkins, *Epic Mythology*, p. 307.

[77]*Mahābhārāta*, 3, 249, 26, 3, 103 (Bombay Edition).

[78]*Ibid.*, 5. 42, 21.

Bhagavatism.[79] But the authors of the epic adapted themselves to the changing religious conditions of the times and elevated him (Vishṇu) to the supreme rank, the *nisṭhā* of all the five religious systems as mentioned above. But Vishnuism becomes infused with a new life only when it is definitely identified with Nārayaṇism or Vāsudevism. Though Vishṇu maintains also a separate and independent existence apart from Krishṇa, the most attractive and interesting feature about him is his transformation into the supreme personal god as Krishṇa-Vāsudeva. It is like the personal development of the Vedanta philosophy, only it is touched here by the personality of the man-god Krishṇa.

Regarding Nārāyaṇa, we know that he is not an ancient deity like Vishṇu. He is mentioned for the first time in the *Brāhmaṇas*. The *Śatapatha Brāhmaṇa* (xii, 3. 4.) calls him Purusha Nārāyaṇa who "at the instance of Prajāpati places all the world and all the gods in him and his own self in all the world and all the gods, thus becoming the power of sacrifice, the universe itself." In the same book (xiii, 6. 1. 1.) it is further stated that to surpass all things he performed a Pañcharātra sacrifice (lasting over five nights) and became supreme and omnipresent. In the *Mahābhārata* (Śānti Parva) he is indentified with Vishṇu and Vāsudeva and is described as all pervading, all generating and with the eternal characteristics of the supreme purusha.[80]

In the epic, the identity of Vishṇu and Nārāyaṅa[81] as the eternal Purusha is an acknowledged fact. In the fourth *prapāṭhaka* of the *Taittirīya Āraṇyaka* mention is made of Nārāyaṇa in connection with Vishṇu and Vasudeva apparently as three phases of the same supreme spirit : *Nārāyaṇāya vidmahe, Vāsudevāya Dhīmahi tanno Vishṇu prachodayāt.*

[79]The sectarian term "Vaishṇava" as a worshipper of Vishṇu, is to be found nearly at the end in the latest portion of the epic, and that also three times only. In the *Mahābhārata* (xviii, 6.96) for instance, we are told *ashṭādaśa purāṇānāṁ śravaṇād yat phalaṁ bhavet/tat phalaṁ samavāpnoti Vaishṇavo nātra saṁśayaḥ//.*

[80]Muir, *Original Sanskrit Texts*, Vol. 4, pp. 33, 43, 223 ff.

[81]The precise solution of the equation is not possible, but it may be said that Nārāyaṇa's connection with sacrifice as Purusha-Nārāyaṇa probably helped his equalization with Vishṇu, the Brāhmanic personification of the sacrifice.

We have seen that the worship of Vishṇu began as early as Rigvedic times, but Krishṇa-Vāsudeva is a later divinity.[82] The Vāsudeva cult cannot be definitely proved on any authentic ground much prior to Pāṇini's time (*c.* 600 B. C.). The earliest source ascribing divinity to the human Vāsudeva is the Ashṭā-dhyāyī *sūtra* (iv. 3, 98) and it is very difficult to say as to when first Krishṇa-Vāsudeva came to be identified with Vishṇu. Vāsu-deva is the name given to Vishṇu in a passage of the tenth *prapāṭhaka* of the *Taīttirīya Āraṇyaka* as noted before, but according to the consensus of opinion this work cannot be earlier than the beginning of the christian era.[83] In the *Bodhā-yana Dharmasūtra* which is an orthodox treatise dating at least as far back as the third century B. C. we find that Garutman is the vehicle of Vishṇu[84] and Keśava is Vishṇu's epithet.[85] On the evidence of Patañjali's *Mahābhāshya* (early second century B. C.), we shall presently see that Keśava was an appellation of Vāsudeva Krishṇa.[86] This shows that the identity of Vāsudeva-Krishṇa with Vishṇu was an established fact by the third-second centuries B. C.

Now we may consider the viewpoints of the *Mahābhārata* and the *Mahābhāshya* of Patañjali. In the *Mahābhārata* which contains a vast collection of heterogeneous materials originating in different sects, Krishṇa has been represented diversely. Inso-far as he is introduced as an actor of the main events of the poem he is made to play a human role and his divine character is not unoften disputed, while also where he appears as a divine bieng, indentified sometimes with Vishṇu and Nārāyaṇa, the supreme spirit of the Brahmanical theology. In the *Sabhāparva* Śisupāla contests his claims to divinity though Bhīshma defends it. In the *Vana* and *Anuśāsana parvas* he is represented as paying homage to Mahādeva and receiving boons and blessings from him. In the *Ādiparva* he and his brother Balarāma are referred

[82]It may be said that a divinity called Vāsudeva-Vishṇu might have existed before the man-Krishṇa while the patronymic Vāsudeva could be identified with Vishṇu.

[83]Ray Chaudhuri, *op. cit.*, p. 107.

[84]*Bodhāyana Dharmasūtra* (11, 5, 24), Govt. Oriental Series, Mysore.

[85]*Ibid.*

[86]Patañjali's *Mahābhāshya* on Pāṇini *sūṭra* 11, 2.34.

to as being born from the two hairs of Hari-Nārāyaṇa.[87] But there are many passages which assert his divinity in unambiguous terms. In the *Udyogaparva* (49-19) it is said that two heroes Vāsudeva and Arjuna who are great warriors, are the old gods Nara and Nārāyaṇa. Traditionally, as Nārāyaṇa, he lives through ages. Even while acting as the ally of the Pāṇḍavas he slays Śiśupāla supernaturally with the discus. In the *Udyogaparva* Sañjaya describes before Dhritarāshtra the divine nature of Krishṇa and identifies him with Nārāyaṇa-Vishṇu thus:

> The divine Keśava by his own abstraction makes the circles of time, of the ages (*yugas*) continually to revolve. This divine being alone is the lord of time, of death, and things moveable and immoveable, this I tell thee as a truth...Keśava is immeasurable. He is to be known as Vāsudeva from his dwelling in all beings, from his issuing as a Vasu from a divine womb .... He is a called Vishṇu because of his pervading nature.... He is called Mādhava, O Bhārata, because of his practices as a muni, contemplation of mind on truth and Yoga absorption.... Born of the Sāttvata race he is called Krishṇa because he uniteth in himself what are implied by two words '*Krishi*' which signifies what existeth and '*na*' which signifies eternal peace .... He is called Nārāyaṇa from his being the refuge of all human beings.... Krishṇa is based upon truth (*satya*) and the truth, is based upon him, and from this truth Govinda is truth therefore he is called Satya. The god is called Vishṇu from striding (Vikramanāt), Jisḥnu from conquering, Ananta from his eternity.[88]

Further in the *Śāntiparva*, Yudhisṭhira addresses a hymn to Krishṇa saying, "Glory be to thee, thou mover of all, the soul of all, thc source of all, Vishṇu, Hari-Krishṇa, Vaikuṇṭha, Purushottama.[89]

[87]Muir, *op. cit.*, Vol. 4, p. 221.

[88]*Udyogaparva*, Eng. Tr. by P. C. Roy, pp. 227 and 228.

[89]*Viśvakarman namaste 'stu viśvātman viśvasambhave Vishṇo Jishṇo Harekrishṇa Vaikuṇṭhapurushottama*/quoted in Muir's *Original Sanskrit Texts*, Vol. VI, p. 223.

R. G. Bhandarkar[90] and a few others hold that Krishṇa's identification with Vishṇu is a post-*Gītā* element. In support of this, Bhandarkar says that when Krishṇa shows his Viśvarūpa (*Bhagavadgītā*, ch. II) to Arjuna, he is twice addressed by the latter as Vishṇu on account of his dazzling brilliance, but Vishṇu here is regarded as the chief of the Ādityas and not as the Supreme Being. In the *Anugītā* portion of the *Āśvamedhika Parva*, it is related that while Krishṇa was returning to Dvaraka, he met on the way the famous contemporary sage Uttanka of the Bhrijgu family. The latter asked him whether he had reconciled the Kurus with the Pāṇḍavas. He replied that the Kurus had perished. This displeased the sage who was apparently a partisan of the Kauravas and he threatened Krishṇa with a curse. To pacify him Krishṇa agreed to explain to him the mystery of his own nature and showed him his universal form *(virāṭa svarūpam)*. This *svarūpa* is similar to the *Viśvarūpa* unfolded to Arjuna in the *Gītā*. In the *Anugītā* this is called *Vaishṇavarūpa*, the name which is conspicuous by its absence in the *Bhagavadgītā*. All this shows according to Bhandarkar that the identity of Krishṇa Vāsudeva with Vishṇu was effected between the period of the *Gītā* aud the *Anugītā*.[91]

With regar d to Bhandarkar's theory it may be stated that the *Udyogaparva*, which comes before the *Anugītā* and also the *Bhagavadgītā* in the epic arrangement, identifies Krishṇa-Vāsudeva with Vishṇu in clear terms. This shows that the identification of Krishṇa-Vāsudeva with Vishṇu took place much earlier than Bhandarkar supposes. Again, it is difficult to agree with Bhandarkar's view that Vishṇu as an epithet of Krishṇa in the *Gītā* (Chapter XI) is referred to as a god of dazzling ligh tor splendour, i.e. as the chief of the Ādityas and not as a Supreme Being. It is to be remembered that the original conception of Vishṇu is as an aspect of the sun-god. His solar attributes did not drop altogether even when he rose to the position of a monotheistic and supreme divinity. This is but in keeping with the idea of an all-god who is considered to be possessed of all kinds of attributes including those assigned to other deities,

[90]Sir R. G. Bhandarkar, *Vaishṇavism, Saivism and Minor Religious Systems*, 1913, pp. 13 ff.

[91]*Ibid.*

though on a particular occasion stress may be laid on a particular set of attributes of such a supreme divinity. Hence, even if Vishṇu is described in the *Gītā* with reference to his solar aspect there is no valid reason to hold he is alluded to in the above context as an Āditya only and not as a supreme deity. It is to be noted here that the identification of Krishṇa-Vāsudeva with Vishṇu is an accepted fact in the epic though it is difficult to say as to when first this amalgamation of the two deities took place, owing to the uncertainty of the date of the major portions of the epic. Anyhow, Vishṇu and Krishṇa-Vāsudeva were looked upon as one and the same deity in the second century B. C. and probably a few centuries earlier as is evident from the inscribed Garuḍa pillar of Heliodoros at Besnagar noticed before, and also from the *Mahābhāshya* of Patañjali (early second century B. C.) to which we shall refer now. Patañjali notices under Pāṇini (ii, 2. 34) a verse which states that the musical instruments were played in the temple of Dhanapati, Rāma and Keśava. Rāma and Keśava are the names of Balarāma and Krishṇa-Vāsudeva respectively. In *Bodhāyānā Dharmasūtrā,* Keśava is an epithet of Vishṇu as noted before. In view of this it may be held that during Patañjali's time Krishṇa-Vāsudeva came to be regarded as identical with Vishṇu. Further, in discussing evidence afforded by the *Māhābhāshyā* regarding the early existence of the drama, Weber notices therein two subjects of dramatic representations, one of the Balibandha and the other of Kaṁsavadha. As one of them, i. e. the Balibandha, has been derived from the Vishṇu legends, it is probably necessary to assume, as Weber points out, that Vishṇu and Krishṇa already stood in close relationship.[92]

Garuḍa is a "sun-bird." The Garuḍadhvaja of Besnagar, erected in honour of Vāsudeva as expressly stated in the inscription, suggests a close relationship between Vāsudevism and sun worship. The Vedic Vishṇu with whom Vāsudeva was identified iu the epic times was, we know, a solar deity. In the Rigveda Vishṇu is mentioned along with the sun[93] and is regarded as one of the Ādityas.[94] Vishṇu's three steps represent, according

[92]*Journal of the Royal Asiatic Society*, London, 1908, pp. 172-173.

[93]*Rigveda*, 1.90, 9; VII, 39, 5; X.65, 1.

[94]In fact, most of the important Vedic divinities were "Ādityas" or

to scholars, the sun's daily course, namely its rise, zenith and setting.[95] Barnett points out that the three immortal steps, namely *dama*, *tyāga* and *apramāda*, mentioned in the Besnagar Garuḍa pillar inscriptions seem to be an attempt to moralise the old mythical feature of the three steps of Vishṇu.[96] Krishṇa-Vāsudeva, the propounder of the Bhāgavata religion is represented in the *Chhāndogya Upanishad*[97] as the disciple of Ghora Āṅgrasa and both the preceptor and disciple are said to have been worshippers of the sun. Grierson rightly holds that the legends dealing with the origin of the Bhāgavata religion are closely associated with sun worship.[98] According to the *Māhābhārata* (*Nārāyanīya* section) the Bhāgavata religion was revealed by Bhagavat himself to Nārada and Nārada taught it to others including the sun, who in his turn communicated it to mankind; here "sun" evidently stands for the adherents of the solar cult or perhaps members of the "solar" or Mānava-Aikshvāku ruling class. The most worshipped of the Bhāgavata or Vaishṇava incarnations is Rāmachandra who was a member of the solar clan in ancient India. Thus we find that the element of sun worship was common to the cults of Vishṇu, Vāsudeva, and Rāma. This might have offered a footing on which the first and second and the first and third, originally different deities and cults, could have been amalgamated into one. Vāsudeva's Garuḍa and Chakra are definitely "solar" symbols, and the Besnagar inscription is a living testimony to sun worship being a chief feature of Bhāgavatism or Vaishṇavism.

It will not be out of place to say that one of the chief contributions of Bhāgavatism or Vaishṇavism is the reconciliation of two traditionally opposed ideological camps, the worshippers of the Nāgas and Garuḍa. To the Nāga worshippers, the earth itself is the divinity, the mysterious and fertile earth which is supported by Nāga Śesha and which draws its sustenance and fecundity from the waters of the ocean. The worshippers of

---

solar. In some sense or other, Vishṇu is regarded as an Aditya in the *Mahābhārata* and *Purāṇas* also, Muir, *op. cit.*, Vol. 4, p. 105.

[95]Wilson's introduction to the English Translation of the *Rigveda*, Vol. 1, p. 53.

[96]Barnett, *Hindu Gods and Heroes*, p. 89.

[97]R. P.Chanda, *The Indo-Aryan Races*, pp. 102 and 103.

[98]*Indian Antiquary*, 1908, pp. 253-4.

Garuḍa are evidently the worshippers of the sun shining high up in the sky. The difference is between the ethereal and the earthly. Vishṇuism closes the difference as is evident from various mythological stories, one being that of the Ananta-śayana of Vishṇu on the waters of the sea.

One of the chief features of the Bhāgavata or the Pañcharātra cult is the worship of the four Vyūhas,[99] Vāsudeva and his several forms, viz. Saṁkarshaṇa, Pradyumna and Aniruddha (elder brother, eldest son and eldest grandson respectively of Krishṇa-Vāsudeva, according to the genealogies in the epics and the *Purāṇas)*. It is taught in detail in the *Nārāyaṇīya* section of the *Mahābhārata.* It is somewhat difficult to set forth the dogma clearly from the rather incoherent and clumsy account in the epic with its complicated phraseology. The main outlines are as follows. Vāsudeva who is Nārāyaṇa or Vishṇu, is identified with the supreme being described as Purusha, Parmātman, Īśvara, or Kshetrajña. That Being, dividing himself, became four persons by successive production. From him who is the summit of all existence, sprang Saṁkarshaṇa from whom came Pradyumna from whom issued Aniruddha. Saṁkarshaṇa is identified with *Jīva* (the living soul), Pradyumna with *Manas* (intelligence) and Aniruddha with *Ahaṅkāra* (egotism or consciousness). The Pañcharātra teaches a chain of emanations as it were. Each emanation except the first became a flame proceeding from another flame.[100]

The date of the *Nārāyaṇīya* section is uncertain. But from other literary and archaeological sources it appears that the Vyuhā system was formulated earlier than the second century B. C. One of the earliest accounts of the above doctrine is to be found in the *Brahmasūtras*[101] (ii, 2. 42-45) as explained by Śaṁkara and Rāmānuja. It is difficult to ascertain the time when the *Brahmasūtras* were written but it will not be far from

[99]For an elaborate discussion of the Vyūha cult see "Early Vishṇuism and Nārāyaṇa worship," *Indian Historical Quarterly*, 1932, Vol. VIII, No. 1. p. 64 ff; "Elements of Hindu Iconography," Vol. 1, p. 234 ff; and *Indian Antiquary*, 1908, p. 261.

[100]Schrader's Introduction to the *Pancharātra and Ahir Budhnya Saṁhitā*, p. 35.

[101]*Utpatyasambhavāt, nacha kartuḥ kāraṇaṁ, vijñānādibhāve vā tatpratishedhāḥ, vipratishedhāchcha.*

the truth to suppose that it was written somewhere near the second century B. C.[102] Patanjali mentions not only Rāma-Keśava but also "Janārdana" with himself as the fourth *(Janardanastvātma chaturtha eva*[103] which indicates probably the four mūrtis of Vāsudeva or Nārāyaṇa. The worship of Saṁkarshaṇa and Vāsudeva are referred to in the inscriptions noted above. D.R. Bhandarkar saw fragments of a column and a *makara* lying a few yards off the Garuḍa pillar of Heliodoros in Besnagar. The fragments might be parts of the Makaradhvaja as has been suggested by him. The *makara* is a symbol sacred to Pradyumna, the son of Krishṇa-Vāsudeva. As the Guruḍa column indicates the worship of Vāsudeva, so from the *makara* column the existence of a temple of Pradyumna can be reasonably inferred.

According to the Vyūha doctrines Saṁkarshaṇa has sprung from Vāsudeva and as such is mentioned after him. But it is to be noted that their position is reversed in the inscriptions noted above; Saṁkarshaṇa comes first and Vāsudeva next. This is to be expected as the inscriptions are historical documents and they could not take liberties with the genealogical tables of the Yādavas given in the epics and *Puraṇas.* This also indicates the fact that Saṁkarshaṇa was formerly a popular independent divinity. The religious leader Saṁkarshaṇa was, we know, looked up to for guidance and held in special honour by Duryodhana, while Krishṇa-Vāsudeva received the honour and devotion of the Pāṇḍavas. Kauṭilya's *Arthāśāstra*[104] speaks of people who were devotees of Saṁkarshaṇa. It says:

> Spies disguised as ascetics with shaven head or braided hair and pretending to be the worshippers of Saṁkarshaṇa may mix their sacrificial beverage with the juice of the Madana plant (and give it to the cow-herds) and carry off their cattle.

These details would indicate that while Krishṇa reformed Vishṇu-worship, Balarāma reformed Rudra-worship both taking in the elements of the ancient Nāga cult as well and that this

[102]S. N. Das Gupta, *History of Indian Philosophy*, Vol. 1, p. 418. The Vyūhas are not mentioned in the Gitā. *Mahābhāshya*, Vol. iii, p. 143.

[103]*Ātmachaturthahasya iti*, a *bahuvrīhi* compound. Kielhorn, *Vyākaraṇa.*

[104]*Arthaśāstra* of Kauṭilya (Eng. Trans.) by Shama Sastri, p. 485.

was at first (as in the earlier epic traditions) a source of the conflict between the two "Dharma-pravartaka" brothers, and their adherents among their kinsmen, the Yādavas as also amongest the allied Kauravas and Paṇḍavas. Thus it appears that side by side with the growth of the Pañcharātra cult, Saṁkarshaṇa and Vāsudeva were also in other circles looked upon as divine personalities of equal independent status, this latter phase in fact is the more natural, since the basic fact of the Bhāgavata religion is the hero worship of the brothers Saṁkarshaṇa and Krishṇa-Vāsudeva among the Vrishṇis and Yādavas. The historical and older traditions lingered for some time even after the worship of Saṁkarshaṇa merged into the larger sphere of the Krishṇa-Vāsudeva worship and the Vyūha system describing Vāsudeva as the supreme self come into being.

4. The Nāga Cult

Neo-Brahmanism has absorbed many indigenous cults and beliefs of which the worship of the Nāga (serpent) deserves special mention.

Animal worship is very common in the religious history of the ancient world. One of the earliest stages of the growth of religious ideas and cults was the stage when human beings conceived of the animal world as superior to them. This was due to the obvious deficiency of human beings in the earliest stages of civilization. Men not equipped with scientific knowledge were weaker than the animal world and attributed the spirit of the divine to it, giving rise to various forms of animal worship. Of all the forms of animal worship the worship of serpents became most popular throughout the length and breadth of the ancient world. The wide diffusion of serpent worship or the Nāga cult is explicable by the fact that serpents occur in every part of the world, and are also the uncanniest of all animals. They naturally became the appropriate symbol for the early people to express their ideas of divinity. Fergusson, who has brought together in his *Tree and Serpent Worship* a large array of facts showing the extraordinary range of serpent worship, remarks:

> There are few things which at first sight appear to us at the present day so strange or less easy to account for than the worship which was once so generally offered to the serpent god. If not the oldest, it ranks at least among the earliest forms through which the human intellect sought to propitiate the unknown powers. Traces of its existence are found not only in every country of the world, but before the new was discovered by us, the same strange idolatry had long prevailed

there, and even now the worship of the serpent is found lurking in out of the way corners of the globe.[1]

So far as the early history of serpent worship in India is concerned, it may be said that it was prevalent originally perhaps among the pre-Aryan people of Indian and it came to be associated also with Aryanism as early as the Vedic *Saṁhitās*.

The earliest representation of the Nāga occurs on the faience seals of Mohenjodaro. It appears there in half-human and half-animal form as suppliants to a deity. In this connection, Marshall remarks that the cobra appears to be distinct from the kneeling suppliant, but the details being blurred, it may be that "the tail of the cobra is intended to be looped round and joined to the feet of the suppliant...and it seems probable that the suppliant in this case is meant to be a nāga".[2] It may be true that the Mohenjodaro Nāga appears as a devotee and not as a deity. But the introduction of a Nāga in the role of a suppliant is in itself a significant fact. It shows that as early as the Mohenjodaro civilization snakes came to be associated with the religious beliefs of the peole.

In the *Rigveda Saṁhitā* the serpent appears sometimes as a demoniacal creature and sometimes as a divine being. Ahi-Vritra was a powerful demon, the foe of Indra. Indra slew this demon and recieved the appellation of Vritrahan.[3] The serpent, however, appears also in the role of a divine being as Ahibudhnya in the *Rigveda Saṁhitā*.[4] The Ahibudhnya represents probably the beneficial side of the character of Ahi-Vritra. It can perhaps be concluded that the conflict between the original settlers of India,

[1]Though the Nāga cult was diffused all over the world, in no other country, however, was it more widely distributed or developed in more varied and interesting forms than in India. It is even now prevalent in India. See Fergusson, *Tree and Serpent Worship*, *Introduction*, p. 1; *Encyclopaedia of Religion and Ethics*, Vol. XI, pp.411–12; Crooke, *Popular Religion and Folklore in Northern India*, p. 11 ff; *Gazetteer of South Arcot District*, 1906, 1. 102.

[2]*Mohenjodaro and the Indus Civilization*, Vol. 1, p. 68, pls. cxvi, 29; cxviii, 11.

[3]*Indra prehi purastvam viśvasyesān ojasā Vritrāṇi Vritrahan jahi* (*Rigveda*, 8. 17. 9).

[4]Hopkins, *The Religions of India*, p. 94; *Naighaṇṭuka*, 5.4; Macdonell, *Vedic Mythology*, p. 153.

whose religion was the worship of Nāgas, and the Aryans whose religious ideas and traditions were different from those of the former had been reconciled. The Ahi-Vritra is the Aryan attitude but the Ahibudhnya seems to have been the indigenous attitude and this was accepted by the Aryans as early as the Rigvedic times.

As Vogel and several other scholars have already pointed out, the *Yajurveda* the *Atharvaveda*, the *Grihya-sūtras* and the epics and the *Purāṇas* contain many passages paying homage to serpents.

The *Maitrāyaṇī Saṁhitā* (ii, 7. 15) states :

Homage be to the snakes which so ever move along the earth, which are in the sky and in heaven; homage be to those snakes which are the arrows of sorcerers and of tree-spirits which lie in holes; homage be to those snakes which are in the brightness of heaven, which are in the rays of the sun, which have made their abodes in the waters, homage be to to those snakes.

The *Atharva Veda* (vi, 56. 1 ff.) says :

Let not the snakes, 0 gods, slay us with our offspring, with our men [*purusha*], what is shut together, may it not unclose; homage be to the god-people....[5] Homage be to Asita, homage to Tiraśchirāja, homage to Svaja [and] Babhru, homage to the god-people.... I smite thy teeth together with tooth, thy [two] jaws together with jaw, thy tongue together with thy tongue, thy mouth, 0 snake, with mouth.[6]

In the above passages quoted from the *Atharva Veda* we find two different sentiments. Certain snakes have been addressed as

[5]Whitney's translation of the *Atharva Veda*, *Harvard Oriental Series*, Vol. 7, first half, p. 323; *Māno devā Ahirvadhitā satokān sahapurushān*/ *Saṁyatam na vispard vyāttam na sam yamannamo devajanebhyaḥ*// *Atharva Veda*, Vol. II, p. 114, Ed. by Sankar Pandurang Pandit.

[6]*Ibid.*, p. 323; *Namostvasitāya namastiraśchirājaye*/*Svajāya babhrave namo namo devajanebhyaḥ*. *Atharva Veda*, Vol. 11, p. 114, ed. by Sankar Pandurang Pandit. *Samtehanmi datā dataḥ samu te hanvāhanu sam te jihvāṁ sambāsnahi āsyam*, *Atharva Veda*, Vol. II, p. 114, edited by Sankar Pandurang Pandit.

devajana which leaves hardly any doubt that they were looked upon as divine beings. On the other hand, the author of the hymn has expressed a desire for their destruction. The two aspects of propitiation and extermination were celebrated simultaneously. This provides us with a clue as to the origin of snake worship. Snake worship, as is well known, grew more from fear than any other cause.

The *Atharva Veda* (Chapter III, 27) associates the serpents with the Vedic divinities as the protectors of the quarters.[7] The Buddhist text, the *Lalitavistara*, includes some well known Nāga kings among the Lokapālas.[8]

Snake worship is varied and complicated in character. Barth observes:

> ...the serpent religions of India form a complex whole and as such is not accounted for viewing it as a simple worship of deprecation. We can distinguish in it: (*i*) the direct adoration of the animal, the most formidable and mysterious of all the enemies of men; (*ii*) worship of the deities of the waters, springs, and rivers, symbolized by the waving form of the serpent; (*iii*) conceptions of the same kind as that of Vedic Ahi and connected clearly with the great myth of the storm and the struggle of light with darkness.[9]

The *Grihya-sūtras* prescribe many rites pertaining to snake worship. They have a two-fold purpose, i. e. honouring and warding off snakes. The *Āśvalāyana Grihya-sūtra* (II, 1. 9) states that the sacrificer should go out to the east, pour water in the ground on a clear spot and offer sacrifice with the formula :

> To the divine hosts of the serpents, svāhā, the serpents which are terrestrial, which are aerial, which are celestial, which dwell in the direction [of the horizon], to them, I have brought

[7]Cf. Whitney's translation of the *Atharva Veda*, Harvard Oriental Series, Vol. 7, p. 133.

[8]*Lalitavistara* (R. L. Mitra's edition), Ch. XXIV, p. 502, *Bibliotheca Indica*, New Series, No. 443.

[9]Augustus Barth, *Religions of India*, p. 166 ff.

the *bali* [sacrificial offerings], to them I give over these *bali.*[10]

Further, it is stated in II. 1.14 of the same text that the sacrificer should offer the *bali* to the serpents in the evening and in the morning till the *pratyavarohaṇa*[11] with the formula, "To the divine hosts of serpents, svāhā."[12] The *Āśvalāyana Grihya-sūtra* (IV, 8.27) says that to gratify the snake the sacrificer should offer them the blood of the sacrificial animal with the formula: "Hissing ones, noisy ones, searching ones, serpents, what here belongs to you, take that."[13] The *Pāraskara Grihya-sūtra* (II. 14, 9) prescribes sacrificial rites to the serpents.[14] All this shows that Nāga worship became part and parcel of the Aryan religion during the *Sūtra* period (*c.* 600-400 B. C.).

The epics throw considerable light on the origin of the Nāgas,[15] their physical features, magic power and sanctity. Both the aspects, viz. the dreadful nature and the divine origin of the Nāgas are emphasized there. Ordinarily, they are prone to anger and are venomous. But they are descibed also as guardians of riches, and the bestowers of health, longevity and offsprings. They are possessed of magic power and they can assume any form they like. Their general abode is in the waters or below the earth in the nether region.

Regarding the hostilities between the Nāga and others there are many stories in the epic-literature. It is well known how Parikshit was killed by the Nāga Takshaka. Janamejaya, to avenge the death of his father, started the snake-killing sacrifice. The Nāga race was saved only by the intervention of

[10] *Āśvālāyana Grihya-Sūtra, Sacred Books of the East*, Vol. XXIX, p. 202.

[11] The *Pratyavarohaṇa* (i. e. the ceremony of redescent) is performed on the full moon of Mārg Śīrsha, on the 14th tithi.

[12] *Ibid., Āśvalāyana Grihya-Sūtra.*

[13] *Ibid.*, p. 257.

[14] Pāraskara *Grihya-Sūtra, Sacred Books of the East,* Vol. XXIX, p. 328.

[15] In the epics, the snakes are described as of divine origin, *Rāmāyaṇa*, III, 14, 28, *Mahābhāratā,* 1.66.70. The general abode of these divine serpents is below the earth, where usually is found Śesha, the Nāga of a thousand mouths who supports the earth from below (*Mahābhārata*, V, 103, 2 ff, VII, 94, 98). It is the endless serpent Ananta lying on the waters, a creation of Vishṇu's illusion, Udakeyśaya (lying on the waters) like Vishṇu himself as Nārāyaṇa, *Rāmāyaṇa,* VII, 104, 5.

Āstīka, the son of sage Jaratkārau, sister of the Nāga king Vāsuki. It appears that there were long-continued hostilities between the Nāgas and the Pāndavas though in the *Mahābhārata* the latter are described as the grandsons of the grandson of the Nāga Āryaka. Krishṇa and Arjuna helped the fire god in destroying the Khāṇḍava forest, which was the abode of the Nāga Takshaka and his son, Aśvasena. It is quite possible that in having helped Agni in the work of destroying the Khāṇḍava forest Arjuna incurred the wrath of Takshaka and his son Aśvasena. In order to avenge Arjuna, Aśvasena magically entered the quiver of Karṇa in the shape of an arrow and intended to kill Arjuna.[16] This also explains why Takshaka, of all the Nāgas, offered to bite Parikshit to death to fulfil the curse of the Brahmin Śriṅgin.

But not all the Nāgas were cruel and dangerous. Both in the *Rāmāyaṇa* and the *Mahābhārāta*, the sanctity of the Nāgas has been emphasized inasmuch as they are attributed a divine origin. This is in continuty of the tradition in the *Athārva Veda* which calls the Nagas "devajanas".

Among the virtuous Nāgas, the names of Śesha, Padmanābha, and several others are prominent. Nāga Śesha, the eldest of the thousand sons of Kadru and Kāśyapa, separated from his brothers and practised self-control and austerities. Pleased with his piety, Brahmā granted him the boon that he would protect the earth from below.[17] In Vaishṇava mythology he is held in very high esteem. He is a creation of Vishṇu's illusion, Udakeśaya lying on the water, like Vishṇu himself as Nārāyaṇa. There is no more common representation of Vishṇu than as reposing on the Śesha, the celestial seven-headed snake contemplating the creation of the world. It was by his assistance that the ocean was churned and *amrita* was produced. Balarāma, the elder brother of Krishṇa, is described as an incarnation of Nāga Śesha. Nāga Śesha is regarded as one of the Prajāpatis in the *Rāmāyaṇa*.[18] He is also called a *deva* with a thousand hands, who

[16] *The Mahābhārata, Karṇaparva.*
[17] *Ibid., Ādiparva,* XXXVI.
[18] *Rāmāyaṇa,* III, 14, 7.

encircles the world and eventually curls himself over Vishṇu, one of the titles being Dadhikarṇa.[19]

The story of Nāga Padmanābha is highly interesting. As described in the *Shāntiparva* of the *Mahābhārata*,[20] he lived in the Naimisha forest in the bank of the river Gomati. He was fond of studies, accomplished on austerities and abstemiousness, of superior moral conduct, was pious in his sacrificial work, a master of liberality, forbearing, of excellent demeanour and good character, truthful, free from envy, gifted with complete self-control, subsisted on leavings, affable in speech, gracious, honest and of great eminence, mindful of benefits, not quarrelsome, rejoicing in the welfare of other beings, and born of a race as pure as the waves of the Gaṅgā. He drew the one-wheeled chariot of the sun god. As the story goes, a Brahmin called Dharma-raya, disgusted with wordly affairs, came to Padmnābha for wise counsel. The Nāga dwelt on the virtues of asceticism which removed all doubts from the mind of the Brahmin. The association of Nāga Śesha with Vishṇu as Anantaśayana and of Padmanābha with the sun seems to be somewhat anachronistic in view of the fact that the vehicle of Vishṇu is Garuḍa, the traditional enemy of the Nāga and the charioteer of the sun is Aruṇa, the deformed halfbrother of Garuḍa.

This shows the synthesizing power of the Brahmanical cults. As we shall see later, Buddhism also absorbed the Nāga cult. All this shows one interesting trend. In the early stage, the Nāga cult was in opposition to other cults, but as a result of social changes the elements of the Nāga cult were absorbed and introduced in other pantheons. In the *Rigveda*, Ahi-Vritra was treated as an enemy of Indra, but gradually it was transformed into Ahibudhnya. The *Mahābhārata* and the *Purāṇas* present a struggle between Krishṇa and Kāliya; Kāliya was subdued, and later on both Krishṇa and Balarāma were treated as Nāga divinities (Keśava Anantaśayana and Balarāma as an incarnation of Śesha).

The Jātakas also refer to the prevalence of snake-worship among the people. In the Champeyya Jatāka we read that as the

[19] *Ibid.*, IV. 40, 49.

[20] J. P. Vogel, *Indian Serpent Lore* (London, 1926), p. 85.

Nāga king Champaka took up his abode on an anthill to keep his vows of the Sabbath day, the passers-by worshipped him and craved for sons through his aid. This practice survives still in many parts of our country. In the Tamil country the childless wives take a vow[21] to install a serpent if they are blessed with offspring.

Apart from the indigenous literary sources, there are notices by foreign writers with regard to the prevalence of serpent worship in India. Aelian writers:

> When Alexander was assaulting some of the cities in India and capturing others, he found in many of them, besides other animals, a snake which the Indians, regarding as sacred, kept in caves and worshipped with much devotion. The Indians accordingly, with every kind of entreaty, implored Alexander to let no one molest the animal and he consented to this.[22]

The above passage is a very important testimony to the prevalence of Nāga worship in India in the fourth century B. C. The Nāga association during this period seems to have been popular also in folk art, as is evident from a number of terracota figurines of the Mauryan period which are preserved in the Patna Museum, Patna.[23] The figurines with Nāga hoods (which have been distinguishing features of Nāga divinities and chiefs and emblems of cult gods like Śiva and Vishṇu) show that the Nāga cult must have been an important element in the

[21]"The ceremony consists in having a figure of a serpent cut in a stone slab placing it in a well for six months, giving it life (prāṇaprashṭhāi) by reciting mantras and performing other ceremonies over it and then setting it up under a pipal tree (Ficus Religiosa), which has been married to Mangosa (Melica Azadi- rachta). Worship consists mainly in going round the tree 108 times. It is then performed for the next forty-five days. Similar circumambulations will also bring good luck in a general way substantially." See the *Gazetteer of South Arcot District*, 1906, i. 102.

[22]M'crindle, Aelian, Ch. XXI; *Ancient India as Described in Classical Literature*, p. 145 ff.

[23]*Archaeological Survey of India, Annual Reports, 1926-27*, p. 139, pl. XXXI; *Pathak Commemoration Volume*, p. 255 ff.

religious history of the period. Further, it may be noted that the snake is a frequent device on punch-marked coins[24] (600 B. C. to 300 B. C.).

There are tangible epigraphic records regarding serpent worship during the early historical period (185 B. C. to A. D. 319). Bühler describes a Kharoshṭhī inscription in the *Indian Antiquary* (Vol. XXV, pp. 141-2) which records[25] that a tank was caused to be made for the worship of all the Nāgas in the year 113 in the bright half of the month of Śrāvaṇa by Thera Nora, son of Dati. The scripts of the inscription agree closely with those of the Taxila copper plate of Patika and of Soḍāsa's inscriptions on the Mathura Lion Capital. Hence the present inscription can be assigned on palaeographical grounds to the first century A.D. Thera Nora, as the name shows, must have been a Greek living in the Gandhāra region where the inscription has been found. The Gandhāra region was inhabited during the early centuries of the Christian era by a large number of Greeks and Bactrian Greeks, some of whom, we know, adopted and patronised Buddhism. The term "Thera" denotes perhaps "Sthavira," a well known Buddhist title. If this is accepted we find here an important instance of the close association of Buddhism with the Nāga cult. Buddhism, as we shall see presently, borrowed from and absorbed many Nāga religious beliefs and as such it was very popular among those whose original cult was Nāga worship.

The Nāgas have been associated with water in various places in Indian literature and art. The Vedic Ahibudhnya, as we have noted above, is the dragon of the "fathomless deep". Thə Anantaśayana of Vishṇu on the coils of the Nāga Ananta in the midst of water points perhaps to the same fact and is the continuation of the tradition of Vedic Ahibudhnya. The association of Nāgas with water is so close that certain scholars have taken them to be water spirits. So the dedication of a tank for snake worship need not cause surprise to us. It is in keeping with the

[24] Allan, *Catalogue of Indians Coins, Ancient India*, p. 299.

[25] *Indian Antiquary*, Vol. XXV, pp. 141-142.

L. 1. *Datia putreṇa Thaī Norena puka-*

L. 2. *ra [ṇi?] Karavita savrasapaṇapuyae*

L. 3. *Vashra Icxiii Śrāvaṇa s[u]dha.*

traditions regarding the habitations of the Nāgas in rivers, lakes and pools.[26]

Mathura has been an important centre of the Nāga cult since early times. The victory of Krishṇa over Kāliya, the story of the incarnation of Śesha as Balarāma, elder brother of Krishṇa and the observance of Nāga rituals by certain prominent inhabitants of Mathura-Vrindavana region seem to bear testimony to the above fact.[27]

Mathura has yielded a large number of Nāga inscriptions and sculptures which can be ascribed with certainty to the early centuries of the Christian era. One of the earliest Nāga inscriptions in this connection is that described by Y. R. Gupte.[28] It is engraved on the lower end of a Nāga image discovered near the village of Bhadal, about six miles from Mathura. The author collects from local traditions that the spot was visited by barren women who made vows to the deities. When they got sons, they came to the place to perform the tonsuring ceremony. The Nāga is represented standing with two Nāgās (female serpents) on either side.

It has a canopy of seven hoods with forked tongues. On the pedestal there are twelve human figures, five males, five female and two boys. They are evidently worshippers. The inscription in question is dated in the year eight of the Kushāṇa era and it records the erection of a tank and a garden in honour of Svāmi Nāga.

[26]Vogel, *op. cit.*, pp. 3 ff. As Bühler remarks, every tank in Kashmir is known by the name nāga, and every small one is called nāgī. The guardian deity of each tank is a nāga; the Vular lake is said to be the residence of the serpent Padma (*Iṇdian Antiquary*, Vol. XXV, p. 141 ff). See also the Mathura inscriptions, *Epigraphia Indica*, Vol. XVII, p. 10 ff. which records the dedication of a tank and garden in honour of Bhagavat Svāmī Nāga.

[27]In the *Harivaṁsa*, *Adhyāys*, XI, XII, it is stated that Nāga Kāliya lived in a pool (lake Kālia) near the river Yamunā, and the neighbouring forests were infested by various nāgas. Kāliya poisoned the water of the pool and Krishṇa became determined to chastise the nāga who rendered the water of the pool undrinkable. Krishna entered into the pool, danced on the hoods of the Kāliyanāga and burst assunder the snake's coils which fettered him. Kāliya, thus tamed, sought Krishṇa's mercy. Krishṇa spared his life but banished him with his kinsmen from the lake.

[28]*Epigraphia Indica*, Vol. XVII, p. 10 f.

Bühler has described in the *Epigraphia Indica* (Vol. 1, p. 390), an important Nāga[29] inscription which records that a stone slab was set up in the place sacred to the Lord of Nāgas, Dadhikarṇa, in the year 26 on the fifth day of the third month of the rainy season by the boys "chief among whom were Nandibala... the sons of the actors of Mathura, who are being praised as Chhandaka brothers". In the inscription, Dadhikarṇa is called Nāgendra and Bhagavat (this title has been used also before the name of Svāmi Nāga noted before). The present inscription states clearly that Nāgendra Dadhikarṇa had a sanctuary set up for himself. The epigraph is written in the Brāhmī scripts of the Kushāṇa period and the slab on which it is recorded was found at the Jamalpur Mound, located about two miles south of the city of Mathura. This was the site where once stood, as Vogel remarks, the Vihāra of Huvishka.[30]

In this connection there is another inscription engraved on a pillar base which might have belonged to Huvishka's Vihāra noted above. It records the gift of one Devilla,[31] the servant of the shrine of Dadhikarṇa. From this inscription it is also clear that there was a shrine or temple for the Nāga deity Dadhikarṇa in Mathura. That Dadhikarṇa was a very prominent Nāga is proved by his name being included in the list of the Nāgas in Hemachandra's own commentary on the *Abhidhāna Chintamaṇi*.[32] He is invoked in the snake spell, the daily prayer, recited by Baladeva and after him by Krishṇa.[33] It appears that the worship of the Nāga was a part of the Bhāgavata ritual practised in Mathura.

Vogel has drawn attention to another very relevant story or instance of a close association between the Nāga and Bhāgavata cults. This is the Puranic story of Akrūra's paying homage to the lord of the Nāgas (Ananta).[34] Deputed by Kaṁśa, Akrūra came to collect from Vraja taxes due to him. Krishṇa and

[29] *Archaeological Survey of India, Annual Report, 1908-1909*, p. 159.
[30] *Ibid.*, p. 160.
[31] *Epigraphia Indica*, Vol. I, p. 381.
[32] *Ibid.*, 160.
[33] *Ibid.*
[34] *Harivaṁśa, Adhyāyā*, XXVII, 5, 36-61.

Baladeva accompanied Akrūra on his journey back to Mathura. On the way, Akrūra got down from the car to the pool of the river Yamunā to offer his worship to the lord of the Nāgas, thousand-headed Ananta having a plough in one hand and his frame supported by a mace.[35] When he dived into the water he saw Krishṇa, dark like a thunder cloud and wearing a yellow robe, seated on the lap of Ananta. His (Krishṇa's) breast was adorned with the Śrīvatsa. Akrūra raised his head and found Krishṇa and Baladeva seated on the chariot as before. He dived again and found them in their divine form.

Further, it is a well known story that when Vāsudeva was carrying the new-born Krishṇa to Gokula,[36] it rained and thundered and Nāgaśesha helped Vasudeva to cross the river Yamunā by warding off the water with his hood.

The above legends may be regarded as containing reference to two significant facts: the one is that by this time the enmity between the Nāga and Bhāgavata worshippers as represented by Krishṇa's fight with Kāliya was over, and the other is that certain elements of Nāga-worship were accepted by the Bhāgavatas inasmuch as Baladeva came to be regarded as an incarnation of Nāga Śesha. Again, Mathura has yielded another very interesting inscription engraved on a Nāga image of Huvishka's time. The image in question was discovered at the village of Chhargaon, 5 miles south of Mathura.[37] The Nāga is represented standing "with his right arm raised over his head as if ready to strike". The left hand is damaged, which probably held a cup in front of the shoulder.[38] The head

[35] *Tasya madhye sahasrāsyam hemtālochchhrita dhvajam/lāṅgala sakta-hastāgraṁ mushlopasritodaram/Harivamsa*, XXVI, 5, 49. In sculptures Baladeva appears with a canopy of serpent hoods as a snake deity and he holds a club (*mushala*) in the right hand and plough in the left, *A Short Guide Book to the Archaeological Section of the Provincial Museum, Lucknow*, by V. S. Agrawala, p. 14; *Archaeological Survey of India, Annual Reports*, 1918-19, pl. xiii *a*.

[36] *Vavarsha parjanya upaṁśu garjitaṁ Sesho navagādvāri nivārayan phaṇāiḥ, Bhāgavata Purāṇa*, X. 3. 49. Dayaram Sahni has recognized the representation of this legend in a Mathura sculpture of the first or second century A. D., *Archaeological Survey of India, Annual Reports, 1925-26*, pp. 183-4.

[37] *Archaeological Survey of India, Annual Reports, 1908-1909*, p. 160.

[38] *Ibid.*

is surrounded by a seven-headed snakehood. The inscription says that the image was set up at a water tank during the 40th year of the reign of Huvishka. It concluded with the prayer, "May the Nāga deity be pleased" (*Priyyati Bhagavā Nāgo*).

In the neighbourhood of Mathura have been discovered a few more Nāga images similar to that of the Chhargaon one. Growse got one such in the Sadabad Tahsil, characterised by a canopy of seven hoods, each hood with a forked tongue.[39] Not far from the village of Itauti, eight miles east from Mathura, Vogel discovered the upper portion of a Nāgī figure about four feet high. This image was known locally by the name of Bhai and placed in the tank of Bai-ka-pokhra. This is perhaps a part of the Nāga image with an inscription of the Kushāṇa period recording the dedication of tank and a garden to the holy Svāmi Nāga published by Y.R. Gupte (*Epigraphia Indica*, Vol. xvii) as noted before.

A few more relics of Nāga worship, though of a little later date, are also interesting. One is a sculptural fragment of the hind portion of a coiled-up snake.[40] The missing portion, as Vogel states, must have been a human bust with a snake hood. The fragment in question contains a short inscription in Sanskrit "*Srī Aśvadevasya Bhuvana-Tripravaraka-putrasaya*". The inscription on palaeographical grounds may be assigned to the fourth century A.D. Tripravaraka is an orthodox Brahmanical designation. The gift of a Nāga image by one belonging to a Vedic Pravara denotes that Nāga worship was intimately associated with orthodox Brahmanism.

Another Nāga statute of the Gupta period is housed in the Lucknow Museum. The arms of the figure are broken, but it is, as usual, accompanied by seven snake hoods. There is a Nāgī on its right-hand side and on the left are two kneeling figures with hands joined in adoration. According to Vogel, it may represent the image of Dadhikarṇa.[41]

[39]*Journal of the Asiatic Society of Bengal*, 1875, Vol. XLIV, pp. 214-15. According to Growse this figure represents Balarāma. Another image of the same type, but much defaced, was found in the village of Khanni, six miles west of Mathura on the way to Govardhana. *Archaeological Survey of India, Annual Reports, 1908-1909*, p. 161.

[40]*Ibid.*

[41]*Ibid.*, p. 163.

Some of the ancient Nāga images are known at Mathura under the name Bai Dauji, i.e. Baladeva. From this it appears that the followers of the Bhāgavata cult tried to spread their religion among the Nāga worshippers, and this was done by the device of describing Baladeva, elder brother of Krishṇa, the founder of the Bhāgavata cult, as an incarnation of Śesha. The inscriptions discussed above prove the popularity of the Nāga cult in Mathura in the early centuries and subsequent times. Similarly, there is archaeological evidence of the popularity of the Nāga cult in other parts of India too. The excavations at Rajgir in the year 1935-36 brought to light some fragments of sculptured stones forming parts of the back portion of a sculpture with two Nāga figures which were unearthed in earlier years. Joined together, they constitute the following panels of sculptures.

(*i*) The lowest panel represents eight Nāga figures standing side by side with an indistinct inscription on the pedestal. (*ii*) Above it is a decorated surface with one niche on each of the two extremities, the left one containing a Nāgi sitting on a cushion in the Bhadrāsana, with her feet resting on a stone pedestal which bears an inscription reading 'Bhaginī Sumāgadhī'. The figure in the right niche is broken and only the canopy of the serpent hood is visible. (*iii*) On the top of these there was another panel of standing figures, only the feet of which have now survived, with an inscription below which suggests that a certain king pleased Maṇi Nāga.[42]

These inscriptions belong to the Kushāṇa period and the sculptures are on Mathura sandstone. Two things are thus clear—firstly, the diffusion of Mathura sculptures to as far as Rajgir in the east, and secondly, the prevalence of Nāga worship in Rajgir, which is also corroborated by literary sources. Budhaghosha speaks of the existence of a beautiful and spacious Nāga world under the Vaibhara mountain. The *Mahābhārata* refers to the temples of two pannāgas or Nāgas, namely Maṇināga and Svastika in Girivraja (*Sabhā-parva* of the *Mahābhārata,* Ch.21, v.9). The Maniarmath is perhaps the site of the temple of Maṇināga mentioned in the epic.[43]

[42]*Archaeological Survey of India, Annual Reports, 1936-37*, p. 46.

[43]Maniarmath is perhaps the site of the temple of Maṇināga mentioned in the epic (*Memoirs, Archaeological Survey of India,* No. 58, pp. 33 ff).

The Nāgas figure prominently also in Buddhist literature and art. In the Brahmanical legends and art of both pre-Buddhistic and post-Buddhistic periods the Nāgas have been treated as independent deities, while in the Buddhistic treatment they are semi-divine spirits or real human beings, who are shown no doubt, sometimes as fierce and rebellious, but who bow ultimately to the supreme, regulative, and persuasive power of Buddha. Vogel, in his *Serpent Lore in India* has drawn attention to most of the Nāga legends in Buddhist works and their representation in art.

One of the greatest miracles of Buddha was the subduing of the Nāga in the fire altar of the Kāśyapa (Jaṭila) brothers. The story goes that after preaching the first sermon at Sārnāth, Buddha came to Gayā (Uruvila) and met the Kāśyapa brother, on whose fire altar[44] was a Nāga divinity. As soon as Buddha entered the fire altar, the Nāga became furious and began to pour out venom. But Buddha subdued him[45] by his own tejas

Further, it may be stated that excavation exposed several brick altars or platforms round the main shrine of the Maniarmath. On and near one such altar were found scattered a large number of pottery jars, some of them being four feet in height. A peculiar feature of these jars is that they have struck on, or in some cases rivetted into their surfaces a large number of spouts some of which are curiously shaped as serpent hoods, goblins and animal figures. It is interesting to note that similar jars with spouts are still used in Bengal in the worship of serpents under the name Manasa. *A Guide to Rajgir* by H. Kuraishi and A. Ghosh, pp. 24 and 45 and pls. IV and V.

[44]The fire-cult is a very ancient institution and it has been put to different uses. Agni as the sacrificial altar is a link with all divinities. As subsequently various cults arose their divinities were sought to be identified with Agni. Since Nāgas are often as lustrous as fire, it is natural that they were associated with the fire cult.

[45]There is one trend here which is noticeable. In the early stage the Nāga cult was in opposition to other cults, but as a result of social changes it was introduced and absorbed in other religious pantheons. In the *Rigveda*, Ahi-Virtra has been treated as an enemy of Indra but gradually it was transformed into Ahibudhnya, and the *Puranas* and the *Mahābhārata* present a struggle between Krishṇa and Kāliya; but Kāliya was subdued and a compromise was effected between the Nāga and Bhāgavata cults later on, resulting in both Krishṇā and Balarāma being regarded as Nāga divinities (Kesava Ananta-śayana and Avatara of Śeshanāga in Balarāma). Similarily the Nāgas were opposed at first to Buddha's teachings but after Buddha's victory over the Nāga of Uruvilva the Kāśyapa brothers were converted to Buddhism.

and put the Nāga in his alms bowl. This legend has found expression[46] in the art of Sanchi, Amaravati and Gandhara. It is to be noted that since one branch of the Kāśyapas was Kādravas or Nāgas, Nāga worship was traditional with certain Kāśyapa Brāhmaṇas. The other branches of Kāśyapas, like the Mānavas or Īkshvākus (to which group the Śākyas belong) were thus cognate to Kādrava Kāśyapas. This explains the readiness with which Buddhism approaches and absorbs the Nāga cult. In Sanchi, the Buddha's presence has been indicated, as is usual with early art, by a stone seat in the altar hall. The five-headed hood of the Nāga can be seen clearly over the seat and the Jaṭilas with matted hair and *valkala* garment represent the three Kāśyapa brothers. In the Amaravati panel illustrating the story, the presence of Buddha is indicated by a pair of footprints in the fire-hut. In Ganda sculptures anthropomorphic figures of the Buddha have been introduced and he is shown in the midst of anchorites (Kāśyapa brothers). On one fragment (No. 2345) in the Lahore Museum he is shown offering the Nāga in the alms-bowl to the eldest Kāśyapa.

The Bhārhut sculptures contain representations of several Nāgarājas. Nāgarāja Erāpatra is shown as making his way to the Buddha, seated under one of the Śirīsha trees together with his wife and daughter to pay their homage to the Buddha. The dragon chief raises his head over the water and his daughter is represented as singing and dancing in order to attract the notice of the visitors who might give information as to the whereabouts of the Master. There are two inscriptions, one recording the name of Erāptara and the other his action "Erāpatra the Dragon Chief" and "The Dragon Chief Erāpatra bows down to the divine Master."[47] On Bhārhut sculptures there is representation of another Nāgarāja, called Chakravāka.[48] He is shown standing in human form with a cobra hood near a lake in an attitude of devotion.

[46]Fergusson, *Tree and Serpent Worship* (1868-1873 editions), pls. XXXII, LXX; Grünwedel, *Buddhist Art in India*, p. 61 ff., Fig. 35; Foucher *Beginnings of Buddhist Art*, pp. 97 ff., pl., IX, 1.

[47]B. M. Barua, *Barhut*, Books I & II, p. 61.

[48]*Ibid.*, p. 62.

Thc taming and conversion of the Nāga King Apalāśla, who was a native of the Swat valley is a favourite theme with the Graeco-Buddhist and other artists of the early centuries of the Christian era. The sculptures depicting the story represent Buddha as turning towards the frightened Nāga accompanied by one or two Nāgīs. The Nāga is shown standing either at Buddha's side or rising from the water of which he is the presiding deity.[49]

The Nāgas are associated also with various events of Buddha's life. When Bodhisattva Gautama was born in the Lumbinī garden, two Nāgarājas, Nanda and Upānanda came and bathed him with two streams of hot 'and cold water. Another Nāga, Muchalinda, protected Buddha at Gaya by spreading his large hood over his head against cold winds and rains. The Nāgarāja Kālika foretold the approaching enlightenment of the Bodhisattva in a hymn of praise. Nāga Elāpatra came from Taxila to Sarnath to seek refuge with Buddha. The legend apparently records the amalgamation of the Taxila Nāga cult with the new movement, i. e. Buddhism. One of the best examples depicting the story is the panel which was excavated by Stein at Sahr-i-Bahlol and is now preserved in the Peshawar Museum. After the Nirvāṇa of the Buddha, a stūpa was built over his relics at Rāmgrāma and the stūpa was guarded by the Nāgas. In the Buddhist accounts we are told that the Devas and Nāgas also got a share of Buddha's relics (i. e. the as yet unconverted Nāga worshippers and Deva-worshippers recognized the greatness of Buddhism). There are a few interesting sculptures representing the theme. All these and several other stories have been represented elaborately in the Buddhist art of early and later periods.[50] The Nāga lore in Buddhist lore and art

[49]T. Watters, *On Yuan Chawang's Travels in India*, Vol. 1. p. 228 ff.; *Divyāvadāna* (edited by Cowell and Neil), pp. 348, 395; for the sculptural presentation of Nāga Apalāla, see *Archaeological Survey Reports, 1906-7*, p. 159, pl. IV; Hargreaves, *Hand Book of Sculptures in the Peshawar Museum*, pl. 5 a.

[50]*Lalitavistara*, ed. by R. L. Mitra, Ch. VIII; *Mahāvastu*, ed. by Senart, Vol. II, p. 23 ff.; Beal, *Buddhist Records of the Western World*, Vol. II. p. 24 ff.; *Sacred Books of the East*, Vol, XIII p. 80; *The Buddha Charita*, *Sacred Books of the East*, Vol. XLIX, p. 135 ff; Watters, *op. cit.*, Vol. II, pp. 20 ff; Fergusson, pl. XCI, 4 (1873 edition), *Archaeological Survey of*

symbolize the great achievement of Buddha in conquering the hostilities of the ancient and primitive Nāga cult and in making the great mass of the Nāga worshipper and people faithful adherents of the reformed religion, i. e. Buddhism.

As in Buddhism and Brahmanical religion, the Nāgas play a prominent part also in Jainism. A striking instance of the Nāga element in the Jaina religion is the snake emblem of Pārśvanātha, the last but one Jaina prophet and also of Supārśva (the seventh Jaina Tīrthaṅkara). It may be stated here that the colossal Jain figure of Gomatesvara [51] at Śrāvanabelgola in Mysore is represented as surrounded by ant hills from which snakes are found to emerge. An allusion is made to Pārśva's association with the snakes. One day Pārśva saw Kaṭha (an ascetic) engaged in fire penance throwing a serpent into the fire-pan. Pārśava saved the snake and it was reborn as Dharaṇa, the wealthy king of the Nāgas and Kaṭha as a result of his cruelty was born as Asura Megahmālin by name. One day while Pārśva was standing in the forest of Kuśāmbi, the serpent king Dharaṇa came in great haste to do honour to Pārśva and he spread an umbrella over his head to protect him from the sun.[52] Nāgas figure sometimes as attendants of Vardhamāna Mahāvīra[53] also. One such specimen is illustrated on a Mathura slab of the Kushāṇa period, containing the representation of Mahāvīra with lions on the pedestal. Vardhamāna is seated under a sacred tree with attendants, one of whom is a Nāga with a canopy of cobra hoods.[54] As in Buddhist sculptures, Nāgas are sometimes represented on Jaina

---

India, Annual Reports, 1906-7, pp. 152 ff., pl. Liii a; *The Catalogue of Sanchi Museum*, p. 21, No. A, 15, Pl. Viii. On a railing pillar of Barhut perserved in the Allahabad Municipal Museum there is the representation of the footprints of Buddha under the canopy of a five-headed Nāga who is called Nāga Muchilinda in the inscriptions on the pillar. The inscription reads: *Munchilindo Nāgrāja Tisiya Veṇkaṭakiya dāna* (*Journal, U. P. Historical Society*, Vol. XVIII, pls. I & II. p. 96); Burgress, *Amaravati;* pls. XXXII, 5, XXXIX, 3; Hargreaves, *op. cit*, p. 45.

[51]Edgar Thurston, *Omens and Superstitions of Southern India*, p. 135.

[52]Bloomfield, *Pārśvanāthacharita* (the life and story of the Jaina Saviour Pārśvānātha), p. 10.

[53]Smith, *Jain Stupas and Other Antiquities of Mathura*, pl. XCI, righthand figure.

[54]*Ibid.*, pl. XCI.

sculptures as worshipping the stūpas. For example, there is a Mathura panel of the Kushāṇa period containing a stūpa and four worshippers one of whom is a Nāga miden.[55]

The word "Nāga" has been used in Indian literature in more senses than one. Firstly, it refers to the ordinary and deified snakes; secondly, to the people who claimed their descent from Nāga parent or parents; and thirdly, to those who are associated with the Nāga cult. The Nāga people have played an important role in the political history of India as the Nāga cult in the religious history. The matrimonial alliances between the Nāga princesses and the members of the Aryan tribes are frequently referred to in the Brahmanical and Buddhist literature. The marriages between Arjuna and Ulūpi, between Jaratkāru the ascetic and Jaratkāru the Nāga maiden (the sister of Nāga Vāsuki) present apt instances in this regard. The five Pāṇḍava brothers are described in the *Mahābhārata*, as the grandsons of the Nāga named Āryaka. The Barhadrathas and Śiśunāgas are also supposed to be Nāga rulers. Kalhaṇa in his *Ṛajataṅgini* describes the love between the Brahmin Viśākha and Chandralekha, the fair daughter of the Nāga Susravas.[56] The Bhuridatta Jātaka describes the marriage of the Prince of Vārāṇāsi with a Nāga maiden. The girl born of this marriage was married to the serpent king Dhritarāshṭra.

According to the Rāyakota grant (ninth century A.D.) the Brahmin Aśvatthāmā (who founded the Pallava race) married a Nāga woman[57] and by her a son called Skandsishya was born. Tradition avers that the ruling line of the Kamboja country had its origin from the union of the Nāga princess Somā with the Brahmin Kauṇḍinya.[58] Ceylon also seems to have been an important centre of the Nāga race and was known as Nāgadipa for a long time.[59]

The word "Nāga" forms a part of various individuals mentioned in the inscriptions of the early centuries of the

[55]Kalhaṇa, *Rājataraṅginī*, I, pp. 201-73; Stein's trans., Vol. I, pp. 34 ff.
[56]*Epigraphia Indica*, Vol. I, p. 392.
[57]*Ibid.*, Vol. XV, p. 246.
[58]B. R. Chatterjee, *Indian Influence in Cambodia*, pp. 3 ff.
[59]*Proceedings of the Indian History Congress*, 3rd Session, p. 215; Vogel, *op. cit.*, p. 119.

Christian era. The names, like Jayanāga, Mahānagā, Nāgabahutikiya, Nāgadatta, Nāgadina, Nāgavatī, Nāgapiya, Nāgarakhita, Nāgasena, etc., are found in the Brāhmī inscriptions of the post-Mauryan period.[60]

During the first to fourth centuries a large part of South India was under the influence of the Nāga cult. Ptolemy[61] mentions the coast of Soringoi and Arouarnoi with their capitals at Orthoura and Malanga respectively. Orthoura, according to Ptolemy, was ruled over by Sornagos and Malanga by Basaronagos. D. C. Sircar holds that Soringoi represents the Chola Maṇḍala[62] and its capital Orthoura is most probably identical with Uragapura or Uraiyur (Uragapura or Uraipur means etymologically the town of the Nāgas). Arouarnoi is supposed to be identical with Kanchimandala. Sornagos is something like Sūryanāga and Basaronagos is Vajra or Varshanāga.[63] This perhaps shows the prevalence of the Nāga cult in South India during the second century A. D.

During the early centuries of the Christian era, there was a considerable Nāga influence in the Andhradeśa also. The Sātavāhanas and their successors, the Chuṭukula Śātakarṇis seem to have belonged to Nāga stock. In this connection Dr. H. C. Raychaudhuri observes :

> There is reason to believe that the Andhrabhritya or Sātavāhana kings were Brāhmaṇas with a little admixture of Nāga blood. The *Dvātriṁsatputtlikā* represents Sālivāhana (Sātavāhana) as of mixed Brāhmaṇa and Nāga origin.[64]

A chief, Śkandanāga by name, ruled in the Bellary District in the reign of Pulumāvi, the last king of the main Sātavāhana line. Nāga Mūlanikā is known to have made a gift of a Nāga, together with her son called Śivaskanda Nāgaśri.[65] Powerful Nāga

[60] *Epigraphia Indica*, Vol. X, index of personal names in Lüders *List*.

[61] M'Crindle, *Ancient India as Described by Ptolemy*, ed. by S. N. Majumdar Sastri, pp. 64-6, 184-5.

[62] *The Successors of the Sātavāhanas*, *op. cit.*, p. 148 ff.

[63] *Ibid.*

[64] *Political History of Ancient India*, 1st edition, p. 220.

[65] *The Successors of the Sātavāhanas*, *op. cit.*, p. 220.

rulers flourished in North India in the early centuries of the Christian era. The Bhāraśive Nāgas, the Nāgas of Mathura, Padmāvatī, and Vidisa regions were powerful princes and issued coins in their names. The marriage alliance between the Bhāraśive Nāgās and the Vākāṭakas was consided so important that it was recorded in all the Vākāṭaka inscriptions. The passage in which this is recorded also tells that before the marriage, the Bhāraśivas performed ten Aśvamedhas on the bank of the Ganges. Bhavanāga, whose daughter was married to Rudrasena Vākāṭaka (*c.* A. D. 340-360) must have been a very powerful king, otherwise his name would not have occurred in Vākāṭaka inscriptions.

While studying a number of Nāga coins, Dr. Altekar holds that Bhavanāga whose daughter was married to Rudrasena Vākāṭaka and who has been described as a Bhāraśiva prince was a Nāgā ruler of Padmāvatī.[66]

As far as we know, the Nāgas of Padmāvātī did not use Nāga symbols on their coins. It is probably due to the fact that with their rise to higher political power they thought it expedient not to confine themselves to the Nāga cult which concerns only a particular race. Moreover, Vaishṇavism and Śaivism had gained a wide popularity and prevalence by the time of the Bhāraśivas and Vākāṭakas, and Guptas. And we know that the Bhāraśivas and Vākātakas were ardent followers of Śaivism. Among the Nāga rulers who issued coins mention may be made of Skandanāga, Brihaspatināga, Devanāga, Prabhākaranāga and Gaṇapatināga, etc. Gaṇapatināga was a contemporary of Samudragupta. The symbols occurring on the coins are the bull, trident, wheel and peacock, etc., but the Nāga symbol noted above is conspicuous by its absence.

Now we may turn to the rulers who adopted Nāga devices on their coins. Snakes were commonly used on the reverse of the coins of Ayodhya rulers like Viśākhadeva, Dhanadeva and Naradatta[67] (second century B. C.). It is interesting to note that one of the obverse symbols on these coins is a bull. The

[66]*Journal of the Numismatic Society of India*, June 1943, Vol. V, pp. 21-7, pl. 1.

[67]Allan, *op. cit.*, pp. 131-4.

bull occurs very frequently also on the coins of Nāga rulers referred to above. This indicates the close association between the Nāgas and Śaivism. Śaivic association with the Nāgas can be traced as early as 4,500 years back. Rai Bahadur R. P. Chanda has drawn our attention to an Indus copper seal with a deity, two devotees and two Nāgas. The deity is seated in a yogi's posture and this is perhaps a figure of Śiva.[68] In the *Mahābhārata*, Śiva has the snake among other attributes. He is called a snake wearer and club bearer, etc. It to be noted that the Nāga symbol occurs on some of the Andhra coins of uncertain attribution.[69] Certain coins of the above series bear a Nandipada on the obverse and a Nāga symbol on the reverse[70] which bespeaks a close Nāga-Śaiva association.

One of the reasons for the association of serpents with Rudra-Śiva is their power of healing.[71] Fergusson remarks, "When we first meet with serpent worship either in the wilderness of Sinai, the groves of Epidaurus, or in the Sarmatian huts the serpent is always the Agathodaemou, the bringer of health and good fortune." That the idea of health was associated with the serpent is shown by "the crown formed of the asp of sacred Thermuthis, given particularly to Isis, a goddess of life and healing."[72] It is said that in return for the sweet sounding lyre, Apollo gave Hermes "the magical three-leafed rod of wealth and happiness." This rod was sometimes entwined with serpents instead of fillets. In this rod we may recognize the phallic symbol of Śiva which is also found sometimes encircled by serpents. Thus, the serpent seems to be one of the most appropriate symbols of Rudra the "healer".[73] Further, snake symbols occur on the tribal coins of the Mālavas,

[68]*Modern Review*, LII, p. 15 ff, pl. ii, Fig. a.

[69]Rapson, *Catalogue of Coins, Andhras, Western Kshatrapas, Traikutakas and Bodhi Dynasty*, p. 53.

[70]*Ibid.*

[71]Śiva is regarded in Vedic literature as the best of physicians, as noted before.

[72]Staniland Wake, *Serpent Worship*, p. 88,

[73]*Ibid.*

Yaudheyas, Kaḍas and on those of Kausambi,[74] and Taxila of the post-Mauryan period.

The above discussion shows that the Nāga race and the Nāga cult were widespread in India and had a great influence on the social and religious life of the people. The popularity of the Nāga cult has survived down the centuries, as is evident from the profuse representations of Nāgas and Nāgis and other Nāga symbols occurring in the Gupta, Mediaeval and later art of India. Even now in different in parts of India, the snake goddess Manasā, whose exploits are mentioned in the folk-literature of India, is worshipped with great reverence.

[74]Allan, *op. cit.*, p. 150, Nos. 16, 16 a, p. 151 ff; Smith, *Catalogue of Indian Museum Coins*, Vol. 1, pp. 170, 183; S. K. Chakravarty, *Ancient Indian Numismatics*, p. 179.

5. *The Survival of Vedic Elements in Neo-Brahmanism*

Neo-Brahmanism or Hinduism is, as already mentioned before, a multiform structure consisting of polygenous religious ideas. It is a synthesis or a combination of the Vedic and non-Vedic, hieratic and popular, native and foreign. The orthodox and popular elements are so intimately woven that we can only separate them by an act of abstraction. The process of synthesis of which Neo-Brahmanism is the result began very early, but it was intensified perhaps from *c.* 500 B.C. when dissenting religions like Jainism and Buddhism were spreading fast on Indian soil. Brahmanism showed a great alertness in adjusting itself to existing circumstances. Notwithstanding the zeal with which the Brahmanical teachers threw themselves into popular theosophy and devotional systems of worship, they were careful enough to preserve the old traditions and hieratic elements. It is true that as time passed, the sectarian and theistic forms of worship gained wider popularity, but the orthodox traditions and ceremonies continued (and in fact are still continuing) in the framework of expanded Brahmanism or Neo-Brahmanism, however limited their influence might have been. If the Epics and the *Purānas* were devoted mainly to popularizing the worship of personal gods and deities, the *Dharmasūtrās* and *Śāstrās* were written to preserve the popularity of the Vedic practices. An attempt has been made here to show from relevant archaeological and other sources the continuity of hieratic elements in the framework of Neo-Brahmanism (the chief characteristics of which are however the worship of personal gods like Vishṇu, Krishṇa, and Śiva) in the period between 200 B.C.-A.D. 300.

Among the patrons of old Brahmanic traditions in the period under review, the name of Pushyamitra Śuṅga[1] (who was a Brahmin of the Bharadvāja gotra) deserves special mention as he is one of the early rulers known to have performed the Vedic sacrifice called the Aśvamedha. Pushyamitra was the Commander-in-Chief of the Mauryan army and he usurped the throne of Magadha by murdering the last Maurya monarch, Brihadratha[2] in c. 185 B.C. India was full of political unrest when he came to the throne. From Patañjali's *Mahābhāshyā* and various other sources it appears that the Yavanas invaded India and penetrated into the heart of the country at this time. Patañjali alludes to their operations against Madhyamikā (Nagari near Chitor) and Saketa (Ayodhya) for he gives the following illustrations of the use of the imperfect tense (to denote an action which though not seen by a speaker was recent enough to have been seen by him) : "*arunad Yavano Madhyāmikām, arunad Yavanaḥ Sāketām*".[3] According to the *Gārgī Saṁhitā* the Greeks reduced Mathura, the Panchala country, Saketa, and even reached Kusumadhvaja (Pataliputra). Pushyamitra stood firmly against the Greek menace and his army under the command of his grandson, Vasumitra, inflicted a crushing defeat upon the Greeks on the bank of the Sindhu.[4]

Pushyamitra seems to have performed this sacrifice after his victorious wars with the Greeks, which is referred to in the *Mālavikāgnimitram* of Kālidāsa. Patañjali perhaps officiated as a priest in the sacrifice as would appear from the passage in the *Mahābhāshyā : iha Pushyāmitrāṁ Yājayāmaḥ*.[5] The Ayodhya inscription of Dhanadeva informs us that Pushyamitra performed not only one but two horse sacrifices.[6] According

[1]Pāṇini and Baudhāyana represent the Śuṅgas as Bharadvājas: *Vikarṇa-Śuṅgachchhagalād Vatsa-Bharadvājā trishu* (Pāṇini *sūtra*, IV. I. 117); see *Baudhāyana-Śrautasūtra*, edited by Caland, Vol. III, p. 429.

[2]Pargiter, *The Dynasties of the Kali Age*, p. 31.

[3]See Patañjali's commentary on the *sūtra*: *parokshe cha lokā vijñāte prayokturdarsana-vishaye*(Kielhorn, *Vyākaraṇa Mahābhāshya,* Vol. II),p. 119.

[4]*Mālavikāgnimitram,* Act V; V. A. Smith, *Early History of India* (1908), p. 198.

[5]*Indian Antiquary*, 1872, p. 300.

[6]*Journal of the Bihar and Orissa Research Society*, Vol. X, pp. 202-8; *Epigraphia Indica*, Vol. XX, p. 57.

to Jayaswal there is a reference to Pushyamitra's horse-sacrifice in the *Harivamśa.*[7] In Book III Chapter II of this text, there is a significant dialogue between Janamejaya and Vyāsa on the future of the Aśvamedha sacrifice. On Janamejaya's enquiry Vyāsa told him that after his Aśvamedha the Kshatriyas would no longer perform it. Being distressed on hearing it Janamejaya anxiously enquired if there was any hope of its being performed in future by anybody else. In reply, Vyāsa observed that a certain Brahmin Senānī (Commander-in-chief) of the Kāśyapa family will suddenly rise to power and perform the horse-sacrifice in the Kali Age[8] (*Audbhijjo—bhavitā Kaśchit Senānīḥ Kāśyapodvijaḥ| Aśvamedhaṁ Kali-yuge punaḥ pratyāharisharishyati*).

Jayaswal and R.P. Chanda think that the Audbhijja (upstart), Kāśyapadvija (Kāśyapagotra Brahmin), Senānī (commander-in-chief) refers to none other than Pushyamitra.[9] Pushyamitra was no doubt an upstart as he could not claim any royal descent or heritage. Regarding the title Senānī, we know that he is represented as such in the *Purāṇas*, in the *Mālavikāgnimitram* and in the Ayodhyā inscription of Dhanadeva. The difficulty, however, lies with the gotra name (Kāśyapa). Pushyamitra who was Śuṅga should have been described as a Bharadvāja and and not as a Kāśyapa. Jayaswal thinks that he is wrongly represented as belonging to the Kāśyapa gotra in the *Harivaṁśa.* His original gotra seems to have been forgotten when the tradition of his horse-sacrifice was recorded therein.[10]

Jayaswal and many other scholars consider the horse-sacrifice of Pushyamitra as marking the revival of Brahmanism, which, as they hold, fell into disuse in the time of the Mauryas (who, in their opinion, were Śūdras), specially in the reign of Aśoka who put a stop to the animal sacrifices.[11] This view, however, has no foundation in facts. It is true that Brahmanism

[7]*Journal of the Bihar and Orissa Research Society*, Vol. XIV, p. 24.

[8]*Ibid.*

[9]*Ibid.*, p. 25.

[10]Dr. H. C. Raychaudhuri holds that Pushyamitra and his descendants belonged to Kāśyapa-*gotra* and their correct family name was "Baimbika" rather than Śuṅga (*Indian Culture*, Vol. III, p. 739 ff, Vol. IV, pp. 363 ff.).

[11]Mahamahopadhyaya Haraprasad Sastri, *Journal, Asiatic Society of Bengal*, 1910, pp. 259-62.

did not find much royal support in the Mauryan age, as its rulers were followers of dissenting faiths, but that does not mean that Brahmanism was out of vogue during Mauryan times. Even in orthodox communities there arose, long before Aśoka, rational thinkers who decried the efficacy of sacrifices and recorded a strict injunction against animal slaughter. With the growth of Upanishadic thought the idea of the efficacy of elaborate ritualism was discarded and emphasis began to be laid on rational contemplation. The *Brihadāraṇyaka Upanishad* prescribes that instead of a horse-sacrifice the visible universe is to be conceived as a horse and meditated upon as such.[12] Krishṇa, son of Devakī, was taught by his teacher Ghora Āṅgirasa that sacrifice may be performed without objectictve means; that generosity, kindness and other moral traits are the real signs of sacrifices.[13] In the *Śāntiparva* of the *Mahābhārata*, it is laid down that no animal should be sacrificed in the Krita age.[14] Further, in the *Nārāyaṇīya* Section it is written that king Uparicara Vasu, a devotee of Nārāyaṇa, arranged under the superintendence of Brihaspati an Aśvamedha sacrifice according to the rules of *Arāṇyāka* without animal sacrifices. There are references also in the *Rāmāyaṇa* regarding the observance of strict nonviolence in certain orthodox āśramas. We read in *Araṇyakāṇḍa* that when Rāma proceeded from the āśrama of Śarabhaṅga to that of Sutīkshṇa and expressed his desire to stay with the latter, the latter (i.e. Sutīkshṇa) described his āśrama "as resorted to by the Rishi-saṅgha, who did not allow any animal to be slain there". At this Rāma said that his habit of hunting would undoubtedly cause pain to Sutīkshṇa and so he could not stay there for long.[15] After a vegetarian meal Rāma proceeded next morning to other āśramas of the Daṇḍaka Rishis.

As already shown, the opinion against animal sacrifice grew with increasing emphasis on meditation and humanitarian

[12] *Brihadāraṇyaka Upanishad*, I. i.

[13] Hopkins, *The Religions of India*, p. 465.

[14] *Mahābhārata*, XII, 340 (Bombay Edition). *Idaṁ Kritayūga-nāma kālaḥ śreshṭhaḥ pravartitaḥ/ahimsyā yajña-paśavo yūgesminna tandanyathā.*

[15] Dr S. C. Sarkar, *Educational Ideas and Institutions in Ancient India* (The 1925-26 Readership Lectures, Patna University), pp. 137-38; *Rāmāyaṇa*, Book III, 7, vv. 17-22.

works. This trend, which found a clear expression in the *Bhagavadgītā* (Chapters IV, XVII and XVIII) and several other religious texts, became the chief source of attraction of the reformation movements, namely Jainism and Buddhism in the sixth century B. C.

Pushyamitra Śuṅga's coup d'etat against Brihadratha Maurya is regarded by Jayaswal and several other scholars as a Brahmanical revolt against the Mauryas. In the opinion of these scholars, the Mauryas (who were followers of the dissentient faiths) were Śūdras in origin, and the introduction of *daṇḍa-samatā* (equality in punishment), and prohibition of animal-sacrifices, etc., by Aśoka were anti-Brahmanical measures, (as already stated above) seeking to deprive the Brahmanical community of the privileges enjoyed by them from time immemorial, and this led to the great dissatisfaction of Brahmanical people, which culminated in the usurpation of the Magadhan throne by Pushyamitra, a Brāhmaṇa of the Bharadvāja gotra.[16]

Jayaswal thinks that the *Mānavadharmaśāstrā* is a product of the Śuṅga-Kāṇva regime, and the extreme hostility of this *Dharmaśāstra* towards the Śūdras, specially Śūdras as rulers and high officials, is indicative of a strong reaction against the Maurya regime. In support of his theory, Jayaswal refers to the high Brahmanical pretensions contained in the *Mānava* code. According to his interpretation the *Mānavadharmaśāstra* (XII, 100), which states that it is the Brahmin (*Vedaśastravid*) who deserves the leadership of the army *(saināpatya)*, sovereignty (*rājya*), the chiefship of the executive (*daṇḍanetritva*) and the overlordship of the whole people (*sarvalokādhipatya*), refers to the achievements of the orthodox Brāhmaṇa hero, the Senāpati Pushyamitra who obtained sovereignty and followed a strong executive policy, while these and many other Brahmanical pretensions in the code were tolerated, for it was composed during the orthodox regime of the Śuṅgas and Kāṇvas.[17]

The view of Jayaswal and others, as stated above, does not seem to be tenable for more than one reason. The date of the

[16] *Journal, Bihar and Orissa Research Society*, Vol. IV, pp. 257-65; *Manu and Yājñavalkya*, pp. 29-43.

[17] *Ibid.*

composition of the *Mānavadharmaśāstra* is uncertain, and whatever its date may be, there is hardly any justification for characterizing it as a Śuṅgan code reflecting a Brahmanical reaction against the Maurya regime. Again, it is doubtful if the Mauryas were at all Śūdras and if the introduction of *daṇḍa-samatā* and the prohibition of animal sacrifices by Aśoka can at all be interpreted as measures promulgated with a view to offending the sentiments of the Brahmanical community.

To interpret Pushyamitra's military coup d'etat against his master Brihadratha Maurya as a Brahmanical revolt against the heterodox Mauryan regime is to ignore in our opinion the antecedents of his career. His deeds and achievements would reveal that what he did was the successful consummation of the exploits of an ambitious general. He was, we know, a militant Brahmin and the commander-in-chief of the Mauryan army. He was the *de facto* if not the *de jure* ruler of the Maurya dominion in Brihadratha's lifetime. Merutungā's *Therāvalī* relates that the Mauryas ruled for 108 years and Pushyamitra for 30 years. The *Purānas*, in general, accord 137 years for the total duration of the Maurya rule. The total of 137 years suits not only the Purānic but also the Buddhist traditions as recorded in the *Mahāvaṁśa*. So it appears that the *Therāvalī*, which more or less concerns the genealogical succession of kings in Avanti (as the *Purāṇas* concern that of the Magadhan kings),[18] has split the Mauryan rule into two parts and the last part of 30 years has been attributed to Pushyamitra. Thus it seems that Pushyamitra had exercised independent powers in the west during the lifetime of Brihadratha, perhaps acknowledging loyalty nominally to the latter during this period.[19] This seems to be supported by the *Vāyu Purāṇa*[20] which also assigns a rule of 60 years to Pushyamitra. Pushyamitra's rule of 60 years is inconsistent with the general statement of the *Purāṇas* which accord only 110-112 years for the total duration of the Śuṅga rule. But this can be explained by supposing that though the duration of the Śuṅga rule was counted in most of the *Purāṇas*

[18] R. C. Majumdar, *Indian Historical Quarterly*, Vol. I (1925), p. 92.

[19] This explains why Agnimitra and Vasumitra were in Vidisa. They were ruling independently in Central India while Pushyamitra went afield for supremacy in Magadha.

from after the death of Brihadratha and the usurpation of the throne by Pushyamitra, the *Vāyu* has included in Pushyamitra's rule also the years during which he ruled independently in the west in the lifetime of Brihadratha.

From the preceding it is clear that Pushyamitra had acquired considerable power before he seized the Mauryan throne, and that his final coup d'etat is the culmination of his ambitious design to bring the whole Mauryan dominion under his control. It seemes to be unwarranted to characterize it purely as a Brahmanical revolt.

Again, as noted above, Pushyamitra, who was a Śuṅga, was of the Bharadvāja gotra. The Bharadvājas were a branch of the Āṅgirasa some of whom, according to the epic-Puranic traditions, were a mixed Kshatriya-Brāhmaṇa people or Brahma-Kshatriyas combining the functions of the Brahmanas and Kshatriyas, and it is quite possible that Pushyamitra's military profession was due to his family traditions, rather than to any extraordinary circumstances. In other words, it would appear that as Pushyamitra belonged to a Brāhamaṇa-Kshatriya or Brahma-Kshatriya family, the use of arms was quite natural on his part and was not forced upon him to meet a special circumstance.

It may not be out of place to say that the *Purāṇas* refer to several royal families as Brahmakshatra or Kshatriya-Brāhmaṇa families amongst which the Paurava family is the most noted. From the Paurava family emanated both Brāhmaṇas and Kshatriyas. The reasons why the Paurava line is called a Brahma-Kshatra family may be due to the fact that Bharadvāja,[21] a descendant of Brihaspati, the Āṅgirasa rishi, was adopted by Bharata, son of Dushyanta, and the Paurava line was continued by the descendants of this Bharadavāja.

[20]*Pushyamitastu Senānīruddhritya vai Brihadratham/Kārayishyati vairajyam samāḥ shashṭhiṁ sadaivatu* (*Vāyu Purāṇa*, Panchanan Tarakaratna's edition, Calcutta, Ch. 99, v. 337).

[21]Bharadvāja begot a son Vitatha by name. Instead of ascending the throne, he consecrated his son Vitatha and then died or returned to the forest. The Paurava line was continued by Vitatha and the Bharatas (Bharadvājas) could assert either Kshatriya or Brāhmaṇa paternity or combine both. See Puranic texts on the point collected by Pargiter, *Ancient Indian Historical Tradition*, p. 159. See also *Matsya Purāṇa*, 49, 27-34; *Vāyu*, 99, 152-158 (Vangavasi edition).

As a result of this mixture, the Bharadvājas in question, as the *Vedārtha-dīpikā* tells us, could assert either Kshatriya or Brāhmaṇa paternity:

Bharadvājā Bharadvājaputrā ityarthah...cha Brihspate pautrāḥ, Dushyanta nripa-putrasya Bharatasya vā pautrāḥ[22]

Again, the *Matsya Purāṇa* says explicitly that from Bharadvāja were descended both Brāhmaṇas and Kshatriyas.

Tasmādapi Bharadvājāt Brāhmaṇāḥ Kastriyā bhuvi|
dvāmushyāyaṇa-kulīṇāḥ smritāste dvividhena cha||[23]

That the descendants of Bharadvāja, such as Suhotras, Sunahotras, Naras, Gargas and Rijiśvans could also optionally claim to be grandsons of Brihaspati or Bharata, is evident from the statement in the *Vedārthadīpikā* (on *Rigveda,* VI, 52) that they belonged to the Bārhasptya gotra of Saṁyu, who is elsewhere said to be the son of Brihaspati.[24] From the fact that they were born in the Paurva line and yet could claim Saṁyu's gotra, it is amply clear that these Bharadvājas were a Kshatriya-Brāhmaṇa people.

Again, the *Purāṇas* declare in explicit terms the Urukshayas, Kapis, Gargyas, Kāṇvas, Priyamedhas, Maudgalyas, Vishṇuvridhas, Hāritas, Śaunakas, and several others as Kshatropetādvijātyaḥ, who combined the traditions of both the Brāhmaṇas and Kshatriyas.[25] In view of all these, it is quite possible that

[22]See *Shaḍgurusishyakrita-Vedārtha-dīpikā-Sarvānukramaṇī-vritti,* Vol. I, part iv, ed. by Macdonell.

[23]*Matsyapurāṇa,* 196, 52 (Vangavasi edition). Pargiter, on the basis of his Puranic studies, thinks that Bharadvāja, son of Brihaspati, was of two generations earlier than Bharata, and the person who was adopted was not Bharadvāja-Vidathin, grandson or great-grandson of Bharadvāja, (Pargiter, *op. cit.,* p. 163).

[24]*Vāyūpurāṇa*, 71, 37-38, 48-49, Vangavasi Edition.

[25]Indian traditions record several other instances of this peculiar combination of Brāhmaṇas and Kshatriyas, besides those noted above. Richīka, the Bhārgava Rishi and grandfather of Paraśurāma married Satyavatī, the daughter of Kshatriya Gādhi (Muir, *Original Sanskrit Texts*, vol. i, p. 349, and it is a well known fact that Paraśurāma himself was a Brāhmaṇa with the profession of Kshatriya, i. e. warrior. Again, Nahusha's son, Yati, relinqui-

Pusyamitra belonged to one such Brahmakshatra family, and as such was a Brāhmaṇa with a Kshatriya tradition.[26]

In this connection it may also be noted that like the Śuṅgas, their contemporaries and successors, the Kāṇvas, Sātavāhanas, Vākāṭakas, Pallavas and Kadambas seem to have belonged to Brahma-Kshatriya or Kshatriya-Brāhmaṇa families. The Kāṇvas, like their predecessors the Śuṅgas, were a branch of the Āṅgirasas, and an off-shoot from the Paurava line and as such can be described as Brahmakshatras. The Sātavāhanas also seem to have been a Brahmakshatra family as they were both Brahmins and warriors. The Vākāṭakas were of the Vishṇuvriddha gotra. Visṇu-vriddha, we know, was a descendant of Māndhātā who was a Kshatriya-Brāhmaṇa. The Pallavas and Kadambas were also Kshatriya-Brāhmaṇa people as their gotras, surnames and military pursuits would indicate.[27] All this would lend support to the Puranic tradition regarding the existence of Brāhmaṇa-Kshatriya or Kshatriya-Brāhmaṇa families in the early period of Indian history. The Brahmanical rulers of the post-Mauryan period, it would appear, were in actuality Brahma-Kshatriya families.

As regards the tall claims of the Brāhmaṇas advocated in the *Mānava* code (II, 135, VIII, 20; I, 100, etc.) it may be pointed out that almost all the *Dharmasūtras* and other *śāstras* uphold

---

shed his kingdom to his brother Yayāti and became a Brāhmaṇa muni, (*Matsya*, 24, 51, Vangvasi Edition). Viśvāmitra by virtue of his austerities became a Brahmarshi and founder of a Brahmin family. Māndhātri, Kāsya and Gritsamada were also Kshatriyas originally, and attained Brahminhood afterwards.

[26]The Brahmakshatra status of the Śuṅgas is fully corroborated by what M. M. Pandit Harprasada Sastri has adduced regarding their *gotra* and *pravars*. He writes, "The No. 25 of the *Bibliotheca Sanskritica* contains a series of works on the *gotras* and *pravars* of the Brāhmaṇas with an introduction by the editor, P. Chentsal Rao. In leaf VII of the introduction we are told that *pravārs* nos. 4 and 5 are pronounced by persons who are born of Śuṅga, a descendant of Bharadvāja by a woman married in the family of Kata, a descendant of the Viśvāmitra" (*Journal*, *Asiatic Society Bengal*, 1912, p. 187). This also shows that the Śuṇgas had Brahmakshatra blood in them.

[27]Pargiter, *The Dynastic History of the Kali Age*, p. 35; *Ancient Indian Historical Tradition*, pp. 246, 255; *Epigraphia Indica*, Vol. 1, p. 398; Vol. XV, p. 248; *Archaeological Survey of Western India*, Vol. IV, p. 180.

the Brahmanic pretensions and contain harsh provisions against the non-Brāhmaṇas, specially the Śūdras. The *Mānava* code is no exception in this respect. The law book of Vaśishṭha[28] maintains an attitude very similar to that of the *Mānava* code regarding the Śūdras, and in some respects the former is more class-conscious and pro-Brahmanic than the latter. Even a secular treatise like the *Arthaśāstra* of Kauṭilya shows certain pro-Brahmanic pretensions in the matter of punishment for crimes. Preferential claims for the Brāhmaṇas are met with also in the *Atharvaveda*. In view of this, it cannot be held that the *Mānava* code, which contains some extravagant claims for the Brāhmaṇas, implies a special Brahmanical reaction against the Śūdras under the leadership of Pushyamitra.

Further, it is also not possible to accept Jayaswal's interpretation[29] of the Verse 100, Chapter XII of the *Mānava* code (*saināpatyam ca rājyam cha daṇḍa-netritvameva ca/Sarvalokādhipatyaṁ cha Vedaśāstra-vidarhati)*. Jayaswal takes the term "Vedaśāstravid" to mean a Brāhmaṇa and according to him the verse refers to the achievements of Pushyamitra Śuṅga who was a Brāhmaṇa, a senāni and king or the executive head of the state. Jayaswal seems to have missed the real import of the verse. The term "Vedaśāstravid" refers to anyone who studied the *Vedas* and there is no justification for applying this verse to denote a particular person. The main theme of the verse is to extol the excellence of Vedic studies, and in tone and spirit it is an imitation of the Atharvan hymn (XI, 5) dwelling on the temporal and spiritual utility of Vedic education. A few passages from the above-mentioned hymn serve to illustrate this point:

> From him [the Vedic student] was born the Brahman, the chief Brahman...together with immortality.... The teacher [is] a Vedic student, the Vedic student [becomes] lord of men [Prajāpati], Prajāpati bears rule [vi-raj]; the viraj [ruler or king] becomes the controlling Indra.... By Vedic studentship,

[28] *Vaśihsṭha Dharma-śāstra, Sacred Books of the East*, Vol. XIV, Chapters XVII, XXIX, XXI.

[29] *Journal of the Bihar and Orissa Research Society*, Vol. IV, pp. 257-65.

by fervour a king defends his kingdom.... By Vedic studentship, a girl wins [vid] a young husband.[30]

The import of the passages quoted above is that Vedic studies impart efficiency both in the spiritual and material spheres of life. It is Vedic studies that make men successful as governors, rulers, etc. Kings qualify themselves for their position by virtue of their Vedic studies. With this we may compare Gautama's *Dharma-Sūtra* (XI.3) which states that a king should have a good grounding in the *Vedas* and *Ānvikshikī* and that he has to rely on the *Vedas* and *Dharmaśātras*, etc. for carrying out his duties. As the *Atharvaveda* extract tells us, even women had to qualify themselves for marriage by prosecuting a course of Vedic studies. In short, Vedic studentship according to this authority, was an indispensable prerequisite for success in every aspect of life.

Thus the meaning of the verse in question (*Mānavadharmaśāstra*, XIII. 100) is in substance the same as that of the Atharvan passages quoted above, and Jayaswal's suggestion that the achievements mentioned therein refer to those of Brāhmaṇa Pushyamitra appears to be without any sound basis.

From the above it is clear that the prohibition of animal sacrifices or animal slaughter as introduced by Aśoka was in no way a novel measure. Hence it is not safe to suggest following Jayaswal and Haraprasad Shastri that Brahmanism fell into disuse in Mauryan times for Aśoka stopped animal sacrifices. The history of Brahmanism, though full of additions and omissions, is one of continuity. That Brahmanism, including its hieratic and orthodox aspect, was in vogue even during the reign of the Mauryas is evident from different sources. The *Arthaśāstra* of Kauṭilya who is considered by many scholars to have been a contemporary of Chandragupta Maurya refers to the Brahmanical deities and practices. The edicts of Aśoka show that there was an orthodox Brahmanical community in his time and he paid reverence to them as he did to the Buddhists, Nirgranthas, and Ājīvikas. The *Mahābhāshya* of Patañjali throws significant

[30]*Atharva Veda* (Whitney's translation), Lanman, Volume 8, pp. 637, 639 ff.

light on the uninterrupted prevalence of Brahmanical rites on a very large scale in the society. Mention has been made by Patañjali in his *Mahābhāshya*, of various sacrifices including Rājasūya and Vājapeya.[31] With regard to the *Pañchamahāyajñas* he states that they must be performed by every householder.[32] That the observance of sacrificial rites was a usual and traditional affair on the part of the Brāhmaṇas in Patañjali's society is evident from such instances in the *Mahābhāshya* as *Gārgyo yajate*, *Vātsyo yajate*, *Dāksheḥ pitā yajate*, etc. Patañjali refers to animal sacrifices in connection with the worship of Rudra[33] (*Pasunā Rudraṁ yajate*). He explains "yūpa" as a wooden post for binding sacrificial animals and says that it should be made of Bilva or Khadira.[34] He mentions both sacrificial lands and priests specially competent for conducting Vedic sacrifices.[35] There is no doubt that he himself was a distinguished Brāhmiṇ and Vedic scholar. He refers also to the practice of drinking Soma[36] which formed an important part of Vedic sacrifices.

All this would show that there were in Patañjalī's time many Brahmin orthodox families and Vedic scholars, Patañjali himself being one of them, and the orthodox rituals and practices were largely observed in society. This presupposes the existence of orthodox practices in preceding generations also. If orthodox Brahmanism fell into complete disuse in Mauryan times there would have been no Patañjali in the Śuṅga period. All that the horse-sacrifice of Pushyamitra shows is that he was champion or patron of Brahmanism and it will be erroneous to describe him as a reviver of Brahmanism when there is no ground to show that it was non-existent in any preceding generation.

Like the Śuṅgas, their successors the Kāṇvas and others observed orthodox rites and practices as prevailing in their time.

[31]Patañjali's commentary on "Tasya dakshiṇā yajñākhyebyaḥ" runs as follows : *Ākhyāgrahaṇam kimartham, tasya dakshiṇā yajñebhya itiyatyuchyamāne ya eva samjñībhūtakā yajñā utapattiḥ syāt. Āgnishṭomikyaḥ rājasūyikyaḥ* (Kielhorn, *Vyākaraṇa Mahābhāshya*, Vol. II, p. 36).

[32]Kielhorn, *op. cit.*, p. 214.

[33]*Ibid.*, Vol. I, p. 339.

[34]*Ibid.*, p. 8.

[35]*Ibid.*, Vol. II, p. 357.

[36]*Ibid.*, p. 248.

Hara-Pārvatī, stone, Gupta, 5th century A.D., U.P. (Indian Museum Collection, Calcutta).

Brahmā, metal, Gupta, 5th century A.D., Mirpurkhas, Sind.

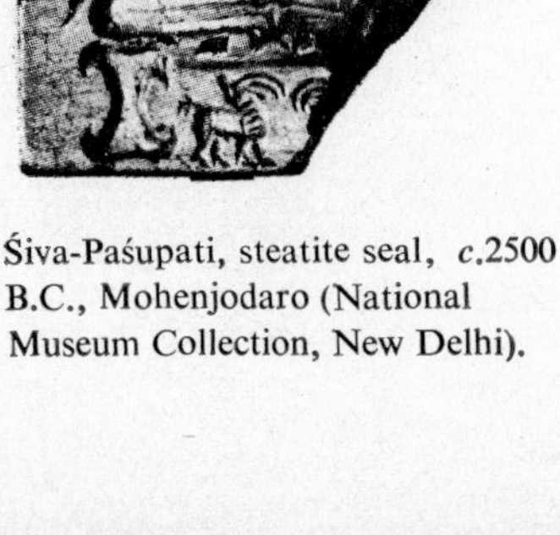

Śiva-Paśupati, steatite seal, *c*.2500 B.C., Mohenjodaro (National Museum Collection, New Delhi).

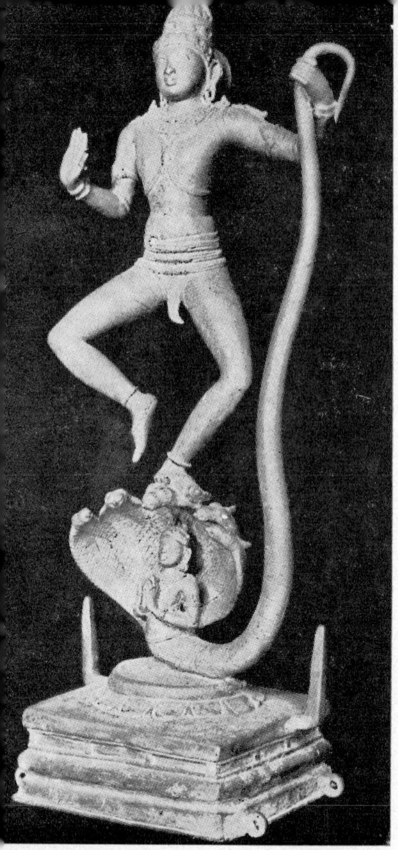

extreme left) Kāliya Krishṇa, bronze, Chola, 10th entury A.D., Tamil Nadu (National Museum Collection, New Delhi).

left) Vaikuṇṭha Vishṇu, metal, Gandhara, 2nd entury B.C., Indische Kunscht, Berlin.

Naṭārāja, bronze, Chola, 10th century A.D., Tiruvarangulam, Tamil Nadu (National Museum Collection, New Delhi).

Sūrya, stone, Eastern Ganga, 13th century A.D., Konarak, Orissa (National Museum Collection, New Delhi).

irth of Buddha and the seven steps, lime stone, kshvāku, 3rd century A.D., Nāgārjunkoṇḍa National Museum Collection, New Delhi).

Nara-Nārāyaṇa, stone, Gupta, 5th century A.D., Deogarh.

Vishṇu, stone, Gupta, 5th century A.D., Mathura (National Museum Collection, New Delhi).

Lakulīsa, 8th century A.D., Cave 29, Ellora, Maharashtra.

(above) Śeshasāyi Vishnu, stone, Gupta, 5th century A. D., Deogarh.

low) The Division of the Relics of Buddha, stone, Śuṅga, 2nd century
C., Bharhut, Madhya Pradesh (National Museum Collection, New Delhi).

.rinegameshī, stone, Kushāna,
.ura, 2nd century A.D.
.aeological Museum Collection,
.ura).

.eme left) Bodhisattva Maitreya,
, Kushāna, 2nd century
. Ahichchhatra, Uttar
.sh (National Museum
.ction, New Delhi).

.r left) Jaina Āyāgapaṭa,
.tone, Kushāna, 2nd century
(National Museum Collection,
Delhi).

.r left) Buddha seated, in
.yamudra, stone, Kushāna, 2nd
.ry A.D. (Archaeological
.um Collection, Mathura).

slab, lime stone,
.āku, 3rd century A.D.,
.rjunakoṇḍa (National
.um Collection,
Delhi). →

Stūpa, 3rd to 1st century
Sanchi. ↓

Kanishka's Relic Casket, metal, Gandhara, 2nd century A.D., Shah-ji-ki Dheri, West Pakistan.

Liṅga, stone, 2nd century B.C., Gudimallam, South India.

Kanishka's coin, showing on the reverse the fig of Buddha, with the legend "Boddo", gold, 2 century A.D. (British Museum Collection).

Pārāsarīputra Sarvatāta as already stated, performed a horse-sacrifice,[37] though he is known also to have built a stone enclosure round the hall of worship of Vāsudeva and Saṁkarshana.

Among the followers of orthodox Brahmanical rites mention may be made here of one Vishṇudeva whose coins (first century B.C.) have been found at Kanauj.[38] On the reverse of one of his silver coins there appears a horse before a sacrificial post or *yūpa* from which it can be reasonably inferred that he claimed to his credit the glory of having performed a horse-sacrifice.[39] Not much is known about him. He can be placed, however, in the first century B.C. on the basis of the palaeography of his coinlegends. Before we proceed, it may be stated that one of the obverse types of early Yaudheya coins (first century B.C. - first century A.D.) is a bull before a *yūpa.* This device can be explained as associated with the Śūlagava sacrifice, i.e., the offering of a bull to Rudra, as mentioned in the *Grihya-Sūtras.* From this it is clear that some of the early Yaudheyas were performers of Brahmanical rites.

Next we may come to the Bhāraśivas and the Vākāṭakas, who, though personally devoted to Śaivism, took keen interest in orthodox Brahmanical rites. The former, who flourished in about the third century A.D., are credited in the Vākāṭaka inscriptions with having performed ten Aśvamedhas and are said to have obtained sovereignty through the satisfaction of lord Śiva as they carried a Śiva Liṅga on their shoulders.[40] The Vākāṭakas, we know, were staunch patrons of orthodox rites. King Pravarasena I who flourished in the latter part of the third century A.D. celebrated four Aśvamedhas and other Vedic sacrifices such as Agnishṭoma, Āptoryāma, Ukthya, Shoḍasin, Atiratra, Vājapeya, Jyotishṭoma, and Brihaspatisava.[41] The personal faith

[37] *Epigraphia Indica,* Vol. XXII, pp. 204-5.

[38] Allan, *Catalogue of Indian Coins* (Ancient India), p. 147.

[39] *Ibid.*

[40] *Aṁśabhāra-sannivesita-Śivaliṅgodvahana-Śiva-suparitushṭa-samutpādita rājvaṁśānāṁ parākramādhigata-Bhāgīrathyāmalajala-mūrddhnābhishiktā-nāṁdaśāśvame dhāvabhritha-snātānāṁ* (*snānānāṁ,* according to Fleet) *Bhāraśivānāṁ* (Fleet, *Corpus Inscriptionum Indicarum,* Vol. III, p. 233 ff- No. 55).

[41] *Agnishṭomāptoryāmokthya - shoḍaśyātirātra Vājapeya-Brihaspaṭi-savā* (Fleet, *op. cit.,* p. 236 ff, No. 55).

of the Vākāṭakas seems to have been Śaivism as was the case with the Bhāraśivas. According to Jayaswal they (i.e. the Vākāṭakas) had Mahābhairava as the royal deity up to the time of Rudrasena I.[42]

During the period under review, orthodox Brahmanical rites and practices were widely prevalent in southern India. The Sātavāhanas and their successors were patrons of Brahmanism like their northern contemporaries. In the Nasik inscription of Vāsishṭhīputra Pulamāvi,[43] Gautamīputra (Sātakarṇi), the celebrated Sātavāhana ruler is described as a great warrior, equal in prowess to Rāma (Balarāma), Keśava and Arjuna, and also as "Eka Bamhaṇa"[44] (a unique Brāhmin) who stopped the intermixture of the four Varṇas and strictly observed Sastric rules. He was an "abode of traditional lore" (*āgamānāmnilaya*) and he properly devised his time and place for the pursuits of the triple object of human activity (*suvibhakta trivarga deśakāla*).[45] This shows that Gautamīputra was a zealous Brahmanical ruler observing Sastric rules. The influence of Vedic Karmakāṇḍa in the early Sātavāhana period is abundantly proved by the Nānāghāt inscription[46] of Queen Nāganikā (first century B. C.) which refers to the performance in the Sātavāhana court of various sacrifices with lavish gifts such as Agnyādheya, Anārambhaṇīya, Bhagāla dāśarātra, Gargātirātra, Gavāmayana, Āptoryāma, Aṅgirasāmayana, Satātirātra, Saptadaśatrātra, Rājasūya, Aśvamedha (two Aśvamedhas) and Āṅgirasātirāta,[47] etc.

Next to the Sātavāhanas the other Brahmanical rulers of Southern India during the period under review were the Ikshvāku prince Vāsishṭhīputra Śrī Śāntamūla, the Pallavas and the Kadambas. In Prakrit inscriptions discovered at Nāgārjunakoṇḍa (Guntur district), Śri Śāntamūla is described as

[42]Jayaswal, *History of India* (A. D. 150-A. D. 350), p. 98.

[43]Bühler, *Archaeological Survey, Western India*, Vol. IV, p. 180 ff., No. 18; Senart *Epigraphia Indica*, Vol. VIII, pp. 60 ff.

[44]For D. R. Bhandarkar's interpretation of "*Eka-Bamhaṇa*," see *Epigraphia Indica*, Vol. VIII, pp. 32-6.

[45]*Epigraphia Indica,* Vol. VIII, pp. 60 f.

[46]*Lüders List*, No. 1112.

[47]*Archaeological Survey, Western India*, Vol. V, p. 60 ff.

a performer of Vedic sacrifices such as the Agnihotra, Agnishṭoma, Vājapeya, and Aśvamedha.[48] Regarding the patronage of Brahmanism by the Pallavas we know that Śivaskandavarman, one of the early rulers of his line, belonging to the first part of the fourth century A.D., celebrated the Agnishṭoma, Vājapeya, and Aśvamedha sacrifices as we read in his inscriptions. The allegiance of the Pallavas to ancient Brahmanical rites is evident also from one of their official charters which describe them as "*yathāvaphārit-āśvamedhānām Pallavānām.*"[49] As for the Kadambas it may be noted that they were a Brahmin family and their first ruler was Mayūraśarman. The Tālaguṇḍa inscription of the time of Śāntivarman informs us that the Kadambas kindled the sacred fire, performed manifold Vedic rites and drank Soma according to the prescribed rules, and Mayūraśaraman himself was adorned with Vedic knowledge, right disposition, and purity.[50] All this clearly testifies to the fact that the Kadambas were ardent followers and supporters of sacrificial Brahmanism.

The increasing popularity of the orthodox rites and practices during the period under review is further attested to by the discovery of the Brahmanical finds in Besnagar, and of several inscribed *yūpas* in the Mathura, Kusambi and Rajputana regions. While excavating a small mound in the close vicinity of the pathway leading from Udayagiri to Khambaba at Besnagar, Dr. Bhandarkar exposed two brick structures[51] which in his opinion resemble the sacrificial *Kuṇḍas* of the Brāhmaṇas. "The resemblance," observes Dr. Bhandarkar, "is observable not only in respect of the sloping sides but also in respect of the

[48]*Mahārājasa Virūpāksha-pati Mahāsena-parigahitasa, Agnihotāgiṭhoma-Vājapeyāsamedha-yājisa* (Śrī Sātamūlasa, *Epigraphia Indica*, Vol. XX, pp. 19 ff.

[49]*Journal of the Bihar and Orissa Research Society*, Vol. XIX, p. 186. The Brahmakshatra status of the Pallavas is indicated not only by their *gotra*, i. e. Bharadvājagotra, but also by the facts of the Darśi copper plates where they are described as Brāhmaṇas who raised their position by the powers of arms and attained the position of the Kshatriya (*Epigraphia Indica*, Vol. I, p. 398).

[50]*Indian Antiquary*, Vol. XXV, pp. 27 ff; *Epigraphia Indica*, Vol. VIII, pp. 31 ff.

[51]*Archaeological Survey of India, Annual Report, 1914-15*, p. 72.

offsets which distinguish them." These offsets are a peculiar feature of *Kuṇḍas*, and are technically called *Mekhalā*.[52] These ;tructures, it may be presumed, represent the old sacrificial *Kuṇḍas* or pots.

Besides the above two, one more pit was found almost at the same level and according to Dr. Bhandarkar it represents a *Yoṇikuṇḍa*.[53] At about the same level in which the *kuṇḍas* were exposed, a silver coin of Mahākshatrapa Īśvaradatta (early part of the third century A. D.)[54] and some Nāga coins of which one belongs to Bhīma Nāga, and three to Gaṇapati Nāga were found. From these considerations the *kuṇḍas* may be dated approximately in the early part of the fourth century A.D. or the middle of the third century A.D.

At about the same level of the *kuṇdas*, Dr. Bhandarkar discovered also walls of two structures which are, according to him, remnants of a sacrificial hall to entertain guests and visitors at the sacrifices. Near the hall he found a seal recording the performance of a sacrifice by one Timitra with *hotā*, *potā* and *mantrasajana*, i. e.…*hymankismen*.[55]

These facts would show that Besnagar was an important stronghold of Vedic Brahmanism during the period under review. We may now discuss certain inscribed *yūpas* which, as noted above, were found mostly in Rajputana, Mathura and Kausambi.

Yūpas are sacrificial stakes to tie and immolate anirmals on the occassïon of various Vedic sacrifices. The sacrifice of animals is a prominent feature of the Vedic sacrifices. Animal sacrifice is a prominent feature of the Vedic religion and has been alluded to in Vedic texts very frequently.

> He who offers living victims will reside high in heaven….[56] The sacrificial fires long for the sacrificer's flesh; he offers to them an animal to redeem himself.[57] By an animal sacrifice

[52]*Ibid.*, p. 73.
[53]*Ibid.*, p. 74.
[54]*Ibid.*, pp. 75 ff.
[55]*Ibid.*, p. 77.
[56]*Vedic Hymns, Sacred Books of the East,* Vol. XLVI, p. 24.
[57]*Śatpatha Brāhmaṇa, Sacred Books of the East*, Vol. XLIV, pp. 117-19.

the sacrificer cenfers upon himself immortal life.[58]

The *Śatapatha Brāhmaṇa* regards *yūpa* as the "crestlock of the sacrifice personified" and contains an elaborate description about its preparation and the ceremonies connected with it.[59] The animal sacrifice is offered to Agni and Soma, etc. but the *yūpa* is said to belong to Vishṇu.[60] This is rather strange in view of the fact that no animal is sacrificed to Vishṇu.[61]

The *yūpa*, according to sacred texts is to be made of wood. There is a well known grammatical example referring to this tradition, viz., *yūpāya dāru*. It is to be noted, however, that only a few selected kinds of wood should be used in preparing the *yūpas*. According to Āpastamba,[62] the sacrificial post is to be made of Palāśa, Khadira, Bilva or Rauhitaka trees according as one desires various results, but in Soma sacrifices preference is given to Khadira.[63] According to Patanjali, a *yūpa* should be made of either Bilva or Khadira. In the *Rāmāyaṇa*, however, we have reference to some other woods also being used in making *yūpas*. In connection with the Aśvamedha sacrifice of Daśaratha, 21 *yūpas* were erected, of which six were of Bilva, six of Khadira, six of Palāśa, one of Śleshmātaka, and two of Devādāru.[64]

About the size of the *yūpas* the texts vary and they prescribe different sizes for different purposes. The *Śatapatha Brāhmaṇa* says:

> When he who is about to perform an animal sacrifice, makes a stake one cubit long, he thereby gains this world, and when he makes one three cubits long he thereby gains the heaven; and when he makes one four cubits long he thereby gains the regions.[65]

58*Ibid.*

59*Śatapatha Brāhmaṇa*, III, 6 4.1.

60*Ibid.*

61*Archaeological Survey of India, Annual Reports, 1910-11*, p.45.

62*Āpastamba Śraut-śutra* (vii.1.16), edited by Richard Garbe, Vol. I, p. 367.

63Keilhorn, *Vyākaraṇa Mahābhāshya*, Vol. I, p. 8.

64*Rāmāyaṇa*, 1.14. 22-25.

65*Śatapatha Brāhmaṇa, Sacred Books of the East,* Vol. XLIV, p. 124,

According to *Kātyāyana Śrauta-sūtra* a *yūpa* may be made from 5 to 15 cubits in length (*Saptadaśa Vājapeya*) and in the Aśvamedha it would be 21 cubits (*Ekaviṁśatiraśvamedhe*).[66] Regarding the shape of the *yūpa* the texts are more or less unanimous. It is laid down that the *yūpa* should be made eight-cornered like the thunderbolt of Indra, because a *yūpa* is a veritable thunderbolt.[67] The *Śatapaiha Brāhmaṇa* says'[68] "It (the *yūpa*) is to be eight-cornered for eight syllables has the Gāyatrī, and the Gāyatrī is the forepart of the sacrifice, therefore it is eight-cornered."[69] Regarding the other features it should be noted that the sacrificial stake should be "bent at the top and bent inwards in the middle."[70] It must have a head-piece (*chashāla*) or top-ring at about eight inches from the top. The *chasāla* should also be octagonal[71] in shape. A *yūpa* resembles in its external appearance a Brahmachārin, so it has a girdle at the centre and a triple *upavīta* across it.[72] It (the girdle-rope) is perhaps "the same as the rope of Varuṇā (*Varṇāya*) *rajju*, with the noose of the sacred order (*ritaśya pāsa*) by means of which the victim is to be bound to the *yūpa*."

Among the earliest of the *yūpas* discovered so far are the Īśāpur stone *yūpas*.[73] These are octagonal except the lower portion which is square. They are are bent at the top but not in the middle, though according to sacred texts a sacrificial stake should be bent at the top and also inwards in the middle. Both the two Īśāpur *yūpas* possess the head-piece or the top-ring and the girdle rope (*rasnā*) with the noose (*pāśa*) is exhibited on both of them and it is (*rasāna*) with the noose (earlier shown on the uninscribed pillar). The epigraph on the other pillar records that it was set up as a sacrificial post by one Droṇala, son of Rudrila, a Brahmana of Bharadvāj gotra, and chanter of holy

[66] *Kātyāyana-Śrauta-sūtra,* VI.1.30, 3I.

[67] *Aitareya Brāhmaṇa, (Bibliotheca Indian Series)* Vol. 1, pp. 234 ff.

[68] *Śatapatha Brāhmaṇa* III, 6.4.27; *Archaeological Survey of India, Annual Reports, 1910-11,* p. 45.

[69] *Śatapatha Brāhmaṇa,* XI, 7.3.3.

[70] *Kātyāyana-Śrauta-sūtra,* VI. 1. 2 ff.

[71] *Epigraphia Indica,* Vol. XXII, p. 44.

[72] *Archaeological Survey of India, Annual Report, 1910-11,* p. 48.

[73] *Ibid.,* p. 40 ff. Īśāpur is a suburb of the city of Mathura.

hymns on the occasion of the *Dvadaśa* sacrifice in the year 24 of the reign of Shahi Vāsishka.[74] Dvādaśa is a sacrificial rite of 12 days. It is both an *Āhīna* and a *Sattra.* The main difference between an *Āhīna* and *Sattra* is that the *Sattra* can be performed by the Brāhmaṇas alone, and an *Āhīna* by any one of the first three *varṇas.*[75] The performer of the *Dvādaśa* sacrifice mentioned in the present inscription was a Brāhmaṇa and hence the sacrifice in question could be the *Dvādaśa* of either type.

A *yūpa* has been discovered at Nandasa in Sāhārā district of of the Udayapur State.[76] This *yūpa,* it should be noted, is entirely round, though according to the texts it should be made octagonal. There are two inscriptions engraved on the Nandsa *yūpa*, dated in the Krita year 282 (the Krita year is perhaps the same as the Vikrama era). The purport of the inscriptions does not seem to be identical. They refer, however, to the performance of an Ekashashṭhīrātra sacrifice by one Śakti-guṇaguru (*Epigraphia Indica*, Vol. XXIV, p. 247).

We have a group of four inscribed *yūpas* set up by the Kshatriya chiefs of Rajputāna.[77] They come from Baḍvā, Kota state, Rajputana. The Baḍvā *yūpas* are octagonal besides the portion underground which is square,[78] like the Iśāpur and Bijyagaḍh *yūpas.*[79] This departure from Sastric injunction is perhaps due to the architectural considerations. "A pillar octagonal above and square at the bottom is more graceful than the pillar octagonal throughout." The architect of the Nandsa *yūpas,*[80] it should be noted, totally disregarded the textual

74*Ibid.,* p. 41. Vāsishka is a Kushana prince who is believed to have ruled between Kanishka and Huvishka

75*Kātyāyan Śrauta-sūtrā*, 1.6.63. *History of Dharmashastras* by P. V. Kane, Vol. II, Part I, p. 153 and footnote. In the Sattras there are no separate priests since the yajamānas themselves are priests. According to Jaimini even the Brāhmanas of the Bhrigu, Sunaka and Vaśishṭha *gotras* are not entitled to perform the Sattras (P. V. Kane, *op. cit.*, Vol. II, Part I, p. 482).

76*Indian Antiquary,* Vol. LVII, p. 53.

77*Epigraphia Indica,* Vol. XXII, pp. XXIV, pp. 251 ff.

78*Ibid.,* Vol. XXII, p. 44.

79Fleet, *op. cit.*, p. 253.

80*Indian Antiquary,* Vol. LVIII, p. 53.

injunctions as he has made the *yūpas* entirely round or circular. The Baḍvā *yūpas* have no girdle in the middle, and like other *yūpas* referred to above they are not endowed with any *upavita*.[81] The first three Baḍvā *yūpas* bear inscriptions in the Krita year 295 and record the erection of these *yūpas* one each by Balavardhana, Somadeva, and Balasimha in connection with the Trirātra sacrifice[82] performed duly by them. Balavardhana Somadeva and Balasimha are sons of one Bala and they are described as Maukhari commander-in-chiefs.[83]

The fourth *yūpa* from Kotah in Rajputana contains an inscription which, as its paleography shows, may be dated in the third century A. D.[84] The object of the inscription is to record that the pillar was set up in connection with the Āptoryāma sacrifice performed by one Dhanutrāta, son of Hastin of the Maukhari clan. The names of Hastin and Dhanutrāta would suggest that they belonged to Kshatriya stock.[85] The whole house of the Baḍvā Maukharīs, it seems, were zealous advocates of the Vedic practices.

We may now discuss the inscribed *yūpa*[86] in the Allahabad Municipal Museum. The pillar has been sadly mutilated, and only one of its facets along with a small part of the adjoining one on its left has been recovered. To judge from the angles of the facets it is clear that the pillar was originally an octagonal one.[87] The characters of the inscription engraved on this *yūpa* resemble the scripts of the inscriptions of Ushabhadāta and Rudradāman. Hence the *yūpa* can be attributed to the second century of the Christian era.[88] This refers to the performance of seven *Soma* sacrifices (technically called *Saptasoma saṁstha*).[89] The

[81] *Epigraphia Indica,* Vol. XXIII, p. 44.

[82] *Ibid.*, p. 52

[83] *Ibid.*

[84] The present inscription does not bear any date, but its scripts agree very closely with those of the other three Badva *yūpa* inscriptions, *Epigraphia Indica*, Vol. XXIV, p. 255.

[85] *Ibid.*, Vol. XXIV, pp. 252 f.

[86] *Ibid.*, p. 245. It was found in the neighbourhood of Kosam, ancient Kausambi.

[87] *Ibid.*

[88] *Ibid.*, p. 246.

[89] Seven *Soma* sacrifices constituting *Saptasoma saṁthā* are Agnishṭoma, Atyagnishṭoma, Ukthya, Shoḍasin, Vājpeya, Atirātra and Āptoryāma.

sacrificer was one Śivadatta who is called in the inscription a trusted minister of a king whose name is not extant.

Two *yūpas* with inscriptions were discovered at Barnal, a small village in Jaipur State, "belonging to the Thakursaheb Barnala about eight miles from Lalsote-Gangapur Fair Weather Road." It is to be noted that the girdle, or the *pāśa* which is executed round the Isāpur pillars is absent in these and also the Baḍvā *yūpas*. The inscriptions on the Barnala *yūpas* bear the Krita years 284 and 335. The Barnala *yūpa* inscription "A" bearing the Krita year 284 records the erection of seven *yūpas*[90] by a person whose gotra was *sohartri* and whose name ended in Vardhana.[91] Dr. Altekar is of the opinion that the sacrificer was a king of the name ending with Vardhana.

The inscription on *yūpa* "B" refer to the performance of five *Gargātrirātra* sacrifices performed by one Bhaṭṭa. The *Gārgātrirātra* sacrifice is an amalgam of *Agnishṭoma*, *Ukthya* and *Atirāta*. The inscription ends with the expression, "May (god) Vishṇu be pleased; may Dharma increase." The name of the sacrificer is not preserved in the whole but his title Bhaṭṭa would show that he was a Brāhmaṇa.[92]

D. R. Bhandarkar discovered a fragment of a *yūpa* at Nagari.[93] The pillar is broken at both ends and bears a mutilated inscription. The words extant in line two of the same read: *sya yajñe Vājapeye yūpo*. This indicates that this *yūpa* was erected in connection with the performance of the *Vājapeya* sacrifice. The scripts of the inscription are of the fourth century A. D.

The *yūpas* referred to above are of stone, though according to sacred texts they should be made of wood. The stone *yūpas* were erected perhaps for a commemorative purpose in imitation of the Mauryan columns.[94] It may be noted here that the orthodox Brahmanical practices spread to Further India also during the period under review. The Batavia Museum contains

[90] *Epigraphia Indica*, Vol. XXVI, pp. 119 and 120.
[91] *Ibid.*, p. 119.
[92] *Ibid.*, p. 122.
[93] *Memoir*, *Archaeological Survey of India*, No. 4, p. 120.
[94] *Epigraphia Indica*, Vol. XXIII, p. 43.

a sacrificial post of stone from Moeara Kaman, Eastern Borneo. It contains an inscription of eight lines in Vengi characters, of king Mūlavarman[95] (*c.* 400 A. D.) ending with: *yupo' yaṁ sthāpito vipraiḥ.*

The above mentioned facts would show that orthodox Vedic practices were widely prevalent in the society. But it should also be remembered that pure Vedism has no practical or independent existence. Brahmanism, as it developed, became a multiform religious system of which Vedism was one of the constituent factors, the others being its more popular elements, the various Brahmanical cults. The manner in which these elements were harmoniously blended with the normal life of the people is illustrated in certain epigraphic records of the normal life of our period. In the Ghoshundi and Hathibada inscriptions, Pārāśarīputra Sarvatāta is represented as an Aśvamedhayāji, performer of a horse sacrifice and also having constructed a stone enclosure for the place of worship called Nārāyaṇa vāṭa for Bhagavat Saṁkarshaṇa and Vāsudeva. Saṁkarshaṇa and Vāsudeva are deities of the Bhāgavata cult. A gift at their place of worship by Sarvatāṭa who performed the Vedic Brahmanical rites, i. e., the Aśvamedha, furnishes a striking instance of the harmonious blending of the orthodox and popular beliefs in the religious life of the people. Similar examples are afforded also by a few more contemporary records.

The Nanaghat cave inscription (first century B.C.) opens with an invocation to Vedic as well as sectarian deities, viz., Indra Dharma, Saṁkarshaṇa, Vāsudeva and the four *lokapālas*, Yama Kuvera, Varuṇa and Vāsava and records also the performance of several Vedic sacrifices as noted before. This shows how the same person offers prayer to the orthodox and also to the post-Vedic sectarian deities. The Bhāraśivas, Vākāṭakas, Pallavas and Kadambas had performed several Vedic sacrifices, though most of them were personally devoted to Śaivism.[96] Similarly, the Ikshvāku prince Śriśantamūla was devoted to the cult of

[95]*Archaeological Survey of India, Annual Report, 1910-11*, p. 40, foot-note; Dr R. C. Majumdar, *Suvarṇadvīca,* Part I, pp. 126 ff.

[96]Fleet, *op. cit.,* Vol. III, pp. 238, 245; *Epigraphia Indica,* Vol. VIII, pp. 31 ff.

Mahāsena (Kārttikeya) as the epithet *Mahāsenaparigrihita*[97] shows, and he performed at the same time Vedic sacrifices like *Aśvamedha* and *Vājapeya*, etc. The Allahabad Municipal Museum *yūpa* inscription mentions one Śivadatta, as we have seen before, as having performed seven *Soma* sacrifices and also made a donation to the temple of Śiva. The epigraph concludes with: *prītimiyan maheśvara iti.*[98]

During the post-Mauryan period, there was a large increase in the foreign element in the Indian population,[99] and it is interesting to know what the attitude of the Brahmanic society was towards the foreign people who settled in India. The ancient Indian society was elastic, expanding and accommodative. The social position was often determined by one's own learning, good qualities and deeds and not by mere birth in a particular family. Further, the Brahmanic society was always eager to widen its bounds and incorporate those who originally professed other cults. Brahminism as a social organization was flexible and based upon the observance of certain rites as laid down in Vedic texts, some early, some late, or in following the precepts of *Sūtras* and *Śāstras* about *Dharma* (social custom) and anybody could be included who could follow some of the philosophical, theosophical or sociological beliefs. In short, birth, race or views were no barriers for entry into the Brahmanic society.[100]

[97]*Ibid.*, Vol. XX, p. 21.

[98]*Ibid.*, Vol. XXIV, p. 251.

[99]There was already a considerable foreign population in India since the sixth century B. C., either domiciled or in various degrees of intermixture with the local people or professedly alien.

[100]It is well known that Vyāsa was born of a Vāśishtha rishi (Parāśar) and Matsya-princes and Parāśara himself was the son of a woman belonging to a community outside the *Varna* system. Again, Viśvāmitra who was originally an "*Aila*" Kshatriya, became a rishi and founder of a Brāhmaṇa gotra. As a man could rise to a higher status by appropriate deeds and spritual efforts, one could in the same way be degraded to a lower caste and position for his misbehaviour. The *Vishṇu Purāṇa* tells us that Nabhāga, a scion of the illustrious Kshatriya line of Vaisali, became a Vaiśya and Prishadhra (also of the Ikshvāku Kshatriya group) was reduced to Sudrahood for offending the priesthood (*Vishṇu Purāṇa*, Vol. IV, 1. 15 ff, edited by Jivandan Vidyasagar). Regarding the elasticity of the Brahmanic society, see D. R. Bhandarkar, *Some Aspects of Indian Culture*, pp. 57 ff.

There is a passage in the *Santi Par va* of the *Mahābhārata*, Section 65, which explains very well the position of the different castes and races in the Brahmanic society. In this passage, Māndhāta asks Indra, "What duty should be performed by the Yavanas, the Kiratas, the Gandharas, the Chinas, the Sabaras, the Barbaras, the Śakas, the Tushāras, the Kankas, the Pallavas, the Andhras, the Madrakas, the Pundras, the Ramaṭhas, the Kambojas, the several castes that have sprung up from the Brāhmaṇas and Kshatriyas, the Vaisyas and the Śūdras that reside in the dominions of the Ārya kings. What are the duties again to the observance of which kings like ourselves should force these tribes that subsist by robbery ? Indra answers, "All these tribes should serve their mothers, fathers, their preceptors and other seniors and recluses living in the woods. They should also serve their kings, and perform the duties and rites inculcated in the *Vedas*. They should perform sacrifices in honour of *pitris* (Manes) and make seasonable presents unto the Brāhmaṇas. They should also perform all kinds of *Pākayajñas* with costly presents of food and wealth."[101]

What follows from the above passage is that the foreigners and people of diverse cults could be admitted into the Brahmanic society provided they observed the Brahmanic *Dharma* (social constitution) as laid down in the sacred texts.

The literary traditions noted above (for earlier periods) are supported by archaeological evidences of our later period, thereby showing the continuity of the Brahmanical tradition of elasticity and expansion. We have a number of inscriptions which show that foreigners were easily incorporated into Brahmanic society. The most striking instance that we can refer to in this connection is that of Śaka Ushavadāta (Rishabhadatta). Rishabhadatta is a purely Indian name, (with a Jaina flavour) so also is that of his wife, namely Dakshamitrā (somewhat Śaivite).[102] Apparently from the name itself Rishabhadatta cannot be recognized as a foreigner. Fortunately the inscriptions throw a good deal of light on the point.

[101]*Mahābhārata Śāntiparva,* Section 65, English translation by P. C. Ray.

[102]Lüders list Nos. 1132 and 1134.

In the Nasik inscriptions[103] and also in one of the Karle Buddhist epigraphs,[104] Rishabhadatta has been described as the son of Dinika and son-in-law of Kaharata Kshatrapa Nahapāna. Dinika and Nahapāna are non-Indian names and Nahapāna was a well-known Śaka ruler of the Deccan and Gujarat. Besides the names of his father and father-in-law which suggest his foreign nationality, Rishabhadatta himself has been expressly described as a Śaka in an epigraph.[105] He was devoted to Brahmanism. A Nasik inscription[106] described him as a liberal and mighty donor to the Brāhmaṇas. He gave away three hundred thousand cows, made gifts of money, went on *tīrthas* on the river Prabhāsa and dedicated 16 villages to the gods and Brāhmanas. He fed annually one hundred thousand Brahmins and provided the Brāhmaṇas with eight wives each at the religious tirtha of Prabhāsa (*Prabhāse Puṇyatīrthe Brāhmaṇebhyaḥ ashṭabhāryāpradena*). He gifted thirty-two thousand stems (plant) of cocoanut trees at the village Nanangola to the congregation of Charakas[107] at Pimdita-Kavada, Govardhana, Suvarnamukha and Ramatirtha in Soparga.

These facts leave no doubt that Rishabhadatta was an ardent follower of Brahmanism and this is corroborated by a few other inscriptions of his. The Nasik inscription No. 12 records his

[103] *Ibid.*, Nos. 113 and 1133.

[104] *Ibid.*, No. 1135; *Epigraphia Indica,* Vol. VIII, p. 85.

[105] *Ibid.*, No. 1135; *Epigraphia Indica,* Vol. VIII, p. 85.

[106] *Epigraphia Indica,* Vol. VIII, pp. 78, 79.

[107] "The communities of Charakas to whom the gift has been made seem to be indentical with those who are named in a stereotyped formula of the Buddhist (Mahāvastu, ii, 412; anyatirthīkacharka parivyājaka) and Jaina texts, namely a certain special category of Brahmanical ascetics; to take "*Charaka*" for Brahmanical students would leave the gift too undetermined and if the Charaka samgha of the *Yajurveda* were meant, the expression would have been made more definite" (E. Senart, *Epigraphia Indica,* Vol. VIII, p. 79). *Charaka* is probably the same class of Brāhmaṇa teachers as the Yājāvaras to which Jaratkāru (a contemporary of Janamejaya Parikshita, 900 B. C.) belonged. It is possible that the medical treatises collected in the so called "Charaka" *Samhita,* belongs to this school of itinerant teachers. Charakas as wandering mendicants are mentioned in the Allahabad Municipial Museum *Yūpa* inscription, l. 15 : *agachchhadbhih Charakairbhoktavyamiti* (*Epigraphia Indica*, Vol. XXIV, p. 251).

donation of 7,000 Kārshāpaṇas[108] to the venerable gods and Brāhmaṇas and his gifts to the Brāhmaṇas on the river Branasa and at Prabhasa have been referred to also in a Karle Buddhist cave inscription (Lüder's *List*, No. 1099).

Besides Śaka Ushabhadāta, there were many other foreigners who seemed to have been adopted into the Hindu fold. The Nasika Buddhist Cave inscription No. 18 refers to the dedication by Indrāganidattā of a cave[109] in mount Tiranhu with a Chaitya-griha and cisterns to universal *Sangha* of monks. Indragnidatta was the son of Dharmadeva, the Yavana. The names Indrāgnidattā and Dharmadeva are definitely Brahmanical names. Again, Vishṇudattā a female *Śaka* and lay devotee of Buddhism, provided money, as is stated in a Nasik inscription,[110] for the treatment of the sick of a local Buddhist sangha. Vishṇudattā was the mother of Gaṇapaka Viśvavarman and daughter of Agnivarman, the *Saka.* The suffix Varman shows that Agnivarman and Viśvanarman were looked upon as Kshtariyas.

During the period under review there were certain foreigners who were devoted to Brahmanism though they did not lose their foreign indentity. This shows that Brahmanism was growing in popularity even among unabsorbed foreigners, i.e. those who were either in the first stage of immigration into India, or were in the borderlands and beyond in the north and west. The best instance in this connection is exemplified in the Mathura inscription of the year 28, edited by Sten Konow in *Epigraphia Indica,* Vol. XXI, p. 55 ff. This inscription is dated the first day of Gurppiya in the year 28 as noted above. Gurppiya, as Konow points, out is the Macedonian month Gorpaios, corresponding to the Indian Proshṭhapāda.[111]

The inscription records a permanent endowment of a sum of 1,000 *purānas* with two guilds, by one who is designated as *Kanasarukamānaputra Kharasalerapati Vakanapati.* The object of the endowment was to feed daily a hundred Brāhmaṇas by the interest realized from month to month, and also to keep

[108] *Epigraphia Indica,* Vol. VIII, p. 82.
[109] *Ibid.,* p. 90.
[110] *Ibid.,* p. 88.
[111] *Epigraphia Indica,* Vol. XXI, p. 56.

some provisions daily for the hungry and the destitute.[112] It is notable that the donor was a foreigner who came to Mathura to create an endowment for the welfare of the Brāhmaṇas and the benefit of the poor. The foreign origin of the donor is implied not only by his title Vakanapati,, but also from the date of the record which is not the Indian but the Greek calendar month. It is to be noted that the gift was made during the rule of Huvishka, for the donor expressly wishes that whatever merit may accrue from his act may accrue to the Devaputra Shāhī Huvishka and also to those to whom the Devaputra is dear.

This patronage of the Brāhmaṇas by one who is of a purely foreign origin shows that Brahmanism was held in high esteem during the Kushāṇa period. This is corroborated by another Brahmanic record from Mathura. This was found engraved on the stone pedestal of an image of which the traces of the left foot alone survived.[113] The pedestal comes from the neighbourhood of the village Mat about nine miles from the city of Mathura, the site from where the well-known statues of Kanishka and Vima Takshana were unearthed. The inscription is broken. However, we learn from it that "there was a devakula[114] of...the grandfather of Devaputra Huvishka" and that this "Devakula" had fallen down. This was repaired by a certain official of Devaputra Huvishka, who, as stated in the inscription, held the title of "Vakanapati" and made provisions for the feeding of the daily guests and Brāhmaṇas.

Among the Satraps of Ujjayini, Rudradaman was the most prominent. His father was Jayadāman, and grandfather, Chashtana. As the names show, the Satrapas of Ujjayini, though of a foreign origin, were gradually Hinduised from the time of Jayadaman. Certain distinctly Hindu names in Rudradāman's line ending with Hindu suffixes are Rudrasinha, Rudrasena, Damasena, Vijayasena, Viśvasiṁha and others. Rudradāman was well-versed in Sanskrit grammar language, music, politics,

[112] *Ibid.*, pp. 55-61.
[113] *Journal of the Royal Asiatic Society*, London, 1924, pp. 403 f.
[114] *Ibid.*

and logic,[115] and he is one of these earlier rulers who took initiative in introducing Sanskrit in official records. Dr D.R. Bhandarkar remarks that so completely Hinduised were the Śaka Satrap families that the other Hindu royal families did not think it polluting or degrading to contract matrimonial alliances with them.[116] A Kanheri cave inscription reveals that the Sātavāhana prince Vāsiṭhīputra Śri Sātakarṇi was married to the daughter of the Mahākshatrapa Rudra who is believed to be the same as Rudradāman of the Junagadh Rock Inscription.[117]

Thus inscriptional evidence is abundant to show that the Brahmanical society during our period was elastic, including and absorbing foreign elements without much difficulty.

The Ābhīras, who, according to D.R. Bhandarkar were a foreign horde, were completely Indianised and adopted Śaivism as their personal creed. In the *Vishṇu Purāna* and *Maushala Parva* of the *Mahābhārata* they have been described as *Dasyus* and *Mlechahhas*.[118] According to the *Purānas* there were ten Ābhīra kings and they ruled for 67 years.[119] An Ābhīra chief, Rudrabhūti by name, is said to have served as the general of a Śaka king of Ujjain. The Gundā inscription which is dated in the Śaka year 103 (A.D. 181), referring to the reign of Rudrasiṁha I speaks of a grant made by Rudrabhūti.[120] The Śaka Satraps of western India were overshadowed for a time by an Ābhīra king named Māḍharīputa-Īśvarasena (third century A.D), son of Īśvaradatta, whose inscription has been discovered at Nasik.[121] The names Rudrabhūti, Īśvaradatta, and Īśvarasena are Brahmanical (Śaivite) names.

According to D.R. Bhandarkar, the migration of the Abhīras into India took place towards the beginning of the Christian

115Junagadh Incription of Rudradamu I, D. C. Sircar, *Select Inscriptions*, Vol. 1, p. 172 f.

116D. R. Bhandarkar, *Indian Antiquary*, 1911, pp. 7 ff.

117*Ibid.*

118*Vishṇu Purāṇa, Bibliotheca Indica Series* (Ed. by R. L. Mitra), chapter XLV, vv. 115, 126, *Mahābhārata, Maushala Parva, xvi*, 7, 223: 8. 270.

119*Pargiter, The Dynasties of the Kali Age*, p. 45.

120*Epigraphia Indica*, Vol, XVI, p. 235.

121*Ibid.*, Vol. VIII, p. 88.

era.[122] The Ābhīras, in our opinion, seem to have settled in India much earlier than Bhandarkar supposes. In the *Mahābhārata* they are mentioned in the *Parvas*,[123] ii, iii, vi, vii, xiv and xvi. In the *Mushala Parva* (i.e. *Parva* xvi) we are told that when Arjuna, after the catastrophe at Dvaraka, was taking the Yādava women, children and old men to Indraprastha, they attacked him (i.e. Arjuna) on the way (in Pañchanada) and robbed most of the women. The Yādava re-exodus to Indraprastha under the leadership of Arjuna is a historical fact and forms a basic part of the *Mahābhārata* episode. The date of this event which took place shortly after the Bharata war would be before 1,000 B.C. if tradition is to be believed. Even if its date is fixed on the basis of the time of the *Mahābhārata* composition, it cannot be much later than the fourth-third century B.C. as the epic nucleus seems to have been complete by this time. The main story of the *Mushala Parva* describing the attack of the Ābhīras upon the Yādavas cannot be dismissed as an interpolation for it forms an integral part of the epic. In the light of this, we can hold that the Ābhīras lived in India several centuries before the Christian era. Our opinion seems to be corroborated by the *Mahābhāshya* of Patañjali who flourished in the early part of the second century B.C.

Pātañjali mentions Ābhīras in his *Mahābhāshya* in the compound Śūdrābhīram while commenting on and illustrating the grammatical aphorism *Sāmānya viśesha vāchinośchadvandābhāvāt siddham*.[124] The very fact that the Ābhīras were considered in Patañjali's time as Śūdras, one of the four varṇas in Indian society, shows that they (i.e. the Ābhīras) settled and were domiciled in Indian soil at least some centuries before the second century B.C. It may be stated here that they are also

[122]D. R. Bhandarkar, "Foreign Elements in Hindu Population," *Indian Antiquary*, Vol. XL (1911), pp. 7 ff; *Some Aspects of Indian Culture*, pp. 4, 62. Sir R. G. Bhandarkar also places the Ābhīra migration into India in the first century A. D. (*Vaishnavism, Saivism and Minor Religious Systems*, p. 34).

[123]Sorensen, *Index of Names in the Mahābhārata*, p. 4.

[124]Kielhorn, *Vyākaraṇa Mahābhāshya*, Vol. 1, p. 252.

called *Śūdras* in certain parts of the *Mahābhārata.*[125] All this would tend to show that D.R. Bhandarkar may not be correct in bringing down the Ābhīra migration into India as late as the first century A.D.

[125]Sorensen, *op. cit.*, p. 4.

6. Jainism

The Jainas claim high antiquity for their religion and enumerate twenty-four Jinas (a term from which the word Jaina has been derived) or Tīrthaṅkaras,[1] i.e., the expounders of dharma. Rishabha is the first and Vardhamāna is the last of these Tīrthaṅkaras. Though nothing can be said definitely about the historicity of the early Tīrthaṅkaras (as the age and stature assigned to them seem to be unbelievable), yet there can hardly be any doubt that Vardhamāna Mahāvīra's two immediate predecessors (Arishṭanemi and Pārśvanātha) were historical persons. Vardhamāna was, in fact, a reformer and not the founder of the Jaina religion as some scholars think him to be.

Regarding Arishṭanemi, we know from Jaina literary tradition that he was born in the Yādava clan of Dvaraka and was a cousin of Krishṇa Vāsudeva and Baladeva (who were leaders of another group of philosophies or religious sects such as the Vaishṇavas). His father, Samudra Vijaya, was king of Dvaraka or Saurīpura and his mother was Śivadevi. The race to which he belonged was called Harivaṁśa. His (i. e.

[1]A Jina or Tīrthaṅkara, according to Jaina belief, is one who has attained omniscience and freedom not by the help of a teacher nor by the revelation of the Vedas but by his own power. He is also given many other epithets, like Mahāvīra, Sarvajña, Kevalin and Arhat, etc. indicating the ideas entertained about him by his votaries.

The twenty four Jinas or Tīrthaṅkaras are Rishabha, Ajita, Sambhava, Abhinandana, Sumati, Padmaprabha, Supārśva, Chandraprabha, Pushpadanta or Suvidhi, Śitala, Sreyāṁśa, Vāsupūjya, Vimala, Ananta, Dharma, Sānti, Kunthu, Ara, Malli, Munisuvrata, Nimi, Nemi or Arishṭanemi, Pārśvanātha and Vardhamāna Mahāvīra.

Arishṭanemis) parentage and family have thus a well-known historical background.[2]

Pārśvanātha is one of the most important Jaina Tīrthaṅkaras. Some regard him as the true founder of the Jaina faith.[3] His father was Aśvasena, king of Benaras, and his mother queen Vāmādevī. He was probably born in about 817 B.C. and died about 717 B.C. He took to the life of an ascetic at the age of thirty. He obtained enlightenment at the foot of an Aśoka tree and preached for seventy years the doctrines of love and fraternity.[4] According to the *Uttarādhyayanasūtra*,[5] he enjoined upon his followers four vows: (*i*) not to injure life; (*ii*) to speak the truth; (*iii*) not to steal, and (*iv*) not to own property, while Mahāvīra added one more, namely, the vow of chastity. Pārśva allowed his disciples to wear a garment but Mahāvīra advocated complete nudity.[6] Thus, Pārśva was a historical person and, as is known, his organization was led by Keśi in the days of Mahāvīra. That Jainism as a religious movement flourished before Mahāvīra's time is proved by a few more facts. "Nirgrantha" or Nigaṇṭha was the name by which the Jainas were originally known, though it was later on applied to denote Mahāvīra's followers particularly. It may be noted here that the *Pitakas* mention very often the Nirgranthas as opponents or converts of Buddha and his disciples. As it is nowhere stated or implied that they were a newly founded sect we may hold that they existed a considerable time before the advent of Buddha and also of Mahāvīra.[7] As Buddhaghosha informs us, Makkhali Gośāla, the founder of the Ājīvika sect, divided the contemporary population into six clans of which the Nirgranthas were one.[8] All this would tend to show the great antiquity

[2]B. C. Bhattacharya, *The Jaina Iconography*, p. 81.

[3]Rhys Davids, *Encyclopaedia Britannica*, 9th edition, Vol. XII, p. 543.

[4]M. Bloomfield, *The Life and Stories of the Jaina Saviour, Parsvanatha.*

[5]Lecture xxiii, *Sacred Books of the East*, Vol. xlv; *Encyclopaedia of Religion and Ethics,* Vol. 1, p. 264.

[6]*Uttarādhyayanasūtra*, Lecture xxiii, *Sacred Books of the East*, Vol. XLV.

[7]*Ibid.*, pp. xxii, xxiii.

[8]*Sāmaññaphala Sutta-Vāṇṇanā* in the *Sumaṅgala-vilāsini*, *Buddhaghosha's* Commentary on the *Dīgha-Nikāya* (Pali Text Society's Edition), pp. 160-65.

of this sect[9] before Vardhamāna Mahāvïra, the twenty-fourth Tīrthaṅkara. Vardhamāna was a great preacher and he showed extraordinary genius in organizing the Jaina Sangha. He was born in Vaisali (modern Basarh) in the district of Muzaffarpur, Bihar. His father, Siddhārthā, was the head of the Kshatriya clan, the Nāṭas or Nāyas of Kollāga,[10] the suburb of Vaisali. Hence Mahāvīra was known also as Vesāliya, i. e. of Vaisali. His mother's name was Triśalā, a daughter of Chetaka, who was then the governing "Rajan" of the Republic of Vaisali. Mahāvīra who was born about 599 B. C. was therefore a highly connected personage.[11] His parents died when he was thirty and he became a monk and took to a life of mortification lasting for twelve years, when he reached the state of omniscience. He died at Pava (Patna District) at the age of 72 in 527 B. C.

In Kollaga there was a religious establishment called the Dūipalāsa Chaitya for the accommodation of the monks of the order of Pārśvanātha to whom the Nāya clan (to which Vardhmāna belonged) professed allegiance.[12] Mahāvīra, on adopting the monk's vocation joined the order of Pārśvanātha. But the observances of that order do not seem to have satisfied his notions of stringency, including nudity.[13] So after one year he separated[14] and, discarding his clothes, wandered about the country of north and south Bihar.

The last 30 years of his life Mahāvīra passed in preaching his religious system and organizing his order of asectics. His order was patronised chiefly by those princes with whom he was connected through his mother, the royal families of Videha, Magadha and Anga. He spent the major part of his life in the

[9]*Majihima Nikāya* (of the Pali Text Society's Edition), p. 250.

[10]Belonging to the Nāṭa clan of Vaisali Vardhamāna is called a *Nāṭaputta*, *Sacred Books of the East*, Vol. XXII, p. xvi.

[11]*Proceedings of the Asiatic Society of Bengal*, Feb. 1898, p. 40 ff.

[12]*Ibid.*, p. 40.

[13]*Ibid.*

[14]Mahāvīra was thus not the propounder of the Jaina religion. He was a monk who espoused the Jaina creed and brought about a reformation in the Jaina church. He may be called in one sense the first schism-maker in the Jaina church inasmuch as he seceded from Pārśva's order.

towns and villages of these regions[15] though he perhaps extended his travels up to Sravasti in the north and Kalinga in the south-east. He won for himself numerous followers among the clergy and the lay clergy.[16] After his death the Jaina order continued to flourish under the rule of the great ascetic's disciple Sudharmā and his successors, as we learn from the study of the Jaina legends.

Mahāvīra and Gautama Buddha, because of their aristocratic descent, had easy access to the royal courts and made many converts from among the members of the royal houses. Mahāvīra met Bimbisāra and his son Ajātaśatru or Kuṇika and was treated by them as well as by others of the royal family with the utmost courtesy and respect. After Mahāvīra's death, Jainism also continued to receive royal patronage as was the case with Buddhism after the death of Gautama Buddha. In fact, the success of both Jainism and Buddhism was largely due to royal support. According to Jain literary traditions, Ajātaśatru's son and successor, Udayī, was a great patron and follower of the Jaina faith. The *Āvaśyakasūtra*[17] and also Hemachandra's *Pariśishṭa-Parva*[18] inform us that Udayaī caused to be built a splendid Jaina temple in the centre of his new capital, Pataliputra. That the Jainas had free access into his court is evident from the fact that he was murdered by one (whose father was dethroned by him) in the guise of a Jaina monk.

Jainism seems to have had abundant influence with the rulers of the Nanda dynasty. The Hathigumpha inscription tells us that the image of a Jina was taken away as a trophy to Magadha by a Nanda who was a Jaina and Jainism came to Kalinga at a very early date.[19] This has also the support of the literary tradition that the Nanda dynasty has a line of Jaina ministers beginning with Kalpaka.[20]

[15]*Sacred Books of the East*, Vol. XXII, pp. xv-xvi ff; *Proceedings of the Asiatic Society of Bengal*, 1890, 40 ff.

[16]The present chapter contains a detailed description of Mahāvīra's church-organisation.

[17]*Āvaśyakasūtrā*, p. 689.

[18]Hemchandra's *Pariśishṭaparva*, Canto VI, v. 181. See also p. lxii.

[19]See p. 153 of the present treatise.

[20]*Āvaśyākasūtra*, p. 692.

The Mauryas succeeded the Nandas on the Magadhan throne. According to the Jaina tradition, a great famine visited Magadha lasting twelve years, during the reign of Chandragupta Maurya. Bhadrabāhu, the leader of the Jain church, left Magadha with a number of his followers and settled in the Carnatic country. The Jains say that Chandragupta Maurya also followed Bhadrabāhu[21] and starved himself to death at Sravana Belgola following the Jaina practice.

The Aśokan Edicts supply the earliest authentic information on the Jainas. Aśoka not only interested himself in Buddhism which he professed in his later years but took care in a fatherly way of all other religions. In Pillar Edict VII he says:

> Some [Mahāmātras] were ordered by me to busy themselves also with Brāhmaṇas [and] Ājīvikas; other were ordered by me to busy themselves also with the Nirgranthas.[22]

The Nirgranthas, as already mentioned above, are the older name of the Jainas and as they are mentioned here along with the other important sects of the land we may conclude that they were of no small importance during Aśoka's time. Aśoka's grandson, Samprati, was a staunch follower of the Jaina religions and showed great zeal in the propagation of this faith. Hemachandra credits him with the creation of a large number of Jaina temples all over Jambudvīpa and he led with great devotion religious festivals and processions in honour of the Arhats during the stay of Suhastin in Ujjayini. This devotion of Samprati was emulated not only by the chiefs subordinate to him but also by the kings of the adjacent kingdoms, with the result that the Jaina faith gained widespread popularity. Samprati's missionary efforts spread to South India as well. Hemachandra tells us that he sent Jaina monks to preach in countries like those of the Andhras and Darmillas[23] (Dravidian countries).

Of the archaeological remains of Jainism pertaining to the Maurya period, mention may be made of a nude torso of

[21]Narsimhachar, *Epigraphia Carnatica*, Introduction, p. 41; Lewis Rice, *Mysore and Coorg*, p. 8.

[22]Hultzsch, *Corpus Inscriptionum Indicarum*, Vol. I, p. 136.

[23]Hemchandra, *Pariśishṭaparva,* Canto XI, vv. 63-102.

polished Chunar stone, which may be described as a Tīrthaṅkara figure in Kāyotsarga posture. Another torso of the same type, but belonging probably to the Śuṅga period, shows the continuance of Tīrthaṅkara worship in Magadha. Both these torsos, found in Lohanipur near Patna town, are preserved in the Patna Museum, Patna. Some Jaina bronzes from Chausa in the Shababad district and those from Machuatand Aluara in Manhum district seem to show the popularity of Jainism in Bihar during the late Śuṅga and Kushāna period.

During the Śuṅga period, Jainism found strong support among the people of Kalinga. As Buddhism became the paramount religion of the Magadhan empire during the reign of Aśoka, so was Jainism in Kalinga during the reign of Khāṛavela. The text of the Hathigumpha cave inscription (deciphered by R. D. Banerjee and K. P. Jayaswal, *Epigraphia Indica*, Vol. XX, pp. 72 ff) shows that Khāravela, who flourished as the overlord of Kalinga in the early part of the second century B. C.,[24] was devoted to the Jaina creed. This record, which furnishes a description of the first thirteen years of Khārvela's reign, opens with an invocation to the Arhats and the Siddhas, two of the common appellations by which a Jaina Tīrthaṅkara or a saint is described.[25] It has to be mentioned that this invocation which quite agrees with the usual Jaina formula of *Namaskāra*,[26] is met with also in Jaina inscriptions of

[24]There is a good deal of difference of opinion among scholars regarding the date of Khāravela. Jayaswal assigns him to the first half of the second century B. C. and holds that he was a contemporary of Pushyamitra Śuṅga. (*Epigraphia Indica*, Vol. xx, pp. 75-6). According to H. C. Raychaudhury, Khāravela is to be assigned either to the third century B.C. or the first century B.C. and in no case could he be a contemporary of Pushyamitra Śuṅga (*Political History of Ancient India*, 4th Ed., pp. 314-15). In the opinion of Rapson, Khāravela belongs in any case to almost the middle of the second century B.C. (*Cambridge History of India*, Vol. I, p. 535). These differences of opinion regarding the date of Khāravela would hardly affect our main conclusion as our task is to give the history of Jainism in Kalingā in the post-Mauryan period (c. 185 B.C.-300 A.D.)

[25]*Epigraphia Indica*, Vol. XX, p. 79.

[26]*Namo arihaṁtāṇaṁ namo Siddhānam/Namo āyariyāṇaṁ namo uvajhāyāṇaṁ/Namo loesavva sāhūṇaṁ*. Compare the Buddhist formula of *vandanā* in the *Peṭakopadesa* : *Namo Sammāsambuddhānaṁ paramattha dassinaṁ silādiguṇa pāramippattānaṁ.*" *Indian Historical Quarterly*, Vol. XIV, p. 462.

Mathura.[27] Hence it is natural to suppose that Khāravela, who paid obeisance to the Arhats and the Siddhas, was an adherent of the Jaina faith.

If the invocation formula of the Hathigumpha inscription be indecisive as to whether Jainism was the personal faith of Khāravela or the person by whom the epigraph was composed for him, the contents of the epigraph when studied fully will leave no doubt with regard to Khāravela's allegiance to Jainism and its wide popularity in Kalinga.

In line 12 of the Hathigumpha cave inscription we are told that Khāravela in the twelfth year of his reign attacked Magadha, made its king Bahasatimitra (whose identity is a matter of great controversy among scholars) bow at his feet and he carried to and set up in Kalinga the image of Jina of Kalinga which was earlier taken away from Kalinga by king Nanda[28] of Pataliputra (4th century B. C.).

The episode of the Jaina idol as narrated in line 12 of the Hathigumpha inscription offers some valuable information with regard to the history of Jainism. Firstly, it shows that Khāravela was an avowed champion of the Jaina faith which is supported by the other contents of the Hathigumpha inscription. Secondly, it tells us that Jainism prevailed in Kalinga as its national faith for some centuries even before Khāravela's time. Thirdly, it leads us to believe that the Nanda invader who carried away the Jina image was interested in the Jaina faith.

The antiquity and popularity of Jainism in Kalinga before Khāravela's time has the support of literary tradition. The Jaina *Harivaṁśa Purāṇa* states that Mahāvīra Vardhamāna

[27]*Archaeological Survey Reports*, XX, pl. V, No. 6 : Namo Arhata Vardhamānasa, Lüders List No. 59.

[28]M(āgadha) (ṁ) cha rājānaṁ Baha (sa) timitaṁ pādevamdāpayati Nanda-rājañītam cha Kā (li) ṁga-Jinam saṁnive(sa) (*Epigraphia Indica*, Vol. XX, p. 80). Dr Barua reads this portion thus : *Mā (gadhaṁ) cha rājānam Baha-(sa)timita (m) pade va (ṁ) dāpa(ya) ti, Nandarāja-Jita Kaliṅga-jana-saṁ (n) i(ve)sam.* Khāravela, compelled Brihaspatimitra, the king of the Magadha people, to bow down at his feet (did something in connection with) the settlements of Kalinga people subjugated by king Nanda (*Indian Historical Quarterly*, XIV, p 480).

preached his religion in Kalinga.[29] Another Jain work, *Āvaśyakasūtra*, says that Mahāvīra visited Kalinga, as the king of that country was a friend of his father.[30] In view of this, there is nothing surprising about the fact that Kalinga had a Jina idol in the days of the Nandas (two centuries after Mahāvīra's nirvāṇa). Since its introduction in Kalinga, Jainism seems to have enjoyed an uninterrupted popularity there. It may be pointed out that the Udayagiri and Khandagiri hills in Orissa are honeycombed with caves and cells which were in use by the Buddhist and Jaina monks from an early time. Though most of the caves were excavated during the second-first centuries B.C.[31] there is no doubt that some of them are much older than Khāravela's time. In this connection Ganguly observes:

> We think we shall not be far from the truth in dating some of the caves even in the 4th or 5th century B.C.—that is, before the period of the Hathigumbha inscription, for the locality where the caves were excavated must have had some sort of previous sanctity preserved in the eyes of the coreligionists.[32]

Further, it is stated in the *District Gazetteer*, Puri, that there settled in that district a large number of Jainas during the rule of Aśoka. Some of the sandstone hills of Udayagiri and Khandagiri contain their hermitage caves with traces of inscriptions in Maurya Brāhmī characters.[33] They all seem to have been excavated for the religious use of the Jaina monks and have been used by them for many a century. Again, the site of the Hathigumpha cave itself seems to bear evidence to the antiquity of Jainism in Kalinga. A royal edict, so that it may serve its purpose, is engraved at a place which is promi-

[29]R. D. Banerji, *History of Orissa,* Vol. i, p. 61.

[30]*Āvaśyakasūtra*, pp. 219-20.

[31]B. M. Barua, *Old Brahmi Inscriptions in the Udayagiri and Khandagiri Caves,* pp. 292 ff.

[32]Manmohan Ganguly, *Orissa and Her Remains—Ancient and Mediaeval,* p. 32.

[33]*Bengal District Gazetteer,* Puri, p. 24.

nent in the eye of the people for some reason or other. The caves in ancient India were holy resorts of the monks and saints. So it may be supposed that Khāravela, who was a Jaina, chose to incise his record there on the obvious ground of the religious sanctity attached to it, for the situation of the Hathigumpha cave cannot be attributed importance of any other kind, viz. commercial or strategic. We have epigraphic evidence to show that the spot was visited by piligrims as late as eleventh century A.D.[34]

It has already been pointed out that Mahāvīra preached his religion in Kalinga. Jayaswal and R. D. Banerji think that the Kumārī hill may be the site where he preached, as they are inclined to believe that the expression *Supavata-vijaya-chaka kumārīpavate* (on the Kumārī hill where the wheel of law had been well revolved, i. e., the religion of Jina had been preached) contains an allusion to that effect.[35] If Jayaswal and Banerji's reading and translation are regarded as authentic, there is no difficulty in accepting the literary tradition of the Jainas regarding Mahāvira's visits to and preaching in Kalinga. Further, the Hathigumpha Cave inscription shows that there were on the Udayagiri hills Kāya Nishīdīs (the relic memorials) as Jaina institutions, in existence from before Khāravela's time.[36] Line 14 of the Hathigumpha inscription refers to the Yāpa professors who were at Kāya Nishīdī (relic memorial) on the Udayagiri hill. The word Nishīdī occurs in Pillar Edict VII of Aśoka and the Nagarjuni Hill cave inscription of his grandson Dasaratha as Niṁsiḍhiyā and Nishīdīyā respectively, The Jainas employ this word in the sense of resting places. The Jainas employ the word in a technical sense, i. e., in the sense of a memorial tomb erected over the remains of a Jaina ascetic. That the Nishīdīs on the Kumārī hill were not merely

[34] *Epigraphia Indica,* Vol. XX, p. 72. On the wall of the Hathigumpha Cave there were a number of medieval records (10th-11th century) consisting mostly of the proper names which shows that the pilgrims regarded this place as a sacred spot as late as the 11th century A. D.

[35] *Ibid.,* Vol. XX, pp. 72, 80. Dr Burua translates this portion of the text as "On the Kumari Hill in the well founded realm of victory" (*Indian Historical Quarterly,* Vol. XIV, p. 480).

[36] *Ibid.*, Vol. XX, LL. 14 and 15, p. 80.

ornamental tombs is evident from the qualifying word Kāya. This shows that the enshrinement of the corporeal relics of the saints was a practice prevalent among the Jainas from an early time as it was the case with the Buddhists. This seems to be also corroborated by the Jaina stūpas discovered at Mathura. All this tends to prove the settlement of the Jainas in Kalinga before Khāravela's time.

Khāravela took a deep interest in Jaina religious doctrines. Line 14 of the Hathigumpha inscription says that in the thirteenth year of his reign he respectfully offered royal maintenance, China clothes (silk) and white clothes to the members of the Yāpanīya Saṁgha (Yāpa-ñavakehi) who "have extinguished the rounds of their lives" by means of austerities at the relic memorial (Kāya-Nashīdī) on the Kumārī Hill.[37] The Yāpana Saṁgha flourished in the south. They are mentioned often in Jaina literature and medieval inscriptions of South India.[38] On the authority of the *Bhadrabāhucharta*, Jayaswal says that the Yāpana Saṁgha were among the numerous disciples of Bhadrabāhu who worshipped his bones, and then finally decided to remain without clothes.[39]

Khāravela's interest in the Jaina faith is indicated also by a few more facts. From the closing portion of line 14 of the Hathigumpha cave inscription as interpreted by Banerji and Jayaswal, we learn that Khāravela as a layman was devoted to worship and that he realized the nature of *Jiva* and *Deha.*[40] *Jīva,* according to the Jainas, is the first category of the fundamental truth of their philosophy. They say that experience

[37]*Terasame cha vase Supavata vijaya chaka Kumārīpavate arahayate pakhina-sam (si) tehi Kāyanisīdīyāya Yāpañavakehi rājabhitini Chinavatāni va (sā) s (i) tāni* (*Ibid.*, Vol. XX, p. 80).

[38]Premi, *Vidvatratnamālā,* i. p. 132; Maliyapundi grant of Chalukya King Ammaraja II (*Epigraphia Indica,* vol. IX, p. 54; *Indian Antiquary,* Vol. XII, p. 20). According to the inscriptional evidence the Yāpakas were a part of the pure Nandigachha community (*Epigraphia Indica,* vol. IX, p. 54).

[39]*Journal of the Bihar and Orissa Research Society,* Patna; Vol. IV, p. 398.

[40]*Pūj-ānurata-uvās (aga) Khāravela sirinā Jīva-deha (siri) kā parikhitā* (*Epigraphia Indica,* Vol. XX, p. 80).

shows that all things may be divided into the living (*Jīva*) and non-living (*Ajīva*), the principle of life is entirely distinct from the body and it is most erroneous to think that life is either the product or the property of the body. It is on account of this life principle that the body appears to be living. This principle is the soul.[41]

The highest goal of a Jaina is Nirvāṇa. But only an ascetic who has renounced the world and has faithfully performed the duties and vows prescribed for him can attain it. Though a layman cannot attain Nirvāṇa, he can undertake duties and share the principles of the Jaina religion which enables him to treat the way which leads to it. From the Hathigumpha inscription it appears that Khāravela was a devoted lay worshipper and that he was able to realize the higher ideals of the Jaina philosophy.

Line 15 of the Hathigumpha inscription states that Khāravela convened a council of the wise ascetics and sages from all directions near the relic depository of the Arhats. The object of this assembly is referred to in line 16 which, according to Jayaswal, states that Khāravela caused to be compiled expeditiously the text of the seven-fold Aṅgas of the sixty-four letters.[42]

According to the Jaina tradition the Jaina canon seems to have fallen into oblivion during the time of the famine which occurred in Magadha when Bhadrabāhu, a contemporary of Chandragupta Maurya (fourth century B.C.) was the leader of the Jaina community. After the famine was over a council met at Pataliputra to collect the canonical scriptures under the leadership of Sthūlabhadra. The council collected the eleven Aṅgas but the 12th was missing. "This twelfth Aṅga contained fourteen pūrvas which Sthūlabhadra was able to supply." During the famine period, Bhadrabāhu, as is well known, migrated to the South with a number of his disciples, leaving the leadership of the Jaina church in the hands of Sthūlabhadra. His party,

[41]S. N. Das Gupta, *History of Indian Philosophy,* Vol. I, p. 188.
[42]*Epigraphia Indica,* Vol. XX, p. 79.
[43]*Ibid.,* Vol. XX, p. 77.

which came back after the famine was over, refused, however, to accept the text of the Pataliputra council and declared the Aṅgas and pūrvas as lost.

From the above it appears that the Jaina canon established at Pataliputra was not an agreed religious canon of the Jainas consisting of two main groups—one represented by Sthūlabhadra and the other by Bhadrabāhu. That Khāravela undertook the compilation of the Jaina canon which is described by Fleet as being lost or scattered since the time of the Mauryas, indicates perhaps that according to the reading of Jayaswal and R.D. Banerji, the works "Angasatikaṁ turiyaṁ" of Aṁgasstikaturiyaṁ are qualified by the adjective "Choyaṭhi" meaning thereby "the seven-fold Aṅgas or Aṅgas in collection of 7 and 4 consisting of letters."[43] The term Choyaṭhi has been given a mysterious interpretation by the Jainas who hold that their sacred literature is made up by 64 letters. J.L. Jaina in his introduction to the *Jīva-Khanda* of the *Gommata Sāra*[44] observes:

> The knowledge of Śruti, Śruta Jñāna may be of things which are contained in the Aṅgas (limbs of sacred books of the Jainas) or of things outside the Aṅgas. There are 64 simple letters of the alphabet; of these 33 are consonants, 27 vowels and 4 auxilliary (which help in formation of compound letters).

The above discussion shows that Khāravela was highly interested in his faith and displayed a good deal of enthusiasm to restore the Jaina scriptures.

Though Khāravela was a patron and follower of the Jaina faith, in his training and policy he did not differ much from other Indian princes. His coronation took place according to Brahmanical rites.[45] He undertook military expeditions and guided himself by the ideals of Brahmanical sovereignty. The principles and methods which he followed in governing his kingdom were quite in accordance with those laid down in

[44] J. L. Jaini, *Gommatasāra,* Introduction, p. 12.
[45] Barua , *Old Brāhmī Inscriptions, etc.*, p. 263.

Brahmanical treatises on Hindu policy. He bestowed gifts on members of other sects as he did on the Jainas. The observance of some of the Brahmanical ideals by Khāravela who was a Jaina, rather puzzled Dr Barua who wrote that so far as this world was concerned Khāravela was a Hindu, and that so far as the other world was concerned, he was a pious Jaina.[46]

In this connection it may be suggested that the general tendency in India is to maintain the ancient rites and traditions. The ancient Vedic ceremonies should not be identified with one set of practices meant for a particular sect. The term Vedic has a wide significance and does not exclusively connote the Brahmanic, though the Brahmanical religion has retained more of the Vedic character than any other religion. The Vedic ceremonies are a mass of social traditions. The kings and princes, to whatever faith they might have belonged, tried to keep up the ancient practices which were embedded in the general structure of Indian culture. Further, it may be stated that the Buddhists and Jainas discarded the ancient or Vedic practices to the extent that they militated against the accepted philosophies. The social practices were left alone. In fact Buddhism and Jainism were more philosophies than religions until very late. Thus it is not necessary to consider Khāravela's coronation ceremony or his gifts to the Brāhmaṇas as being inconsistent with his religious outlook even from the strict Jaina standpoint.

Jainism seems to have been the religious faith also of other members of Khāravela's family, including his chief queen and his successors. The Svargapura Cave[47] inscription records that the cave was dedicated to the Kalinga recluses of the Jaina faith by his chief queen who is described as the daughter of the high-souled king Lalārka Hasti Sāha or Hastisiṁha.[48] We have a number of Udayagiri Hill inscriptions of Khāravela's successors recording their dedication of caves to the monks

[46]Barua, *op. cit.*, p. 263.

[47]The upper story of the Manchapuri cave is popularly known as Svargapuri. It has been referred to by R. L. Mitra and Fergusson as Vaikunthapuri Cave.

[48]Barua, *op. cit.*, p. 57, see also f. no. 1, p. 57.

[49]*Indian Historical Quarterly*, Vol. XIV, pp. 160-66; *Epigraphia Indica*, Vol. XIII, p. 159 f.

The inscriptions which belong to 200 B. C. 100 A. D. do not specify as to which particular religious sects the monks receiving gifts belonged. But in view of the preponderance of the Jaina faith in Khāravela's time it is quite natural to suppose that the recipients of gifts mentioned in these inscriptions were mostly of the Jaina faith.

Jainism in Western and Southern India

Western India is one of the early strongholds of the Jainas. Dvaraka is the birthplace as well as the main centre of the missionary activities of Arishṭanemi, the twenty-second Jaina Tīrthaṅkara. Samprati, a grandson of Aśoka, whose dominion included the Avanti region, was a devout follower and patron of the Jaina religion as noticed before. As the *Kālakāchārya-kathānaka* and the Jaina recension of the *Vikramacharita* show, Jainism continued to flourish here during the post-Mauryan period too. According to the *Kālakācharyakathānaka* the Jaina saint Kālaka came to Ujjayini with his followers to preach his doctrines. It so happened that Kālaka's sister, Sarasavatī, also reached there after some days with a party of nuns. Gardabhilla, the king of Ujjayini, as the story tells us, was so infatuated with the beautiful Sarasavatī that he carried her off. When Kālaka failed to rescue his sister, he went to the land of the Śakas (where the princes are called Shāhīs and their over-lord Shānano Shāhī)[50] and persuaded 96 Śaka princes to invade Ujjayini. Gardabhilla was defeated in the encounter and Kālaka placed one of the Śaka princes on the throne. After a time, as we are told in the story, there arose a king of Mālava named Vikramāditya who overthrew the Śakas, ruled gloriously and established an era of his own. Subsequently, another Śaka king arose and overthrew the dynasty of Vikramāditya. When a hundred and thirty-five years of the Vikrama era had elapsed, this Śaka king started an era of his own.

[50]This title in its Greek and Indian form was adopted by the Śaka kings of the Punjab, Maues and his successors who belong to the first century B.C., and it appears in the form Shaonano Shao on the coins of Kushana rulers. This shows that the Kālaka story has a historical background.

According to certain eminent historians, Gardabhilla and Vikramāditya (who is in their opinion perhaps the founder of the Vikrama era of 57 B.C.) were actual historical persons reigning in the first century B. C. and the Kālaka story reflects the history of this period.[51] If this is conceded, we can hold that there was a good deal of Jaina influence in western India in Gardabhilla's time[52] (i. e. early part of the first century B. C.). It may be noted that there were three saints of the name of Kālakāchārya, and one was separated from another by an appreciable period of time. As is generally held, it was Kālaka II who was the uprooter of Gardhābhilla. The year of Kālaka II is by all authorities said to be 453 B.C. of the Vīra era in which years it is stated in a stanza appended to several manuscripts of Dharmaprabhasuri's version that he took (*gahiya*) Sarasvatī.

Coming to Vikramāditya, the successor of Gardhabhilla, we find that the Jainas claim him as one of the patrons and followers of their religion. The Jainistic recension of the *Vikramacharita* represents Vikrama as listening to the instruction of the Jaina saint Siddhasena Divākara, with great interest.[53] The *Jainapaṭṭāvalīs* tell us that Siddhasena Divākara converted Vikrama to his faith in 470 Vīra era (i. e. 57 B. C.).[54] As to the archaeological evidence of Jainism in this period, though not necessarily of western India, mention may be made of an interesting bronze image of Pārśvanātha standing in the Kāyotsarga posture. There are snake hoods over his head. The image is preserved in the Prince of Wales Museum of Western India, Bombay. Though its findspot is not known, on a stylistic basis it can be attributed to the first century B. C.

[51]Sten Konow, *Corpus Inscriptionum Indicarum*, Vol.II, p. XXVII; Smith, *Oxford History of India,* 1919, p. 151; Edgerton, *Vikrama's Adventure* (Jainistic Recension), Part I, p. Lvii, ff.

[52]The *Purāṇas* refer to the Gardabhillas and make them precede the Śakas, Pargiter, *Dynasties of Kali Age*, p. 45; N. Brown, *The Story of Kālaka,* p. 6.

[53]Edgerton, *Vikrama Charita,* Harvard Oriental Series, Vol. 26, pp. 26, 251-254; Vol. 27, p. 233 ff.

[54]Paṭṭāvalīs of Kharataragachchha, *Indian Antiquary*, Vol. XI, 1882, p. 247.

According to Jaina Paṭṭāvalīs, there flourished in western India in the first century B. C. several Jaina saints besides Siddhasena Divākara, who were noted for their learning and missionary zeal. Among them mention may be made of Vriddhavādin, Vajra and Pādalipta. Vriddhavādin[55] is regarded by the Jains as a saint of great repute and a Guru of Siddhasena. Vajra,[56] who belonged to the Gautama gotra, was born in 496 Vīra era (31 B. C.). The name of his father was Dhanagiri and that of his mother Sunandā. He learnt the eleven *Aṇgas* and went from Dasapura to Bhadragupta at Avanti to study the 12th, i. e. the *Drishṭivādāṅga.* He was the last Jaina saint to possess knowledge of the complete *Pūrvas.* He spread the Jaina religion in the South. Pādalipta was a contemporary of Vikrama Vriddhavādin and Siddhasena Divākara.[57] Jaina traditions associate him with the foundation of Palitana city.[58] According to Haribhadra Suri he spent most of his time in Manyakheta in the south and did away with all the bad religions there.[59]

Architectural remains would show that Jainism continued to flourish in Western India as a popular religion during the subsequent centuries. As scholars hold, some of the caves at Junagadh (Gujarat) were occupied by the Jainas during the third century A. D. This is indicated by a stone inscription in one of these caves. This inscription, which belongs to the time of the grandson of Kshatrapa Jayadāman mentions such Jaina terms as Kevalī. Even if it is presumed that this inscription was brought from some other place, the Jaina association of these caves is amply testified to by the occurrence of the Jaina symbols carved on Cave No. K. These symbols include the Śrīvatsa, Bhadrāsena, Nandipada, Mina-Yugala and Kalasa. It is well known that such auspicious symbols occur also on the Jaina Ayāgapaṭa of Mathura.[60]

55 *Indian Antiquary,* Vol. XI, p. 245 ff.

56 *Ibid.*

57 *Ibid.*, p. 251.

58 Jhaveri, *Nirvāṇakalikā,* Introduction, p. xi ff.

59 *Samyktvasaptati*, vv. 96, 97, quoted in the Mysore Archaeological Report, 1923, pp. 10-11.

60 *Ibid.*, *Mysore Archaeological Report*, 1923, p. 11.

Jainism seems to have been popular in the north-western parts of undivided India during the early century of the Christian era. According to Sir John Marshall, two of the stūpas at Sirkap, Taxila, were of the Jaina faith. Further, it may be mentioned here that Jaina traditions speak of a dharmachakra set up by Bahubali, son of Rishabhanātha, at Taxila.[61]

Jainism seems to have been a popular faith in the South also in our period. The *Samyaktvasaptati* states that there were many Jaina saṁghas in the South noted for their good qualities, during the first century B. C. when Pādalipta came to preach his doctrines in Manyakheta.[62] Some of the Sravana Belgola inscriptions contain references to the Jaina heirarchy and succession of Jaina teacher in South India.[63] The order generally followed is: Kuṇḍa Kuṇḍa (Koṇḍa-Kuṇḍa), Umāsvāti, Balākpaiñcha, Samantabhadra, Śivakoṭi, Devanandi and others. Of these teachers, the following, viz. Kuṇḍa Kuṇḍa, Umāsvāti, Samantabhadra and Balākapaiñcha, seem to have lived during the post-Mauryan period.[64]

Kuṇḍa Kuṇḍa was a great Jaina preacher and is held in high esteem even now among the Jainas as is evidenced by the fact that at all meetings of Jaina savants in India a reading opens with the verse:

Maṅgalaṁ bhagavān vīro maṅgalaṁ Gautamo ganin
Mangalaṁ Kuṇḍakuṇḍāryo, *Jainadharmostu maṅgalaṁ.*

Kuṇḍa Kuṇḍa was a reputed author. He is said to have composed in Prakrit a large number of works including *Pañchāstikāya*, *Pravachana-sāra*, *Samādhitantra*, *Jñāna-tattva Prajñāpana*, 10 *Bhaṭis*, and 84 *Pāhuḍas*.[65]

There is a good deal of controversy regarding the date of Kuṇḍa Kuṇḍa. Some scholars place him in the sixth century

[61]H.D. Sankalia, *Archaeology of Gujarat*, Bombay, 1941, p. 41.

[62]U.P. Shah, *Studies in Jain Art*, 1955, p. 10.

[63]*Epigraphia Carnatica*, Vol. ii, edited by R. Narasimhachar, 1923, pp. 85, 87, Introduction, 64 (40), p. 13; Lewis Rice, *Mysore and Corg*, p. 104.

[64]A.N. Upadhyay, *Pravachanasāra*, pp. XXIVff; Faddegon, *Pravachanasāra of Kuṇḍakunda*, pp. XIX ff.

[65]*Epigraphia Carnatica*, 1923, pp. 85, 87.

A.D. while others take him back to as early as third century B.C.[66] The views of these scholars are based upon insufficient data and cannot be accepted as reliable. It is to be mentioned here that a line of Digambara teachers constituting the Sarasvatī Gachchha or Nandigaṇa or Desigaṇa of the original church (*mūla saṅgha*) founded by Mahāvīra is constantly cited in the Mysore inscription as the Kuṇḍakuṇḍa *anvaya*.[67] In the *Paṭṭāvalīs* of the *Anvaya* Kuṇḍa Kuṇḍa[68] is mentioned as the third pontiff of the line, with date corresponding to 8 B.C.-44 A.D. In view of this we may hold that Kuṇḍa Kuṇḍa flourished in the second part of the first century B.C. and the early half of the first century A.D.

Regarding Umāsvāti (who was also known as Gridhrapiñcha) we have no tangible evidence to fix his date. As tradition regards him both as a contemporary of Kuṇḍa Kuṇḍa, he and his disciple and successor[69] may be regarded as living in the first or second century A. D. He is credited with a learned work called *Tattvārthasūtra*. He wrote in Sanskrit whereas Kuṇḍa Kuṇḍa wrote in Prakrit.

Balākapiñcha is said to be a direct disciple of Umāsvāti and as such he may be taken to have flourished somewhere in the second century A. D.[70] Not much is known about him.[71]

Samantabhadra, who is said to have flourished in the second century A. D., was a Digambara monk of considerable repute. A Sravana Belagola inscription tells us that he invited opponents to refute his views at Pataliputra, Malwa, Sindh, and Thakka, which shows that he travelled far and wide to preach the Jaina faith.[72]

Jainism in Mathura

During the period under review, Mathura was a flourishing

66 *Indian Culture*, Vol. VII, no. I, p. 41.

67 *Epigraphia Carnatica*, Inscriptions of Sravana Belgola, Index.

68 Hoernle, *Indian Antiquary*, Vol. XX, pp. 341-61, XXI, pp. 57-84.

69 *Indian Culture*, Vol. VII, No. 1, p. 43; Faddegon, *Pravachanasāra of Kuṇḍakuṇḍa*, pp. XIV-XV.

70 *Indian Culture*, Vol. VII, p. 43.

71 *Indian Culture*, Vol. VII, No. 1, p. 43.

72 H.L. Jain, *Jaina Śilālekha Samgraha*, part 1, No. 54, p. 102.

centre of Jainism in northern India, as Kalinga was in the south east. Archaeological evidence of Mathura throws a flood of light on the history of the Jaina religion, community and organization for several centuries from before the Christian era down to the mediaeval period. To understand the importance of Mathura as a centre of Jaina religion, art, and iconography[73] during the period under consideration, we may refer in brief to the results of archaeological excavations carried on at Kankalitila and other Jaina mounds by Cunningham and Dr. Fürher.

Cunningham's excavations at Kankal itila yielded important results. He found here a large number of broken statues of Jaina Tīrthaṅkaras, crossbars of railings and pillars, mostly inscribed. Brick walls and and pavements also were discovered but unfortunately no plans or drawings of these are available now.[74] On the basis of these discoveries Cunningham held that Kankalitila was the site of some important Jaina buildings which existed during the rule of the Indo-Scythians. This is supported by the fact that all the twelve inscriptions which he discovered belong to the Kushana rule from 5 A.D. in the reign of Kanishka to 98 A. D. in that of Vasudeva.[75]

The last and most fruitful excavations at Kankali and its neighbourhood were carried out by Dr Fürher during the years 1889-91 and 1896. Dr Fürher's discoveries are full of importance and interest inasmuch as they reveal the antiquity and wide popularity of Jainism in Mathura for several centuries before the Christian era and also throw abundant light on Jaina history during the Indo-Scythic and subsequent periods.

Amongst Fürher's discoveries in 1889-89 as enumerated in the Lucknow Provincial Museum Report, ending 1 March 1889, mention may be made, so far as early pieces are concerned, of ten inscribed statues of several Svetāmbara Jinas of the Indo-Scythic period, thirty-four pieces of scuplture forming parts of a magnificent Svetāmbara Jaina temple of the time of the

[73]Vogel, *Catalogue of the Archaeological Museum at Mathura*, p. 11.
[74]*Ibid.*
[75]*Ibid.*

Kushana King Huvishka,[76] six bases of Buddha statues inscribed and dated in the regnal years of the rulers, Kanishka, Huvishka, and Vasudeva, an inscribed statue of the Bodhisattva Amogha-Siddhārtha of the first century A. D., ten inscribed Buddhist statues of the Indo-Scythic period, a rich sculptured door-Jamb of a Buddha temple, twenty-four inscribed sculptured panels, some of which are inscribed in characters of the Indo-Scythian period, in addition to many cross-bars and railing pillars.

Fürher's work in 1889-90 exposed a Jaina stūpa and a Jaina temple belonging to the Digambara sect. In the course of this excavation were exhumed eight images of Tīrthaṅkaras, one hundred and twenty of stone railings, and many miscellaneous sculptures and and numerous inscriptions of which seventeen belong to the Indo-Scythian (Kushana period) from 5 A.D. to 86 A. D.[77]

Excavations in the winter of 1890-91 were highly successful and far surpassed the results of the two previous years. The Provincial Museum Report for 1890-91 shows the acquisition from the Kankali mound of 737 fine pieces of sculptures including well executed and beautifully finished panels, doorways, toraṇas, columns, and Tīrthaṅkaras. Among the sculptures 62 bear inscriptions with dates varying from 150 B. C. to 1023 A.D. On a beautifully carved Toraṇa there is a short inscription which seems to be written in characters more archaic than those of Dhanabhūti's record on the Barhut gateway. Again, there is another inscription which is written in two lines on an oblong slab containing the name of the founder of one of the temples excavated during the year 1889-90. This record is in the scripts of the beginning of the Christian era. These two inscriptions considered together would show that there were two Jaina temples in Mathura, one dating back to the early part of the second century B. C. and the first century A. D.[78] The existence of pre-Christian Jaina sanctuaries or establishments in Mathura is indicated by few more old inscriptions and several

[76]V.A. Smith, *op. cit.,* p. 2.
[77]*Ibid.,* p. 3.
[78]*Ibid.,* pp. 2-4.

other facts. Among these old Jaina inscriptions the earliest is that of Uttaradāsaka recording his gift of an ornamental arch. This inscription is written in the early scripts and Prakrit of the pure Pali type. On palaeographical and linguistic grounds it can be attributed to the middle of the second century B.C. or earlier.[79] The next inscriptions to be mentioned in this connection are the dedicatory records of Śivamitra and Āmohinī. The epigraph of Śivamitra is written in archaic script and it may be attributed to a period earlier than Kanishka,[80] though nothing can be said about its exact dating. Āmohinī's inscription is dated in the year 42 of the reign of Mahākshatrapa Soḍsa who is believed to have reigned in the first century B.C.[81]

All this would show the association of the Jainas with Mathura in centuries earlier than the Christian era. Further, Dr Fürher mentions in his Museum Report for 1890-91, a pilaster with an Indo-Scythic inscription which has been cut out of an ancient nude Jina statue. Further, there came to light a small Jaina statue which was carved out of the back of a sculptured panel with a rather archaic inscription on its obverse.[82] Thus it is evident that the architects of this Jaina temple of the Indo-Scythic period made use of the materials of an older Jaina temple in Mathura, existence of which seems to be proved by the above evidence. The antiquity of Jainism in Mathura is further attested to by an inscription[83] which Fürher found incised on the statue of a Tīrthaṅkara (Aranātha) set up in samvat 78 or 79 within the precincts of a stūpa which was believed to have been built by the gods when the inscription was engraved. The inscription reads thus:

(L.1.) *Sam 79 var. 4 di=20 etasyan purvvāyām Koṭṭiyegaṇe bâiṛayam sākhāyaṁ; (L. 2) Ko Aya Vridhahasti Arhato Nandi [ā] vartasa pratimām nivartayati...B...bhāryyaye Śrāvikāya (dināye) dānāṁ pratimā vodve thūpe devanirmite pra......*[84]

[79]*Epigraphia Indica,* Vol. II, p. 195.
[80]*Ibid.*, Vol. 11, p. 396.
[81]*Ibid.*, Vol. II, p. 199.
[82]V.A. Smith, *op. cit.*, p. 3.
[83]*Ibid.*, p. 4.
[84]*Epigraphia Indica*, Vol. II, p. 204.

The inscription is written in the Kushāna script and the date or the Samvat is 79. It is difficult to ascertain as to what era the year 79 refers to. It is, however, possible that the date belongs to the era used by the great Kushāna kings to whose reign the inscription was executed in 157 A. D. if the year 79 is reckoned to be 78 A. D.

It is interesting to note that the Vodva Stūpa is referred to in the inscription as having been built by the gods.[85] This shows that in 157 A.D. (the time when the inscription was incised) the Vodva stūpa was considered so ancient that it was regarded as the work of the gods, i. e. its origin was totally forgotten. The stūpa is therefore supposed to have been built several centuries before the Christian era. The *Tīrthkalpa* or *Rājaprasāda* of Jinaprabha[86] throws ample light on the antiquity of the stūpa. This work, belonging to the fourteenth century A. D., is based upon ancient materials and traditions discovered by Bühler. According to this :

> ...the Stūpa was originally of gold adorned with precious stones and erected in honour of the 7th Jina Supārśvanātha by the goddess Kuverā at the desire of two ascetics, Dharmaruci and Dharmaghosha. During the time of the twenty-third Jina, Pārśvanātha, the golden Stūpa was encased in bricks and a stone temple was built outside.[87]

The *Tīrthkalpa* further records that 1,300 years after "the Nirvāna of Māhavīra the stūpa was repaired and dedicated in honour of Pārśvanātha by a person called Bhaṭṭisūri". If the Nirvāṇa of Mahāvīra is assumed to have taken place about 527 B. C. the restoration of the stūpa would be in the seventh century A. D. and its original erection in the time of Pārsvanātha would not be later than the seventh century B.C. If this tradition is believed, the Vodva stūpa is perhaps the oldest known

[85] *Ibid.*

[86] A.A. Smith, *op. cit.*, pp. 12-13. A legendary account of this stūpa is found also in the *Yaśatilaka Champū of Somadevasūri*, Vol. 11, p. 315, *Jaina Antiquary*, Vol. VIII.

[87] V.A. Smith, *op. cit.*, p. 13.

stūpa so far. It reveals thereby the antiquity of Jainism in Mathura.[88]

Dr Fürher's Museum Report for the year ending 31 March 1896 furnishes further material with regard to the history of Jainism in Mathura. He observes:

> The Archaeological Surveyor, Western Provinces and Oudh, forwarded 57 ornamental slabs of great finish and artistic merit and 15 uninscribed bases of Tīrthaṅkaras which formed part of an ancient Jaina Stūpa dating from the 2nd century B. C.

These sculptures came out in the course of excavations at the site adjoining the Kankali mound.

The Mathura sculptures and inscriptions referred to above fall into distinct groups, viz. those of the pre-Kushāna period and others of the Kushāna period. This shows beyond doubt that Jainism flourished in Mathura several centuries earlier than the Christian era and maintained its popularity there during the Indo-Scythic rule. We shall proceed now to discuss two important points in Jaina history, viz., the Jaina church organisation and schism in the Jaina church during the post-Mauryan period in the light of evidence afforded by the post-Mauryan Jaina inscriptions of Mathura.

Jaina Community and Jaina Inscriptions of the Post-Mauryan Period

Mahavira left behind him a well organized Jaina community consisting of monks, nuns, lay men and women. Among his followers there were fourteen thousand monks. He divided them into nine gaṇas or schools and placed a Gaṇadhara at the head of each school. Besides the monks, he had a large number of followers and according to the Jaina tradition about thirty-six thousand renounced their homes to take to a monastic life. At the head of the nuns was Chandanā, a counsin or aunt of

[88] *Epigraphia Indica*, Vol. II, p. 204.

Mahāvīra. The third and fourth orders of Mahāvīra's community consisted of lay men and women respectively.

Jainism is primarily a philosophical ethical system intended for ascetics. Ascetics alone can reach the highest ideal which according to Jainism is Nirvāṇa or Moksha, "the setting free" of the individual from Saṁsāra by observing the right faith, right knowledge and the right path. It should be noted that Mahāvīra provided a place for the laity also. Though they do not leave the world and dedicate their lives to the search of the truth which a Jaina teaches, yet they can undertake the duties that would ultimately lead to Nirvāṇa. The five great vows which an ascetic has to undertake are : *Ahimsā Asatya-tyagā* (vow against untruthfulness), *Asteyavrata* (non-stealing), *Brahmacharya* (chastity) and *Aparigrahavrata* (renunciation of all love for anything or any other person).[89] Besides the above, a Jaina monk or Śramaṇa has got to observe various other rules of conduct to enable him to appreciate the three jewels—right knowledge, right faith, and right works.[90] Mahāvīra prescribed twelve vows for lay worshippers which would suit household life and at the same time lead to the highest goal of an ascetic.

The vows[91] narrated by Mahāvīra to his disciples are as follows : *Prāṇātipāta Viramaṇavrata* (never intentionally to destory a Jīva that has more than one sense), *Mrishāvāda Viramaṇavrata* (vow against falsehood and exaggeration), *Adattadāna Viramaṇavrata* (vow against stealing or taking a thing which is not given), *Maithuna Viramaṇavrata* (vow of absolute chastity to one's own wife), *Parigraha Virāmaṇvrata* (vow of curbing the desires), *Diśivrata parimāṇa* (vow of setting bounds to one's travels), *Upabhogaparibhoga parimāṇa* (setting a limit to the number of things one may use), *Anarthadaṇḍavrata* (guarding against unnecessary evils), *Sāmayika* (meditating every morning, afternoon, and evening), *Deśāvakāśikavrata* (not going beyond

[89]Stevenson, *Heart of Jainism*, pp. 235 ff.

[90]"Right knowledge is in fact knowledge of the Jaina creed" (Stevenson, *Heart of Jainism*, p. 245). "By right faith a Jaina understands the full surrender of himself to the teacher, the Jina, the firm conviction that he alone has found the way of salvation and only with him is the protection and refuge to be found." Bühler, *Indian Sects of the Jainas*, p. 5.

[91]Hoernle, *Uvāsago Dasāo*; Stevenson, *Heart of Jainism*, p. 25 ff.

the limit fixed in any of the four directions in mind or body), *Poshadhavrata* (spending by a lay man some of his time as a monk), *Atithisamvibhāgavrata* (supplying to a Nirgrantha any of the fourteen things which an ascetic is allowed to use—food, drink, fruits, betelnuts, clothes, pots, blankets, towels, and things which can be lent and returned, such as seats, benches, beds, quilts, etc., and medicine).[92] Before a layman is fit to accept these vows he has got to renounce *Pañca Atichāra* : *Śankā* (doubts), *Kānkhā* (the desire to belong to another faith), *Vitigichchā* (questioning about the reality of the fruits of Karma), *Parapā haṇḍa Paraśamsā* (praising hypocrites) and Parapākhaṇḍa santhana (association with hypocrites). What has been advised by Mahāvīra to Jaina monks and lay men apply *mutatis mutandis* to Jaina nuns and lay women respectively.

We have a large number of dedicatory inscriptions ranging from the year 5 to 98 of the era of the Indo-Scythic kings Kanishka, Huvishka, and Vāsudeva, which reveal the existence of a well organized Śvetāmbara community with its four-fold order inhabiting Mathura in the first-second centuries A.D. The inscriptions refer not only to the pious gifts of the donors but supply also the names of the monks or nuns at whose exhortation the gift was made. Further, it is usual with the dedicatory epigraphs of the Kushāna period to give the list of the teachers and the schools to which they belonged. They are described by their titles *Vāchaka* (reciter), and *Gaṇin* (head of a school), etc. The schools are called *gaṇa* (companies); the sub-division, *kula* (families) and *Śākhā* (branches). It is interesting to note that a large number of Gaṇas mentioned in the inscriptions are met with in the *Kalpasūtra* of the Śvetāmbaras, which maintains a list of the number of patriarchs and the schools they founded.

Some of the important *gaṇas*[93] with their *kulas* and *śākhās* found in the inscriptions are Koṭṭiya (Koḍiya), Vāraṇa, Ārryaudekiya, Veśavādiya, etc. The importance of these inscriptions lies particularly in the fact that they corroborate the literary traditions as given in the Śvetāmbara texts and they show that

[92] *Ibid.*, p. 218.
[93] *Sacred Books of the East*, Vol. XXII, p. 292 ff; *Epigraphia Indica*, Vol. 1, pp. 371-97; Vol. II, pp. 195-212, 311.

the Śvetāmbara community which had an important stronghold in Mathura during the Indo-Scythic period had an independent organization prior to the Christian era.

It is interesting to note that the order of nuns of the Śvetāmbara Saṁgha was a very active organization in Mathura in this period. There can be no doubt, as Bühler shows, that Ārya-Samghamikā,[94] and Āryavasula,[95] Ārya Kumāramita,[96] Balavarmā, Nandā and Akakā,[97] as well as Āryāsāmā[98] were nuns who displayed considerable religious activities. In the inscriptions they are described by their title Āryā (venerable) and as disciples, Śiśini, either of a monk or of a nun who is in her turn a female disciple of some monk. Their main duties seem to have been to give religious instruction to the women and to persuade them to make or offer gifts of Tīrthaṅkaras, pillars and pedestals in the shrines.[99] The inscriptions record various gifts which were made at their instance or request (Nirvartana).

As regards persons who are not monks but presumably lay men and women and ordinary followers, the specifications of their social position which is sometimes added in the inscriptions, possess some interest. The donors of the images, pillars and other things in the Jaina shrines and spots of Mathura belonged to various strata in social life including bankers,[100] village

[94]*Epigraphia Indica,* Vol. 1, No. II.

[95]*Ibid.,* No. XI.

[96]*Ibid.,* No. VII.

[97]*Ibid.,* No. XI.

[98]*Ibid.,* No. XIV.

[99]There is only one instance in Mathura in which a nun acts as a guide to a monk. In the inscription No. VII, *Epigraphia Indica*, Vol. 1, pp. 385-6, we find that Kumāramitā induces her son Kumārabhaṭi to make a gift of the image of Vardhamāna. Kumārmitā seems to have become a nun after the death of her husband as she is shown as having a son. The existence of Jaina nuns and lay women in Mathura can be traced also from another Mathura inscription which Cunnigham describes in the *Archaeological Survey Reports*, XX. p. 37, pl. V, No. 6. The inscription contains the expression *Chaturvarṇa Sangha* which implies the *Chaturvidha Sangha* of the Svetāmbaras consisting of monks, nuns, lay men and lay women.

[100]*Lüders List*, Nos. 24, 41.

headmen,[101] workers in metal,[102] caravan leaders,[103] perfumers,[104] dyers[105] and even courtesan.[106] This shows that during the period under review Jainism was prevalent at every level of society. One of the important features of Jainism is its claim to universality, which it shares in common with Buddhism. It opens its arms to all irrespective of their social strata. "In the stereotyped introductions to the sermons of Jina it is always pointed out out that they are addressed to the Aryan and non-Aryan. Thus, in the *Aupapātika-sūtra* it run as follows:

> *Tesim savvesim āriyamanāriyanam agiles dhammaṁ āikhai*[107]
> (To all these, Aryans and non-Aryans, he [the Jina], taught the law untiringly.)

This principle of universality is fully justified by the epigraphic records and is in accordance with the principle, viz. the conversion of low castes, such as gardeners, etc. which is not uncommon even in the present day.

Schisms in the Jaina Church and Jaina Inscriptions of the Post-Mauryan Period

One of the remarkable events in the history of the Jaina church is the schisms which divided the Jainas into various sects and groups. The first great schism seems to have been led by Mahāvīra himself inasmuch as he separated from the order of Pārśvanātha and organized his own order of monks distinct from that of the the former. This is evident also from the fact that even today there are Jainas who trace their spiritual descent from Pārśva and not Mahāvīra. The second blow to the Jaina church came when Jamāli, the son-in-law of Mahāvīra, left him with 500 monks and founded a new sect called Bahurayas.[108] The next

[101] *Ibid.*, No. 48.
[102] *Ibid.*, Nos. 29, 53 and 54.
[103] *Ibid.*, No. 30.
[104] *Ibid.*, Nos. 39, 68, 76.
[105] *Ibid.*, No. 32.
[106] *Ibid.*, No. 102.
[107] Dr Ernst Leuman, *Das Aupapatikasūtra*, p. 61.
[108] *Bhagavatīsūtra*, 9. 33, 383-7. Gosāla left Mahāvīra before he attained

epoch making division took place during the time of Bhadrabāhu who was a contemporary of Chandragupta Maurya. According to Jaina tradition there occurred during the leadership of Bhadrabāhu a famine of great severity, as noticed before. Seeing that the evil would provoke offences against "ecclesiastic rules", Bhadrabāhu migrated into Karnāta country with a portion of his disciples. Over the other portion that remained in Magadha, Sthūlabhadra assumed the headship. On the return of peace and plenty, the emigrants came back to Magadha, though Bhadrabāhu remained back. The famine brought many changes in the manners and customs of the monks in Magadha. Those who went to the South maintained strict principles of monastic life while their brethren seemed to have undertaken white robes as their clothes and grown less vigilant in their monastic rules. The Jainas who came back from Karnāṭa branded their non-emigrant brethren as heretics.

During the time when the famine took place, the Jaina canon seemed to have fallen into oblivion. Towards the end of the famine the monks of Magadha assembled at Pataliputra during the absence of Bhadrabāhu and collected the Jaina scriptures consisting of *Aṇgas* and *Pūrvas*. The monks who came back from the South refused to accept the newly established canon[109] and declared the old scriptures as lost.[110] This difference laid the foundation of disunity between the party of Sthūlabhadra and that of Bhadrabāhu, though it did not result in a definite schism at once.

Regarding the schism which brought about the division of the Jaina community into two sharp and distinct groups as Svetāmbaras and Digambaras, there are several conflicting Jaina traditions. According to the Digambara Āchārya Devasena, the Svetāmbara Samgha came into being in Vallabhipura in Saurashtra 136 years after the death of Vikrama. The origin of the Svetāmbaras is, in the opinion of Devasena, due to the wicked

Jinahood. Gosāla's desertion cannot be called a schism strictly, though it shook to some extent the prestige and integrity of the Jaina Church for the time being.

[109] *The Cambridge History of India,* Vol. 1, p. 165.

[110] *Ibid.*, p. 166.

and loose-charactered Jinasena who was a disciple of Āchārya Śānti.[111] The Svetāmbaras attribute the origin of the Digambaras to one Śivabhūti, who was in the service of the king of Ratha Vihara, and became a Jaina ascetic and received on the day of his initiation a blanket from the king as a farewell present. He was so enamoured of it that he refused to discard it in spite of his preceptor's instructions. The latter tore it to pieces one day in Śivabhūti's absence. He was angered when he came to know of this, and broke away to form the Digambara sect. His first two disciples were Kauṇḍinya and Koṭṭavīra. His sister Uttarā also wanted to follow him. Thinking that a woman should not go about naked, he dissuaded her saying that a woman "cannot obtain Moksha".[112]

The date of this schism according to the Svetāmbaras is 609 years after Mahāvīra,[113] or 82 A.D., while the Digambaras place it 136 years after Vikrama, i.e., 79 A.D. (taking the difference of time between Mahāvīra's Nirvāṇa and Vikrama as 470 years).[114] Though both the Digambara and Svetāmbara traditions agree more or less on the date of this schism (the difference being only of three years) both Jinachancra and Śivabhūti seem to be fictitious persons as the annals of both sects disclaim the fact of any such person belonging to them.

The final schism took place, according to certain Digambara traditions, in the second council which was held in Vallabhī (in Gujarat) under the presidentship of Devardhagaṇi. This council took place 980 (or 993) years after the death of Mahāvīra, probably in 454 or 467 A.D. The Digambaras attribute the origin of the whole Svetāmbara canon collectively known as *sidhānta* to this council of Vallabhī.[115]

Whatever may be the date of the final schism the process of disintegration began a few centuries from before the Christian era and the division which took place in the time of Bhadrabāhu and that of Śivabhūti brought into being two main

[111] *Darsanasāra of Devasena* (ed. by Premi), vv. 11. 13.

[112] *Āvaśyakasūtra*, p. 324; Stevenson, *Heart of Jainism*, p. 79.

[113] *Āvaśyakasūtra*, p. 323.

[114] Hoernle, *Uvasāga Dasāo*, p. IX.

[115] See Jacobi's Introduction to the translation of the *Āchārañga Sūtra*, *Sacred Books of the East*, Vol. XXII.

groups (the Digambara and the Svetāmbara) in the Jaina church with most of the peculiarities which serve the basis of demarcation between the two. Regarding the Svetāmbaras in the latter Indo-Scythic period, we have definite proof in numerous inscriptions discovered at Mathura. Most of them are engraved on the statues and pedestals of the Tīrthaṅkaras and are ascribed to the reign of Kanishka, Huvishka, and Vāsudeva. That the donors of these sculptures belonged to the Svetāmbara sect is evident from the fact that the inscriptions refer to the gaṇas or the list of teachers and pontiffs agreeing with that of the Sthavirāvalī in the *Kalpasūtra* of the Svetāmbaras.

As an example, we may refer to an epigraph which is dated in the year 9 of the reign of Kaniskha.[116] It states that the statue in question was dedicated by a Jaina lay woman, Vikaṭā, at the instance of her religious guide, Nāganandin, who belonged to the Koṭṭiya gaṇa. The Koṭṭiya gaṇa, as mentioned in the *Kalpasūtra*, was founded by Sutthiya or Suthita, the eighth successor of Vardhamāna, who died in the year 313 after Mahāvīra, i.e. in 154 B.C. Further the Jaina inscriptions show the religious activities of the Jaina nuns.[117] It is well known that only the Svetāmbaras admitted women into their order. The Digambaras refused to give them admission on the ground that they were incapable of obtaining Moksha.[118] The existence of the Svetāmbaras as a distinct group can be inferred from the four-fold synod of Kālaka II (contemporary of Gardabhilla) at Ujjayini, which consisted of monks, nuns, lay men and women.

The facts show that the Svetāmbaras had a distinct organization prior to the Christian era though their final separation from the Digambaras might have taken placed as late as the fifth century A.D. under Devardhigaṇi.

[116]*Lüders List*, No. 22, Samvat 9

[117]*Epigraphia Indica,* Vol. 1, pp. 382 ff. It is not necessary to look upon the admission of nuns among the Svetāmbaras as an imitation of Buddhist teachings, for women were admitted into some of the Brahmanical orders also (Bühler, *Indian Sect of the Jainas,* p. 4). See also *Sacred Books of the East*, XXV, p. 317.

[118]Stevenson, *Heart of Jainism*, p. 79; *Journal of the Bombay Branch of the Royal Asiatic Society*, Vol. XXVII, p. 84.

The Svetāmbara group represents, in fact, the tradition of the Pārśvanātha school which was developed about 200 years before Mahāvīra and of which Kasi and Sametasikhara (mount Pārśvanāṭha) in Magadha were the main centres. In a sense the schism between the Svetāmbara and Digambara commences from the reform of Mahāvīra himself in the sixth century B.C.

The Worship of Images in Jainism

The ideal of a Jaina ascetic is the attainment of Nirvāṇa. An ascetic, in his striving for Nirvāṇa, endeavours to suppress the natural desires of a man, and worship the higher powers. But it is not possible for a lay worshipper to cling to the ideal of an ascetic which requires stern and austere discipline. So the religious feelings of the Jaina laity, it is natural, centred round the founders of the religion (i.e. the Tīrthaṅkaras). This gave rise to the worship of the Jainas in Jainism and we know that the affections of the Buddhist laity were similarly directed (i.e. to the worship of religious heads and saints).

It is difficult to say when first the Jainas took to the practice of worshipping images. Stevenson states that an image of Mahāvīra was installed in Upakesapattana[119] during the leadership of the Jaina leader Prabhava (fourth century B. C.). That image-worship was in prevalence among the Jainas about the same time is supported by archaeological evidence. The Hathigumpha inscription of the Jaina king Khāravela records that he took back from Patliputra the Jaina idol which was carried off by one of the Nandarājas from Kalinga.[120] This shows that the Nandas who ruled in the fourth century B.C. had predilections towards Jainism,[121] that Kalinga was an ancient centre of Jaina faith, and Tīrthaṅkara images were made for worship as early as the days of the Nandas. It may be noted here that among the Patna Museum exhibits there are two nude mutilated statues[122] found in Lohanipur, Patna

[119]Stevenson, *op. cit.*, p. 69.

[120]*Journal of the Bihar and Orissa Research Society*, Vol. 111, part IV, p. 458.

[121]C. J. Shah, *op. cit.*, p. 129.

[122]*Journal of the Bihar Research Society*, 1937, pp. 130-32.

Town. One of them is polished in a manner characteristic of the Mauryan age and can be roughly attributed to the third century B. C. and the other, on stylistic grounds, to the second century B. C. It is quite possible that they represent some Tīrthaṅkara images of that period. The author of the *Arthasāstra* seems to refer to the Jaina gods in Jayanta, Vaijayanta and Sarvārthasiddhi.[123]

Most of the important caves, viz. Ananta, Rani and Ganeśa Gumphas in Orissa were excavated in the second century B. C. The Ananta Gumpha contains symbols like the Triśūla and Svastika on its back wall. Moreover, the courtyard of the cave possesses images of many Jaina deities and saints.[124] The Ranigumpha is elaborately decorated with scenes of human activities some of which may represent Jaina religious festivals.[125] These facts would show that image worship was popular among the Jainas several centuries before the Christian era.

Mathura was a very important seat of the Jainas during the period under review. The archaeological excavations[126] there have laid bare the remains of a Jaina stūpa, temples and sculptures ranging usually from the second century B. C. to the third century A. D. The Mathura sculptures have placed at our disposal immense and varied materials with regard to the study of Jaina deities. They represent most of the Tīrthaṅkaras including Rishabha, the earliest one, which shows that the belief of the Jainas in all the 24 Tīrthaṅkaras was an established fact during the period under review.

The Tīrthaṅkara images are purely Indian conceptions and do not betray any foreign influence. One of the striking features of the Jaina figures is their nudity which distinguishes them from Buddha and Buddhist images. Nudity, however, is true only of the Digambara images, whereas the Śvetāmbaras clothe their figures. The Jinas bear symbols not only on the palms and soles but also in the centre of their breasts.

[123]*Arthaśāstra*, Mysore Oriental Series, p. 61.
[124]C. J. Shah, *op. cit.*, p. 152.
[125]*Puri, Bengal District Gazetteer*, p. 254.
[126]Vogel, *op. cit.*, p. 11; V. A. Smith, *op. cit.*, pp. 2-3.

The hair is usually arranged in short curls in the shape of spirals turned towards the right as also the case with most Buddha images. But in the earlier specimens we find sometimes a different treatment. The hair assumes the appearance of perwig or it hangs down on the shoulders in strange locks. In contradistinction with Buddha, the earlier Tīrthaṅkaras have neither Ushṇīshas nor Urṇā but those of the latter part of the middle ages have a distinct excrescence on the top of the head.[127]

A very interesting type of the Tīrthaṅkara images of our period in Mathura is that of the Jina quadruple which is known in Jaina inscriptions and literature as *Sarvato-bhadrikā pratimā.* They consist of "a block square in section"[128] with a Tīrthaṅkara carved on each of the four faces. There is no injunction, however, as to the particular Tīrthaṅkaras to be figured there, but generally the most important ones are chosen. A quadruple image of an "unnamed Jina perfectly nude" is represented on an inscribed sculptured panel found in Kankali mound in Mathura.[129] The epigraph records that it was the gift of Kumāramitā, the first wife of Śreshthin called Veṇī. The figure was made at the request of the venerable Vasulā, a female pupil of the venerable Saṅghamikā who was in turn a female pupil of the venerable monk Jayabhūti. The inscription has been assigned to the Kushāna Period on palaeographical grounds.[130] From the same site, the Kankali mound in Mathura, we have another very interesting representation of an inscribed Sarvato-bhadrikā pratimā of our period. The Jina shown there is Pārśvanātha with traces of his snake canopy. The inscription states that this four fold image was dedicated by one Sthirā for the welfare and the happiness of all creatures. This inscription also belongs to the Kushāna period.[131]

We may refer now to a few early specimens of other types of sculptured representations of Jaina Tīrthaṅkaras in Mathura.

[127]Vogel, *op. cit.*, p. 42.
[128]*Ibid.*, pp. 42-3.
[129]V. A. Smith, *op. cit.*, p. 46; *Epigraphia Indica*, Vol. 1, p. 382, No. 11.
[130]V. A. Smith, *op. cit.*, p. 46.
[131]*Epigraphia Indica*, Vol. II, p. 210.

An elaborate sculpture containing the figure of a seated Jaina was found in the Kankali mound in February 1890. Unfortunately the head of the figure is missing. The Jina is shown with numerous attendant deities. On the pedestal are two lions and two bulls. From the presence of the bull it is evident that the Jina depicted here is Ādinātha or Rishabhadatta. The inscription (defaced) at the base seems to be in some early script.[132]

Another specimen of an Ādinātha figure belonging to the Kushāna period is to be seen on the Mathura Museum Panel No. B 4. The inscription states that the figure was set up in a Jaina monastery by a lady in the year 84 of the reign of Shahi Vāsudeva,[133] the Kushana king. The relief in front of the pedestal contains a Dharma Chakra on a pillar being worshipped by human devotees including the male and female as well.

A mutilated figure of Aranātha[134] is found represented on a sculptured panel found in the Kankali mound in the year 1890-91. It belongs to the Kushāna period. The Jina is shown standing by the side of a wheel placed on a Triśūla with a piece of cloth in his left hand. Naminatha and Neminatha, the 21st and 22nd Jaina Tīrthaṅkaras seem to have been represented along with Pārśvanātha and Mahāvīra on a broken sculptured panel which might have formed part of the decoration of a Toraṇa Pillar[135] of a Jaina monastery in Mathura during our period. There is a fine specimen of a Neminātha figure[136] in the Mathura Museum which Vogel has described in his catalogue of the Mathura Museum antiquities; Neminātha is seated "cross-legged in the attitude of meditation" on the throne. The throne rests on two pillars and a pair of lions. Behind the pillars are two figures with hands joined in adoration. From the throne an ornamental cloth hangs down between the two lions. Below it there seems to be a wheel.

[132] V. A. Smith, *op. cit.*, p. 55, pl. cvxiii.

[133] Vogel, *op. cit.*, p. 67.

[134] V. A. Smith, *op. cit.*, pl. vi.

[135] *Ibid.*, pl. XVII.

[136] Vogel, *op. cit.*, pp. 77, 81.

There is a conch-shell (symbolic of Neminātha) on the plain rim of the pedestal.

The Jaina legends introduce very often the story of Krishṇa Vāsudeva and his family. In the *Antagaḍa Dasāo*[137] we are told that some members of Krishṇa's family joined the Jaina Sangha at the instance of Arishṭanemi, and Krishṇa also, as the legend goes, was proclaimed by him, that is Arshtanemi, to be the 12th among the Tīrthaṇkataas who would arise in the Duḥshama Sushama age. There is a sculptured panel[132] of Mathura which represents an ascetic receiving homage from the female devotees. The inscription records that the panel was a gift of the wife of a person called Dhanahastin. It bears the year 95 of the Kushāna king Vāsudeva's reign probably. The word Kaṇha Śramaṇa[139] occurs in bold type between the head of the ascetic and that of the lady devotee to the proper right. This Kaṇha may be the Krishṇa Vāsudeva of the Jaina legend. Whether the Jaina viewpoint regarding Krisḥna Vāsudeva and his family is accepted or not, this much is true that Jainism and Vaishnavism came in close contact with each other during the time of Arishṭanemi who was a cousin of Krishṇa and Baladeva. Because of the family relationship between Arishṭanemi and Krishṇa Vāsudeva, Jainism was co-existent with Vaishṇavism since Arishtaṇemi's time in places like Dvaraka, Central India, and the Yamuna Valley, the sphere of Yādava influence. Arishṭanemi's emblem is a conch which may be reminiscent of his relationship with the Vaishṇavite family of Krishṇa and Balarāma.

Pārśvanātha occurs very frequently in the Mathura art of our period. We have already referred to his representation as sarvatobhadrikā Pratimā. We shall consider some specimens of his figure belonging to our period. As already stated, the Prince of Wales Museum, Bombay, contains an early figure of Pārśvanātha with snake-hoods over the head. Though its findspot is not known, on a stylistic basis, it can be attributed to the first century B. C. The Mathura Museum Panel B. 70

137 *Antagaḍa Dasāo* (Oriental Translation Fund), pp. 61-2.
138 V. A. Smith, *op. cit.*, pl. XVII, p. 24.
139 *Ibid.*, p. 24.

represents a stele[140] with nude Jina figures standing one each on the four sides. Three of these figures have been provided with haloes; the fourth one is represented with a seven-headed Nāga hood.[141] This fourth figure represents, no doubt, Pārśvanātha. The Mathura Museum Panel B. 71 also contains a representation of Pārśvanātha with a similar Nāga hood. Both these figures belong perhaps to the period under review.

Vardhamāna Mahāvīra is the most popular of all the Tīrthaṅkaras. There are innumerable sculptured representations of his figure in Mathura and other centres of Jaina faith. We shall, however, for our present purpose refer only to two Vardhmāna images found in the Kankali mound in Mathura which belong perhaps to early centuries of the Christian era. In one panel he is shown seated under his sacred tree[142] with several attendant figures, one of whom is a Nāga with a canopy of cobra hoods. There is a defaced inscription on the pedestals of his image which begins with "Namo"[143] in early script. The other image in question is seated under a small canopy with two attendants, one on either side.[144] Both the Vardhamāna figures are seated in dhyānāsana posture, and have, besides the attendants, two lions on the pedestal and angels or Gandharvas hovering in the air and offering garlands.

The Jainas were primarily founder worshippers, but their mythology includes besides the 24 Tīrthaṇkaras a number of other deities. One of the most important deity of this class is Naigamesha who is represented on the obverse of a fragment of a Jaina sculpture discovered at Mathura.[145] The inscription incised on the panel is written in scripts of the beginning of the Christian era. The deity (Naigamesha) is goat-headed and seated on a low seat in an easy attitude. He is shown with his face turned to the right, as if addressing another personage, but the whole image has been lost.[146] To his right are three female

[140] Vogel, *op. cit.*, B. 70.
[141] *Ibid.*, B. 71.
[142] V. A. Smith, *op. cit.*, p. 49, pl. XCI, right hand figure.
[143] *Ibid.*
[144] *Ibid.*, p. 49, pl. XCI, left hand figure.
[145] *Ibid.*, p. 25, pl. XVIII.

figures standing and an infant is shown close to the knee. The deity is called in the inscription "Bhagavat Nemeso."

Nemeso of the present inscription is a variant of the name of the deity Harinegamesi in the *Kalpasūtra,* and Naigameshin in other works.[147] In Jaina religious art he is depicted as a figure either with the head of a ram or antelope or a goat. In the Mathura sculpture which is the subject of discussion here he is found bearing a goat's head. Cunninghan discovered four mutilated figures of Naigamesha which he failed to identify and described them simply as deities with an ox's head.[148]

According to Bühler the sculpture depicting Naigamesha with female figures and a small child refers most probably to the legend which narrates the exchange of the embryo of Devanandā and Trisalā.[195] The legend in the *Kalpasūtra* in short is this. Māhavīra took the form of an embryo in the Brāhmaṇī Devanandā's body. Thinking that an Arhat ought not to be born in a low Brahmanical family, Indra directed Harinegameshi, the divine commander of infantry to transfer Māhavīra from the body of Devanandā to Trisalā, a lady of the Kshatriya family who was also with a child. Harinegameshi carried out successfully Indra's order.

In Jaina mythology Naigameshin is regarded also as a deity of procreation. The *Antagaḍa-Dasao* refers to the story of how lady Sulasā propitiated Naigameshin and conceived through his compassion.[150] The ancient Jainas represented Naigameshin in both male and female forms as presiding over childbirth. The sculptures of the Mathura Museum, Nos. 2547 and E. I. represent the diety in his male aspect, and sculpture No. E 2 (of the same Museum) in her female aspect as the goat-headed goddess.[151]

The Jaina pantheon includes deities like Sarasvatī, Gaṇeśa, etc. which figure prominently in the Hindu pantheon also. We

146*Ibid.*

147*Ibid.*

148*Archaeological Survey Reports*, Vol. XX, p. 36, pl. IV, figs. 2-5.

149*Epigraphia Indica*, Vol. II, p. 314.

150*Antagada Dasão* (Oriental Translation Fund), pp. 36 and 37.

151V. S. A. Agarwala, *Hand Book to the Sculptures of the Curzon Museum, Mathura.*

have from the Jaina mound of Kankalitila two headless female statues. One of them has not been identified,[152] the other is the figure of Sarasvati.[153] The goddess is seated on a rectangular pedestal with her knees up. She has a manuscript in her left hand and the right hand, which was raised, is lost. There is a small attendant on either side. The inscription on the pedestal consists of seven lines in the Indo-Scythic script.[154]

Besides the figures of Tīrthaṇkaras and other deities of the Jaina pantheon, the Mathura sculptures of the Kankali mound bear isolated symbols and designs auspicious to the Jainas, such as the Svastika, Vajra, shell, bull, elephant, goose and antelope, etc.[155] Svastika to the Jainas is the emblem of Supārsvanātha, the 7th Jina; the Vajra is that of Dharmanātha, the 15th Jina; the shell is the cognizance of Neminātha, the 22nd Jina; the elephant of Ajitanātha, the 2nd Jina; the goose of Sumatinātha the 5th Jina, the antelope of Śāntinātha, the 16th Jina, and the bull of Rishabhanātha, the 1st Jina; all these would show that the art of the Kankali mound was thoroughly imbued with the spirit of Jainism.

A dharmachakra and Kalpavriksha[156] are among the Jaina antiquities found in Chausa (Shahabad District, Bihar) now preserved, as stated above, in the Patna Museum, Patna. The dharmachakra is supported by two nude female figures (Yakshiṇīs) similar in style to the Sanchi ones. They issue forth from the mouth of crocodiles with upturned fish tails.

The Kalpavriksha or the Aśoka tree is one with various branches and leaves. On its top is seated a female figure carrying a bowl in her hands. The association of a female figure with trees reminds us of the Śālabhāñjikā or Vanadevatā motifs of ancient India.

Both the dharmachakra and the Kalpavriksha, on stylistic grounds, may be ascribed to the second-first century B.C.[157]

[152]V. A. Smith, *op. cit.*, pl. X cix, left hand figure.
[153]*Ibid.*, right hand figure.
[154]*Ibid.*, p. 57.
[155]*Ibid.*, pls. XXviii, LXXI, LXXII, LXXIV and LXXV.
[156]H. K. Prasad, *'Jaina Bronzes in the Patna Museum'*, *Shri Mahavira Jaina Vidyalaya*, Bombay, pp. 276 ff.
[157]*Ibid.*

Along with the dharmachakra and the Kalpavriksha mentioned above were also found sixteen bronze images of Tirthaṅkaras. Of them, ten are standing and six seated.

The standing Tīrthaṅkara images resemble in execution the corresponding ones of the Kushana period from Mathura. They are all nude, and stand in the Kāyotsarga posture. With the exception of one Pārśvanātha image, none of them bears any *lāñchaṇa*. Further, they are represented singly without the *śāsanadevatās* (i.e. the Yakshas and Yakshiṇīs) or Chauri-bearers which seem to have come into vogue in the Gupta period.

From the Gupta period onwards, we find that the Jaina sculptors have regularly appended the Yakasha and Yakshiṇī figures to the sculptures of the Tīrthaṅkaras. Thus it may be concluded that the *lāñachanas* as well as the Yaksha figure might have remained as isolated and in a germinal state and then actual association with the Jaina images did not take place in the Kushan age of India art.[158]

The seated Tīrthaṅkara images from Chausa belong to the Gupta period. The wide popularity of Jainism in Bihar during the subsequent periods is attested also by the Jaina images found in Aluara (Manbhum District, Bihar). These bronzes are twenty-nine in number, twenty-eight of which are Tīrthaṅkara images, while the remaining one shows the goddess Ambikā.

[158]*Ibid.*

7. Buddhism

Buddhism, like Jainism, arose in the sixth century B.C. in the wake of Upanishadic speculations. This religion centres round the teachings of Gautama the Buddha, one of the greatest thinkers and reformers that the world has ever known.

The age (i.e. the sixth century B.C.) into which Gautama was born was one of religous ferment. He and his contemporaries, Vardhamāna Mahāvīra in India, Zoroaster in Persia, Socrates in Greece, and Confucius and Loa tse in China were the intellectual luminaries of the epoch, who by their sublime thoughts and teachings ushered in an era of critical understanding and spiritual enquiry.

As is well known, Gautama revolted against the existing orthodox Brahamanical system predominated by rituals and the ceremonies involving animal slaughter. He also deprecated the caste supremacy of the Brāhamaṇas. He was, however, not destructive in his outlook. Gifted with extraordinary intelligence and analytical powers, he accepted the best of the existing system and rejected what he did not consider useful or beneficial to a man to gain knowledge and emancipation. In formulating his religion, he was largely influenced by the liberal thinking of the Upanishadic sages, the prevailing idea of knowledge and Yoga practices (leading to mental concentration), the theory of Karma[1] and the value of a mendicant life. At the

[1]*Karma* or one's own deeds influence the destiny of a being. All except those who have gained the highest spiritual knowledge, are subject to the effects of good and bad deeds. Almost all sections of people in India believe in the law of ***Karma.***

same time time he denied the authority of the *Vedas* and declared the Vedic sacrifices as useless. In short, he was a great reformer whose system brought ethical principles to the forefront, emphasising the value of morality, concentration, and wisdom. As he influenced very greatly the religious thought in India, his advent has been rightly considered an event of phenomenal importance. He discovered a way of life[2] which can be followed "regardless of time, place and prevailing culture". He showed the path which leads to the cessation of suffering and attainment of knowledge and emancipation.[3]

It was not some of the Brahmanic practices alone which were repugnant to Buddha, but he deprecated also the unethical thinking and theories of the non-Vedic teachers, mostly of Aṅga and Magadha of eastern India. The number of such teachers was quite numerous.[4] Of them, the names of Purāṇa Kassapa, Makkhali Gosāla, Ajita Keśakambalī, Pakudha Kachchhāyana, Sañjaya Belaṭṭhiputta and Nigaṇṭha Nāṭaputta were the most famous.[5]

Purāṇa Kassapa advocted the doctrine of Akriyāvāda (theory of non-action). According to him, no good or bad results accrue from pious or impious acts. In the *Majjhima-nikāya*, Purāṇa's teachings have been condemned as leading to moral depravity.[6]

Makkhali Gosāla, the founder of the Ājīvika sect, advocated fatalism. He held that everything was fixed and it was beyond man's power to alter or improve his position by his own exertion. Emancipation is a natural process which comes after a series

[2]Sir Charles Eliot, *Hinduism and Buddhism* (London 1952), Vol. 1, pp. XIX ff.

[3]The time of Gautama's advent was suitable for carrying reforms. Within the Brahmanical framework itself, changes were taking place. Side by side with the followers of orthodox Brahmanism, there arose Upanishadic thinkers who advocated the value of simple rituals and meditation in the place of the complicated *Karmakāṇda* or ritualistic system of big sacrifices involving animal slaughter.

[4]The Jaina texts put the number of such teachers as 363, but the Buddhist sources as 62 or 63.

[5]For an excellent exposition of the doctrines of the non-Vedic teachers, See B. M. Barua, *Pre-Buddhist Indian Philosophy*, pp. 279 ff; and N. Dutt, *Early Monastic Buddhism*, Vol. I (Calcutta 1941), pp. 35 ff.

[6]N. Dutt, *op. cit.*, pp. 35, 36; Sir Charles Eliot, *op. cit.*, Vol. II, p. 99.

of migrations from one existence to another. This doctrine is called *ahetuka* or *akriyādrishṭi* in the *Majjhima-nikāya.* The *Añguttara-nikāya* considers this doctrine as opposed to *Karma* (deed), *Kriyā* (action) and *Vīrya* (energy).[7]

Ajita Keśakambalī taught the doctrine of annihilation at death. After death the body disintegrates and merges in the elements, viz., earth, water, air and fire of which it was formed, and the *Indriiyas,* i.e. sense powers, pass into *ākāśā,* i.e. space. Thus, according to Ajita, there is no rebirth or transmigration. No acts, good or bad, produce any results. The *Majjhima-nikāya* declares Ajita's teachings as materialistic, leading to improper thoughts and actions. Sañjaya-Belaṭṭhiputta was an agnostic or sceptic and he was condemned as he refused to give definite answers to fundamental questions and even to those relating to moral responsibility.[8]

Pakudh Kachāyana holds the seven elements, such as earth, water, fire, air, pleasure (*sukha*), pain (*dḥukha*), and soul (*jīva*) as uncreated and permanent. Hence no action good or bad is effective. The doctrine of Pakudha has been desribed as *Akriyāvāda* or *Sāśvatavāda* by the Buddhists.[9]

The doctrines of the Nigaṇṭhas have been referred to in the Buddhist texts as consisting of four restraints: to keep free from passion and desire, to keep aloof from all kinds of traffic, to get rid of all kinds of *parigrahas* (ideas of possession), and to remain absorbed in knowledge and meditation on self. Since the Nighaṇṭhas laid emphasis on extreme physical mortification, the Buddhists considered their own system to be better than the former.[10]

It is thus apparent that there were many religious thoughts and doctrines current during the Buddha's time. While Brahmanism, though never completely free from ritualistic ceremonies, developed during this period the theory of Ātman and Brahman (relationship betwen the individual soul and universal soul) and their identity, the non-Vedic systems held

[7]*Ibid.*

[8]*Ibid.*, pp. 36-7, Sir Charles Eliot, *op. cit.*, p. 99.

[9]*Ibid.*

[10]N. Dutt, *op. cit.*, pp. 40 ff.

various theories of non-action, fatalism, etc. Some ascribed everything to chance and denied causation.

Gautama found none of these systems satisfactory. Though he retained some of the accepted doctrines of his time, his main emphasis was on non-craving, good conduct, concentration, and wisdom. He held that in the phenomenal world everything is bound by a cause, and he preached the noble eightfold path or middle path which leads to the cessation of suffering and attainment of *Nirvāṇa* or knowledge. His teachings produced a deep impression on the minds of the people and spread not only throughout the length and breadth of India, but became popular in the neighbouring countries, like Afghanistan, Central Asia, China, Korea, Japan, Ceylon, Nepal, Tibet, Burma, Thailand, Viet Nam, Indonesia, etc.

The life of Buddha presents a fascinating story. The facts of his life are, however, to be gathered from various sources,[11] as there is no connected account left in any particular place or text.

According to traditions preserved in various texts, Gautama Buddha was born in Lumbinī, now in Nepalese territory. His father was Śuddhodana, one of the ruling chiefs of Kapilavastu. His mother was Māyā who died seven days after his birth. He was brought up by his stepmother Mahāprajāpati, who was his mother's younger sister. His childhood name was Siddhārtha, Gautama being his family name. The learned Brahmins examined the signs on his body and predicted his future greatness as a perfectly accomplished Buddha or as a universal monarch.

As prophesied, Gautama became more and more contemplative and indifferent to worldly matters as he grew. Afraid of this, Śuddhodana married him at the age of sixteen to a beautiful girl called Yaśodharā in order to turn away his thoughts from renunciation, built beautiful palaces and gardens for him and provided him with all the other luxuries of life.

[11]E. Thomas, *The Life of Buddda as Legend and History* (London, 1952), pp. 1 ff; Sir Charles Eliot, *op. cit.*, Vol. 1, pp. 129 ff; N. Dutt, *op. cit.*, Vol. 1, pp. 104 ff; H. Kern, *Manual of Buddhism* (Varanasi, 1968), pp. 12 ff; see also the author's anonymous work, *The Way of the Buddha* (Publications Division, Govt. of India), pp. 289 ff.

Gautama, according to legends, spent a life of worldly pleasusures till a turning point came at the age of twenty-nine when on successive occasions, as he drove on his chariot through the pleasure garden, he saw an old person, a sick person, a dead body and a cheerful Sannyāsī. These encounters convinced him of the futility of living any longer a life of ease and comfort. He became determined to renounce the world and lead the life of an ascetic to escape from misery and old age. To add to the conflict within him a son was born to him. He considered the birth of a son as an additional bondage to life and called him Rāhula (an obstacle).

Seven days after Rāhula's birth, Gautama left home at the dead of night to find out the means of overcoming worldly miseries. Journeying from place to place, he reached Rajagriha, the capital of the Magadhan king Bimbisāra. From there he came to Āḷāra Kalāma and later Udrka Rāmaputra, two renowned philosphers of the time. In a short time he mastered all that they taught him regarding the different stages of meditation. But this did not satisfy him and he left them to find a path of deliverence through his own exertions. With this determination he came to Uruvela near Gaya and there selected a delightful spot near the river Neranjara for his meditation. There he practised severe austerities for six years and was reduced to a skeleton. Yet real knowledge eluded him. He then realized that the practice of austerities was not the way to achieve knowledge. He, therefore, began to partake of food for the sustenance of his body. Then as he sat having resolved to attain enlightenment, Māra, the enemy of liberation upset him in various ways.[12] But Mārā failed to distract his mind and fled away with his hosts. Bodhisattava Gautama then sank into deeper contemplation. "He acquired in the first watch of the night the knowledge of previous existences, in the middle hour of the night the divine vision, in the last part of the night the knowledge of causative process. Thus he attained omniscience."

On having attained knowledge, Gautama, now called Buddha, was in doubt whether he should preach the profound truth he

[12] E. J. Thomas, *op. cit.*, p. 74.

had discovered to anyone in this world steeped in darkness. Then Mahāsahampati Brahmā appeared and exhorted him to preach the doctrine to his erstwhile five companions who left him at Gaya to settle at Sarnath. He addressed these monks as follows:[13]

> These two extremes, O Monks, are not to be practised by one who has gone forth from the world. What are the two ? That conjoined with passion, low, vulgar, common, ignoble, and useless and that conjoined with self-torture, painful, ignoble and useless. Avoiding these two extremes, the Tathāgata has gained the knowledge of the Middle way, which gives insight, knowledge and tends to calm, to insight, enlightenment, Nirvāṇa.
>
> Now this, O Monks, is the noble truth of pain : birth is painful, old age is painful, sickness is painful, death is painful. Contact with unpleasant things is painful, separation from pleasant things is painful, and not getting what one wishes is painful, in short the five Skandhas of grasping is painful.
>
> Now this, O Monks, is the noble truth of the cause of pain, that craving, which leads to rebirth, combined with pleasure, and lust, finding pleasure here and there, namely the craving for passion, the craving for existence, the craving for non-existence.
>
> Now this, O monks, is the noble truth of the cessation of pain, the cessation without a remainder of that craving, abandonment, forsaking, release, non-attachment.
>
> Now this, O monks, is the noble truth of the way that leads to the cessation of pain: this is the noble eightfold path, namely, right views, right intention, right speech, right action, right livelihood, right effort, right mindfulness, right concentration (*Dharmmachaka - ppavattana - Sutta*-K*athā*, *Mahāvāgga*).

On hearing the sermon, the five monks, namely Koṇḍañña, Vappa, Bhaddiya, Mahānāman and Assaji attained the knowledge and received the ordination (*Upasampadā*).

[13]E. J. Thomas, *op. cit.*, p, 87.

Buddha then gave to these monks a discourse on the "non-existence of soul".[14] On hearing the words of the Buddha, all five monks became free from *āsavas*, i.e. they attained full enlightenment as arhats.

With the first sermon delivered to the five monks at Sarnath known as the *dharma-chakra pravartana* i.e. setting in motion the wheel of law, started the missionary activities of Buddha, which lasted for forty-five years.

His wisdom and personality drew adherents from all sections of the people. He was received with the highest regard wherever he went. Among his followers were some of the prominent rulers of the time, such as king Bimbisāra of Magadha, and Prasenajit of Kośala. Ajātaśatru (son of Bimbisāra) who was not well-disposed towards him in the beginning became repentant afterwards and adopted his teachings. The Bhārhut panels of the second century B. C. contain representations of Ajātaśatru and Prasenajit paying homage to Buddha indicated symbolically. The new faith acquired a wide popularity in the lifetime of the Master himself. As the textual and other traditions show, Buddhism gained a strong foothold in Kapilavastu, Magadha, Kasi, Kosla and Videha, in the countries of the Bhaggas and the Koliyas, in Anga, Champa, Kosambi, Mathura, Avanti and several other countries.

Gautama Buddha was no less an organizer than a preacher. He established the monastic order on a strong footing with a set of rules to be followed by his disciples. While the rules for

[14]"The body, monks, is soulless. If the body, monks, were the soul, this body would not be subject to sickness, and it should be possible in the case of the body to say, 'Let my body be thus, let my body not be thus.' Now, because the body is soulless, monks, therefore the body is subject to sickness and it is not possible in the case of the body to 'Let my body be thus, let my body not be thus'.

"Feeling is soulless...perception is soulless...the aggregates are soulless."

"Consciousness is soulless. For if consciousness were the soul, this consciousness will not be subject to sickness, and it would be possible for consciousness to say, "Let my consciousness be thus, let my consciousness not be thus..."

"Thus perceiving, monks, the learned noble disciple feels loathing for the body, for feeling, for perception, for the aggregates, for consciousness." See *Anattalakkhana-sutra,* E. J.Thomas, *op. cit.*, pp. 88-9, Buddha's embodying sermon on the marks of non-soul.

the monks were difficult and many, those for the laymen were few, namely the *pañchaśīlas*.

The life of Buddha, though otherwise peaceful, was disturbed by the mischievous activities of his cousin Devadatta. The latter attempted to take away the leadership of the church by killing Buddha with the help of Ajātaśatru, son of Bimbisāra. The plot of Devadatta failed. As stated above, Ajātaśatru became repentant and sought refuge in Buddha.

Several other events took place during the last days of Buddha. The Śākya clan of Kapilavastu to which Buddha belonged was exterminated by Viḍūḍabha, son of Prasenajit of Kośala. Ajātaśatru made preparations for the conquest of the Visalians. But the war was averted at Buddha's instance. Shortly after these events, Buddha, who was then about seventy-nine years of age, left Rajagriha and came to Nalanda with a large retinue of monks. Thus began his last journey.

From Nalanda, he came to Pāṭaligrama, where he gave a discourse to the laity. From there he came to Koṭigrāma and then to Nadika. At all these places he delivered discourses on duty, self-transcendence and insight. From Nadika he came to Vaisali, where he lived in the mango grove of the well-known courtesan, Āmrapālī. At her request he took meals at her house and she made a gift of her mango grove to the order which was gladly accepted. From there the Blessed One came to Veluva where he had an attack of severe illness. Not wishing to die without leaving his words to guide the Bhikkus, he overcame his illness through his own powers.

He exhorted the monks of Vaisali saying: "Subject to decay are compound things, strive with earnestness. In no long time the Tathāgata will attain *Nirvāṇa*."[15]

Journeying from place to place Buddha came to Pava, where he was invited to a dinner by Chunda, a hereditary smith. Immediately afterwards he had an attack of dysentery. Buddha bore the pain with patience and came to Kusinara. On the way, he converted a young Mallian named Pukkusa who was formerly a disciple of Aḷāra Kalāma. On reaching Kusinara he

[15]See the author's anonymous work, *The Way of the Buddha* (Publications Division, Govt. of India), p. 304.

lay down on a couch spread between two śāla trees by Ananda. The trees burst into blossoms although it was not the flowering season and spirits hovered round the bed.

The last hours were spent in giving useful counsel and instructions to Ānanda who was weeping at the impending death of the Master. "Do not weep," he said to Ānanda. "Have I not told you before, monks, that this is in the the very nature of things near and dear to us that we must part from them. All that is born, brought into being, and put together carries within itself the seeds of dissolution. How then is it possible that such a being should not be dissolved. Be earnest in effort and you too shall be free from the great evils and from ignorance."

As the last watch of the night drew near, the Lord said to his brethren: "Subject to decay are all compound things; strive with earnestness." These were his last words. Then he passed through a series of trances and entered into Mahāparinirvāṇa, "the stage of the cessation of consciousness and feeling."

Very little is known of the history of Buddhism after the death of Buddha till the rise of Aśoka. According to tradition, however, a few weeks after the Buddha's death, a council was held at Rajagriha under the presidentship of Mahākaśyapa. The immediate object of this session seems to have been to rehearse the *dharma* and *Vinaya* rules to prevent arbitrary interpretation or misinterpretation of them by any unscrupulous monks like Subhadra and the like. Five hundred monks including Ānanda were admitted into the council, and as desired by Mahākāśyapa, Upāli narrated the Vinaya rules and Ānanda recited the dharma or *Sūtras*. Thus the first council seems to have determined in a systematic way the creed of the church after the passing of the Master.[16] The expenditure for this council was provided by king Ajatasatru of Magadha.

The chief propagators of the faith during this time seem to have been Mahākāśyapa, Ānanda and Rāhula. As to Ānanda, Buston[17] writes that he entrusted his disciple to propagate the faith after his death. Further, he is said to have converted

[16]See *2500 Years of Buddhism* (Publications Division, Govt. of India), p. 34 ff; N. Dutt, *op. cit.*, Vol. 1, p. 324 ff.

[17]See Obermiller's translation of Buston's *History of Buddhism, II*, p. 88.

before his death 500 Brahmanical anchorites including Madhyāntika who preached the religion in Kashmir.[18] Buddhism does not seem to have received much royal patronage during the rule of the next few monarchs of Magadha, namely, Udāyibhadda, Muṇḍa, Nāgadāsaka and Susunāga.[19]

The next important event in the history of Buddhism is the second Buddhist council held during the rule of Kālāsoka, son and successor of Susunāga. This council was held as a protest against the unorthodox views of the Vaisali monks with regard to the ten points of discipline. The ten points of indulgence opposed to the Vinaya rules are : (1) Siṅgiloṇa-Kappa (carrying of salt in a horn for future use); (2) Dvaṁgula-Kappa (taking food after midday); (3) Gāmantara-Kappa (the practice of going to a neighbouring village and taking a second meal there); (4) Āvāsa-Kappa (the observance of the Uposathas in the different places in the same parish); (5) Anumati-Kappa (asking for a *post facto* sanction of a deed); (6) Āchiṇṇa Kapp (the use of precedents as authority); (7) Amathita-Kappa (the drinking of buttermilk after meals); (8) Jalogiṁ pātum (the drinking of fermented palm-juice); (9) Adasakaṁ-Nisīdaṇam (using as a seat a rag which has no fringe); (10) Jātarūparajataṁ (the acceptance of gold and silver).[20]

These rules are not in conformity with the Pātimokkha (monastic code) the monks are to follow strictly. So the laxity of the Vaisali monks was highly opposed by the orthodox group of the Church, especially by venerable Yaśa of Kausambi. When his appeal to the Vajjian monks failed, he contacted through messengers the monks of Paṭṭheya and Avanti, and he came himself to discuss the matter with the venerable Sambhuta Sanavasi at Ahygamga. In the meantime sixty Theras of Paṭṭheya and eighty Theras of Avanti also arrived in Ahogamga to discuss the questions. As the questions were hard and subtle, it was decided to elicit the opinion of the Saṅgha-Thera, Revanta

[18]As to the condition of Buddhism during the period in question, see N. Dutt, *op. cit.*, Vol. II, pp. 1-4.

[19]N. Dutt, *op. cit.*, Vol. II pp. 30 ff.

[20]See *2500 Years of Buddhism* (Publications Division, Govt. of India), pp. 41 ff.

who used to reside in Soreyya. Both the rival groups of monks, i. e. Yasa and his party on one side and Vajjian monks on the other, met Revata at Sahajāti. But as the matter could not be settled there, a council was held at Vaisali. This council was attended by seven hundred monks. But a committee of eight members, four from the orthodox party of the west (i. e. Yasa's party) and four from the unorthodox party of the east (i. e. the Vajiian monks) was formed to go into the dispute. The ten points were discussed and declared unlawful.

Thus the monks of the eastern party (i. e. Vaisali and Magadha) were excommunicated. But the members of this party were in majority and they held another council and supported the ten points. They were now called the Mahāsaṅghikas (the party of the great assembly) and the western party as Sthaviravādin. From this time Magadha was the centre of the Mahāsaṅghikas and Śrāvastī the centre of Sthaviravāda. The second council is said to have been held in 386 B.C.

Kālāsoka's son and grandson, Surasena and Nanda, seem to have patronised Buddhism. Surasena supported the Bhikkus of different regions and offered gifts to the Chaityas. King Nanda also seems to have made lavish gifts to the Chaityas. According to the *Mañju-śrī Mūlakalpa* Nanda embraced Buddhism towards the end of his reign and died as a true Buddhist.[21]

Nanda was dethroned by Chandragupta Maurya who started the celebrated Maurya dynasty. Chandragupta Maurya and his son Bindusāra do not seem to have had any special predilections towards Buddhism. The next ruler, the great Emperor Aśoka, became deeply interested in the religion and contributed much to its growth and diffusion.[22] Tradition avers that Aśoka was cruel and aggressive in his early days, but ultimately he took refuge in Buddha, Dharma and Saṅgha. In fact, the reign of Aśoka was a landmark in the history of Buddhism. The patronage of so powerful a king who is said to have adopted Buddhism during his ninth regnal year after the Kaliṅga war (which involved a huge massacre and bloodshed) proved to be a great stimulus to the growth and spread of the faith.

[21]N. Dutt, *op. cit.*, Vol. II, p. 23 ff.

[22]D. R. Bhandarkar, *Asoka*, pp. 68 ff.

As his incripitions would indicate beyond doubt, Aśoka paid visits and did honour to the places associated with the events of Buddha's life. According to the Rock Edict VIII he repaired to Sambodhi (the place of Buddha's enlightenment in Gaya) in the tenth year of his reign. He continued his *dharma-yātrā* (pious tour) also subsequently as is evident from the Nigliva and Rummindei pillar inscriptions in the Nepal *terai*. The Nigliva pillar inscription speaks of his visit in his fourteenth regnal year to Rummindei and the enlargement by him of the second stūpa of the Buddha Kanankamuni. The Rummindei pillar inscription informs us of his visit in the twentieth regnal year to the place of Buddha's birth in Lumbinī. On the occasion of this visit he granted exemption of the village from the payment of the religious cess. He also declared that this village was to pay one-eighth of the produce as land revenue instead of one-sixth according to the prevailing practice.

His deep interest in the religion is also revealed by the contents of the Minor Rock Edicts. The Minor Rock Edict No. 1 speaks not only of his intimate association (at the time of the issuing of this Edict) with the Buddhist Saṅgha, but also contains the text of his order for the expulsion of the heretical monks. The Minor Rock Edict III (The Calcutta Bariat Edict) speaks of his deep faith in the Buddha, Dharma and Saṅgha and refers to the sacred texts presented by him for the monks and nuns, lay men and women.[23] The reading of these texts would elevate their mind and soul. Further, his edicts on pillars at Sarnath, Kausambi and Sanchi issue a stern warning to the monks who would cause dissension in the Church. "Whosoever breaks up the Church, be it monk or nun, shall be clad in white raiment and be compelled to live in what is not a residence [of the clergy]. Thus should this order be respectfully communicated to the congregation of the monks and the congregation of the nuns."[24]

Aśoka appointed special officers called *Dharma-mahamatras* who were to look after the spiritual well-being of the people. His message of concord, tolerance, piety and morality seems to

[23]D. C. Sirar, *Inscriptions of Aśoka* (Publications Division), p. 15,
[24]D. R. Bhandarkar, *op. cit.*, pp. 83 ff.

have been well received also in the dominions bordering his empire. His own son Mahendra went to Ceylon to preach the gospel of the Buddha. It is said that his daughter Sanghamitrā also joined her brother in missionary activities.

Aśoka is also credited with the erection of an enormous number of stūpas over the holy relics of the Buddha. That the Buddhist religion and its church engaged the close attention of Aśoka is also evident from the accounts of the third council[25] held under his aegis at Pāṭaliputra. It appears that the points of disagreement over the interpretation of the Vinaya rules deepened further between the Māhasaṅghikas and the Thervadins in his time and he was anxious to maintain the integrity of the Saṅgha. We have already seen that the Mahāsaṅghikas emerged as a powerful body after the second Buddhist council, held in Vaisali during the time of Kālāsoka and as the time passed, their popularity seems to have extended towards the other regions of India. Gradually, their main centre of activities shifted to the Andhradeśa.

This council is mentioned only in the Aṭṭhakathās and the Ceylonese chronicles. Hence, according to certain scholars, this council seems to have been a sectarian affair only of the Theravādins. As the accounts go, Aśoka and his preceptor Moggaliputta Tissa, in order to stop the growth of the schisms and heretical doctrines among the monks, convened an assembly of the bhikkhus of different groups. Those who set forth false doctrines, such as of the external soul, etc. were expelled, and those who held that the religion taught by Buddha was one of Vibhajjavāda were hailed to be followers of the true doctrine of Buddha. Thus, the Buddhist Church was purged of the heretical group of monks, and Tissa became the head of the the Theravāda community.[26]

Moggaliputta Tissa then convened a council of a thousand Theravādi monks and compiled the Tripiṭaka with their help. The doctrines of the heretical monks were also discussed in this council and were declared unacceptable and discarded. Thus the *Kathāvastu*, refuting the heretical doctrines, was compiled.

[25] N. Dutt, *op. cit.*, Vol. II, pp. 264 ff; *2500 Years of Buddhism,* pp. 45 ff.
[26] *Ibid.,* pp. 258-274.

An important outcome of this council was the despatch of missionaries to different countries for the propagation of Buddhism. As related in the *Mahāvaṁśa* (Ceylonese chronicle) Moggaliputta Tissa deputed for this purpose Majjhantika (or Madhyāndina) to Kashmīr-Gandhāra; Mahādeva to Mahīsha-maṇḍala (Mahishmati, south of Vindhyas); Rakhhita to Vana-vāsī (North Canara); Dhammarakkhita (a Yonaka) to Aparanta (i. e. Alor, Broach, and Sopara); Mahādhammarakkhita to Maharashtra; Mahārakkhita to Yona countries (foreign settle-ments in the North-Western Frontier province of undivided India); Majjhima to Himavanta; Sona with Uttara to Suvarna-bhūmi (probably a place in India); and Mahinda to Tambapaṇṇi (Ceylon).[27]

The story of the missionary activities of the above monks during Asoka's time seems to be by and large true. The discovery of a relic casket (second century B. C.) at Sanchi lends support to it inasmuch as the inscription on the casket refers to Majjhima and Kassapagotia as acharyas or propagators of the faith in the Himalayan countries.[28]

From the preceding it appears that the reign of Aśoka was a glorious epoch in the history of Buddhism. He was not only personally interested in Buddhism, but also did much for its propagation in India and outside. He supported the Theravāda doctrines and took measures preventing the Saṅghabheda or dissension in the church.

The sons and successors of Aśoka do not seem to have been much interested in Buddhism. The last of the Mauryan rulers was Brihadratha Maurya who was assassinated by his general, Pushyamitra Śunga, who seems to have championed the cause of Brahmanism. Certain Buddhist texts describe Pushyamitra as having destroyed many Buddhist stūpas and Viharas. Regarding the persecutions of the Buddhists traditions differ and it is not possible to determine to what extent Pushyamitra was respon-

[27]*Ibid.*, pp. 264 ff.

[28]Lūder's list Nos. 654-656 (Sanchi) and 157-158 (Sonari); Cunningham, *Bhilsa Topes*, pp. 119 ff, 286 ff, 313 ff; Marshall, *Monument of Sanchi*, I, pp. 289; Fleet, *Journal of the Royal Asiatic Society*, 1905, pp. 6 ff; Ajoy Mitra Shastri, *An Outline of Early Buddhism* (Varanasi, 1965), p. 57.

sible. Whatever it may be, Buddhism does not seem to have experienced any great setback during this period inasmuch as it saw the erection of many stūpas in Bharhut, Bodhgaya and many other places. One of the stūpas at Sanchi excavated in the nineteenth century was found to contain the relics of two important disciples of Buddha, Sāriputra and Maudgalyāyana.[29] The sculptured panels of Sanchi and Bharhut contain many representations of Jātaka stories, the previous lives of Buddha and scenes from Buddha's last life.

The Śuṅgas were succeded in the north by the Kāṇvas who, like their predecessors, had no special predilection for Buddhism. But their contemporaries in the south, i.e. the Sātavāhanas, seem to have extended their support to and bestowed munificence on the Buddhist establishments in Amarāvati and the neighbouring regions.

Whatever may be the dynastic changes in India after the fall of the all-India empire of the Mauryas and whatever may be the personal faiths of the kings, Buddhism by this time was firmly established all over India (as is attested by the literary and archaeological sources) including the foreign dominions of the north and northwest.

As is well known, the Indo-Greek ruler, Menander (*c.*114 B. C.) was deeply influenced by Buddhist philosphy. Some scholars believe that he was converted to Buddism by the venerable Nāgasena, a great Buddhist philospher of the Sthaviravāda school. The famous Pali book *Milindapañha*, and the questions of Milinda, seem to lend support to this view. This book contains Milinda's (Menander's) questions and Nāgasena's answers to them.[30]

Before we proceed, it may be of interest to recall the Tibetan historian Tāranāth's account[31] of the spread of Buddhism in

[29]Rhys Davids, *Buddhist India* (Calcutta, 1955), p. 161.

[30]Menander was apparently a king of the Kabul valley. He, however, made his conquests into the heart of India as far as Ayodhya and Saketa. According to tradition, Nāgasena came to Sagala to meet Menander. See, Kern, *op. cit.*, p. 118; R. C. Majumdar, H. C. Raychaudhuri and Kalikinkar Datta, *An Advanced History of India* (London, 1949), p. 114.

[31]N. Dutt, *Aspects of Mahayana Buddhism and Its Relation to Hinayana* London, 1930), pp. 23 ff.

India during post-Mauryan India. Though Tāranāth's account cannot be verified from any other source, yet there is nothing improbable in what he says. According to Tāranāth, Upagupta, the celebrated Buddhist monk of Aśoka's time, was ordained at Mathura by Dhitika who was a native of Ujjayini, Dhitika spread the religion far and wide. He converted the Tukhara king Minara and Buddhism was firmly established in Tukhara as a result of the missionary activities of the monks from Kashmir. These monks received support from Minara and his son Imhasa.

After the conversion of Minara, Dhitika, as Tāranāth continues, came to Kamarupa (Assam) and established the religion there. After this he came to preach Buddhism in Malava and Ujjayini in the West. Dhitika's spiritual successor was Kala or Krishṇa and the latter's disciple was Sudarsana. They preached Buddhism in Sindh and Kashmir. Krishṇa is also credited with the task of spreading the faith in south India, Ceylon and China. He was followed by Posadha.[32]

Reverting to historical discussions based mainly on epigraphical sources, it may may be pointed out that Buddhism continued to receive the attention of the people including the foreign population of north-west India during the period subsequent to Menander's reign. The Swat Relic Vase Inscription records the establishment of the relics of the Lord Śākyamuni for the purpose of the security of many people (*bahujana-sthitaye*) by Theodoros, the Meridarkh.[33] This, according to the palaeography of the letters, is one of the oldest Kharoshṭhī inscriptions and can be safely placed in the first century B. C.

Meridarkh, as Konow has suggested, is a Greek title. So, it is apparent that Theodoros belonged to a period of Greek rulers preceding the Parthians and Śakas. He was probably a district officer in a region which included the Kabul territory or Arachosia or Gandhara.[34]

[32] *Ibid.*

[33] Sten Konow, *Corpus Inscriptionum Indicarum*, Vol. II, Part I (Kharoshṭhi Inscriptions), Calcutta, 1929, pp. 2-6.

[34] *Ibid.*

The Taxila copper plate inscription in Kharoshṭhī also mentions a person (name lost) with the title Meridarkh, who together with his wife founded a stūpa in honour of his mother and father for the presentation of respectful offering.[35] Further, the Kharoshṭhī inscription of the Tirath Rock on the border of Swat Kohistan, ascribable to *circa* first century B. C. on palaeographic grounds, also points to the popularity of Buddhism in the realm of Greek supremacy.[36]

It is interesting to note that the inscription in question occurs below a pair of footprints, which are of Buddha (*Bodhasa Sakamunisa Padani*). In his account of Udyana, Fa-hien refers to a spot where Buddha came and left the footprints "which are long and short according to the ideas of the beholder". Hiuen Tsang also speaks of a large flat stone with Buddha's footprints. He locates it on the north bank of the Swat river "thirty li to the south west of the spring of Naga Apalala, the reputed source of the river".[37]

Among the Sakas also, there were many who were devoted to Buddhism. The Taxila copper-plate of Patika would show that in the year 78, during the reign of the Great Moga, Patika, son of Kshaharāta, Liaka Kushulaka established in Taxila a relic of the lord Śākyamuṇi and a Saṅghārāma, through Rohinimitra, who was overseer for Saṅghārāma, for the worship of all Buddhas, for the increase of the life and power of the Kshatrapa.[38]

Liaka Kushulaka held sway in and near Taxila. He was a Śaka ruler while Moga was the Saka suzerain. Palaeographically, the inscription is to be attributed to the end of the second century B. C.[39]

Again, it may be mentioned here that Ayasia Kamucâ, the chief queen of the Mahākshatrapa Rajuvula established the relic of Lord Śākyamuṇi, the Buddha, a stūpa and a Saṅghārāma for the order of the four quarters of the Sarvāstivādins.[40] Palaeo-

[35] *Ibid.*
[36] *Ibid.*, pp. 8 and 9.
[37] *Ibid.*
[38] *Ibid.*, p. 23 ff.
[39] *Ibid.*
[40] *Ibid.*, pp. 31-49.

graphically the inscription is to be attributed to *c*. 5-10 A. D. It is significant to note that the record ends with honour to all the Buddhas, the Law, the order and the Śakastāna.

The above records show beyond doubt the popularity of Buddhism, especially of the Sarvāstivādins, in the north-western region. In the interior of India, i. e. in Madhya Pradesh, Uttar Pradesh, and Bihar as well as in the south, especially in the Andhra country, there grew up as already noted above, in the second-first century B.C. many Buddhist stūpas with railings and monasteries which show how deeply a large portion of the Indian population were interested in popularising the faith. In north India, the early centuries of the Christian era ushered in a new epoch in the history of Buddhism. This period, as a result of the patronage of the Kushanas witnessed the spread of the religion in Central Asia and China. Further, it saw also doctrinal developments leading to the emergence of the Mahāyāna Buddhism to be described later.

The greatest of the Kushana rulers was Kanishka. According to the numismatic evidence, he was eclectic in his religious outlook. Towards the end of his career he seems to have accepted Buddhism as his personal faith. Whatever it may be, his deep interest in the religion is indicated by various archaeological and literary sources including the testimony of the Chinese pilgrims. His services to Buddhism can to a very great extent be compared to those of Aśoka the Maurya who preceded him by about 300 years.

Kanishka ruled over a vast empire comprising Kabul, Gandhara, Sindh, North-Western India, Kashmir, and a part of Madhyadesha as far as Magadha. The *Rājatāraṅgiṇī*, the *Kalpanāmanditikā* and the Chinese (later Han) annals seem to refer to Kanishka's political sway in Khotan. Hiuen Tsang's account also describes Kanishka as governing a territory even to the east of Tsung-ling mountains.[41] Further, Hiuen Tsang refers to the Central Asian princes as being kept as hostages in Kanishka's court.

[41] B. N. Puri, *India Under the Kushanas* (Bharatiya Vidya Bhavan, Bombay, 1960), pp. 37 ff.

Kanishka built his capital in Peshawar which was an important centre of Buddhist art and religion. He erected there a large stūpa which has been described in glorious terms by the Chinese pilgrims. Cunningham and Foucher located the Kanishka Stūpa in the mounds of the Shah-ji-ki-Dheri outside the Ganj gate of Peshawar. Dr Spooner in the course of his excavations of the mound has confirmed this location of the stūpas as suggested by Cunningham and Foucher.[42]

The stūpa was destroyed and rebuilt several times. As found in the excavations, its base is square, measuring about 195 feet on each side, "with massive towers at the corners" and projections bearing stair-cases on each of the four faces. The sides of the stūpa were embellished with stucco sculptures. According to the Chinese pilgrims, the stūpa was surmounted by an iron-pillar with twenty-five gilded discs.[43]

Dr Spooner who discovered the extensive ruins of the stūpa found in it a relic chamber containing an inscribed metal relic casket with sacred bones. The inscription states that the "casket was made for the acceptance of the teachers of the Sarvāstivāda sect" and that one Agisala was architect in Kanishka's Vihāra.[44] Kanishka's allegiance to Buddhism is indicated also by the presence of the Buddha figure on some of his coins.

The greatest event of Buddhist interest during Kanishka's reign was the summoning of a Buddhist council under his patronage. This council, known as the Fourth Council in Buddhist tradition, was held to settle the doctrinal differences affecting the Buddhist Saṅghas. The tradition of this council is preserved mainly in the account of the Chinese pilgrim Hiuen Tsang.

It is said that in order to ascertain the true doctrine, Kanishka, at the instance of the venerable Pārśva, convoked a council attended by 500 monks representing various sects into which the Buddhists came to be divided this time. The venue of the council was either Jalandhar or Kashmīr. Kanishka built a

[42]Sten Konow, *op. cit.*, p. 135 ff.
[43]*Ibid.*
[44]*Ibid.*

monastery for the monks and invited them to compose commentaries on the *Tripiṭakas*. The Council "composed 100,000 stanzas of *Upadeśa śāstras* explanatory of the canonical *sūtras*, 100,000 stanzas of *Vinaya-vibhāshā śāstras*, explanatory of the Vinaya, and 100,000 of *Abhidharma-Vibhāsā śāstras*, explanatory of the *Abhidharma*.... King Kanishka caused the treatises, when furnished, to be written out on copper plates and enclosed these in stone boxes which he deposited in a tope made for the purpose."[45]

According to certain traditions, Aśvaghosha, the author of the *Buddhacharita*, the *Saundarānanda*, and the *Sāriputraprakaraṇa* (the fragments of the *Sāriputraprakaraṇa* have been found in Central Asia) seems to have flourished in the court of Kanishka, in the first century A. D. His *Buddhacharita* (Doings of Buddha) written in ornate Kavya style describes the life of Buddha from his birth to enlightenment. The *Saundarānanda* describes the conversion of his step brother, Nanda. The *Sāriputraprakaraṇa*, which has survived in incomplete form was a play or drama of nine acts, having the conversion of Śāriputra and Maudgalyāyana to Buddhism. The Chinese and Tibetan sources attribute a few more works, including the *Gaṇḍīstotra* and *Vajrasūchi* to Aśvaghosha.[46]

Kanishka was succeeded by his son Huvishka. The latter, like his father, was eclectic in his religious outlook, and Buddhism flourished side by side with other religions during his reign. A Buddhist pillar inscription ascribed to the year 47, records the gift of the monk Jīvaka (who was a native of Udiyana) to the Vihāra of Mahārāja Rājātirāja Devaputra Huvishka.[47]

Huvishka's successor was Vāsudeva. Though he seems to have been completely Hinduised in his outlook, Buddhism and Jainism continued to enjoy popularity during his reign. Two records of Vāsudeva's reign are significant with regard to the history of Buḍdhism. One of them from Mathura dated in the year 67 of Vāsudeva's reign mentions the erection of an image

[45]Sir Charles Eliot, *op. cit.*, Vol. II, pp. 78, 82; M. Winternitz, *History of Indian Literature* (English Translation, Calcutta, 1927), Vol. I, p. 284 ff.

[46]*Ibid.*

[47]*Indian Antiquary,* Vol. XXXIII, 1904, p. I01; B. N. Puri, *op. cit.*, pp. 58 and 68.

of Śākyamuṇi for the acceptance of the Mahāsaṅghika teachers.[48] The other record of the year 77 records the gift of the monk Jīvaka of Udiyana at the Vīhāra of Devaputra Huvishka. This monk seems to be the same as one who made a similar gift[49] at Huvishka's monastery in the Kushana year 47.

The Kushana power began to decline during the rule of Vāsudeva as a result of the onslaught of the Sassanian Shahpur I. During the early centuries of the Christian era, Buddhist activity on a large scale was concentrated in the Andhradeśa. It coincided with the rise of Nāgārjuna, the propounder of the Mādhyamika school of philosophy. It is well known how the Mahāsaṅghika school came to be established in South India.

Nāgārjuna, considered to be the first man to have explained the Mahāyāna philosophy in a systematic manner in the *Prajñāpāramitā-sūtra*, was born in Vidarbha or south Kosala towards the end of the second century A. D. He is credited with preaching Buddhism in Orissa and south India. According to Tāranāth he constructed monasteries in Orissa and other countries and was responsible for the erection of railings around the shrine of Dhānyakataka.

Professor R. Kimura summarizes the other facts[50] about Nāgārjuna's life from various sources as follows:

> At last he came to Kosala, his native place and made that place the centre of his propagandism. At that time the king of Kosala was Sadavāhana or Satavāhana, who belonged to the Andhra dynasty. Hiuen Tsang tells us that Satavāhana greatly prized and esteemed Nāgārjuna when he was at the Saṅgharāmā built by Aśoka, king Satavāhana provided him with a city gate hut. For the sake of Nāgārjuna, the King is said to have tunnelled out the Brahmagiri Rock and built a

[48]*Epigraphia Indica,* Vol. XXX, pp. 183-184.

[49]B. N. Puri, *op. cit.*, p. 59; *Epigraphia Indica*, Vol. IX, p. 243 ff; Lüders List No. 62.

[50]*Journal of the Department of Letters* (University of Calcutta), Vol. I, 1920, pp. 27-8. The Sātavāhana King mentioned here may be Gautamīputra Yajñaśrī. The association of Nāgārjuna with the celebrated Buddhist site of Nāgārjuna-Koṇḍa during the second-third centuries A. D. has not been borne out by archaeological excavations.

big rock temple which was 300 li distant from the Brahmagiri Rock. He also wrote may Śāstras and commentaries. Under the patronage of Satavāhana he refuted all heretical doctrines and clarified the Mahāyāna system. Southern Kosala became the centre of Buddhism at that time and after Nāgārjuna, Kanadeva or Aryadeva, an eminent disciple of Nāgārjuna became a great teacher not at all inferior to his master.

Aryadeva, who also was a Brahmana of Southern India and flourished in the middle of the third century A.D. helped Nāgārjuna in the propagation of the Mādhyamika doctrine.

From archaeological and other sources it is evident that Buddhism was popular over an extensive region in Southern India during the period under review. The major Buddhist sites of the region include Bhaṭṭiprolu, Amaravati, Jaggayyapeta, Nāgārjunakoṇḍa, Goli,) Garikapadu, Guntapalli, Ghantasala Salihundam and several other places.[51] Most of these places are situated in the Guntur and Krishna districts of the Andhra Pradesh. In the Repelle Taluk of the Guntur District, there was erected a Stūpa entirely of solid brick. During excavations in 1922 by A. Rea, many interesting objects including three inscribed votive caskets, each having a stone and crystal reliquary with relics and jewels were found. The Brāhmī scripts of the inscriptions on the caskets would attribute them to about the time of Aśoka.[52]

Amarāvati, also in the Guntur District, was a very important centre of Buddhism[53] from the second century B. C. to the early third century A. D. The Mahāsaṅghikas seem to have migrated here soon after the second Buddhist Council of Vaisali. The famous Stūpa of Amarāvati called Mahāchetiya in inscriptions was first built about 200 B. C. Later it was enlarged till it was

[51]R. Subrahmanyam, *Salihundam* (Hyderabad, 1964), p. 1; K. R. Subrahmanyam, *Buddhist Remains in Andhradesa*, Andhra University Series III, 1932, p. 1 ff.

[52]Aiyappan and P. R. Srinivasan, *Guide to Buddhist Antiquities* (Madras Govt. Museum, 1960), p. 49 ff; *Epigraphia Indica*, Vol. II, pp. 323.

[53]C. Sivaramamurti, *Amaravati Sculptures in the Madras Govt. Museum* (Madras, 1956), p. 27 ff.

completed about 250 A. D. It is held that a grand railing was added to it by Nāgārjuna's endeavour about 150 A.D.

As in the case of the railings of Bharhut and Sanchi in northern India (second-first centuries B. C.) the railings of Amaravati contain beautiful carvings depicting scenes from Buddha's life.

The inscriptions on the Amaravati sculptures throw considerable light on the history of Buddhism. They mention monks (*bhadatas*), elders (*theras*), mendicants (*pendapatikas*), lay worshippers (*Uvāsaka* and *Uvāsikās*), disciples, male and female (*antevāsika* and *anihevāsikās*), preachers of law (*dhammikas*) and various others as donors. Further, various schools of Buddhism are mentioned in these inscriptions. They are the Chetiyakas, Rajagirikas, Siddhathikas, Pubbaseliyas, and Avaraseliyas.[54]

Almost of the same period, i. e. the early phase of the Amaravati stūpa (i. e. the second century B. C.) is the stūpa of Jaggayyapeta on the bank of the Krishna of which some sculptured fragments have survived. The style of these sculptures is similar to those of the early phase of Amaravati.

Excavations at Nāgārjunakoṇḍa have brought to light extensive ruins of structures, carvings and inscriptions of *circa* third and fourth centuries which throw considerable light on the history of Buddhism in South India. Apart from the secular and Brahmanical structures, more than thirty Buddhist establishments came into existence here during the rule of the Ikshvāku kings, Vāsishṭhiputra, Chāmtamlūa in South India, Maṭharīputra Vīrapurushadatta, Vasishṭhīputra Ehuvala Chāmtamūla, and Rudrapurushadatta.

All the datable Buddhist structures came into existence between the sixth and the eighteenth regnal year of Vīrapurushadatta. The Mahāchaitya of Nāgārjunakoṇḍa built in the sixth regnal year of Vīrapurushadatta received the patronage and munificence of the pious lady Chāṁtaśrī, the sister of Vāsishṭhīputra Chāṁtamula.

The Mahāvihāra and the apsidal chaityagriha (stūpa shrine)[55] meant for a much smaller stūpa, were set up respectively in

[54]C. Sivaramamurti, *op. cit.*, p. 271.

[55]H. Sarkar and B. N. Misra, *Nagarjunakonda* (New Delhi, 1966), pp. 22-3.

the fifteenth and eighteenth regnal years of the same king for the Aparamahāvihāraseliya sect. Some structures near-by must have come into existence between the sixth and the fifteenth regnal years, for one Bodhisri, a lay worshipper from Govagama, donated an apsidal stūpa shrine in the fourteenth regnal year of Vīrapurushadatta to the Ceylonese monastery on the Chuladhaṁmagiri.

The inscriptions of Nāgārjunakoṇḍa mention at least five Buddhist sects: the Theravādins, Mahāvihāra-vāsins of Ceylon, the Mahīśāsakas, Bahuśrutīyas and Aparamahāvihāraseliya. The existence of the Ceylonese Buddhist sects and monks in Nāgārjunakoṇḍa is proved beyond doubt by the inscriptions.

The Buddhist ruins of Goli, Ghantasala and Gummididuru, and several other remaining sites also speak of the wide popularity of Buddhism in Southern India during the second-third centuries A.D.

In Western India also, Buddhism was popular over a wide region as the various archaeological remains would support. At Ajanta, some of the caves, 9 and 10, were excavated during the second-first century B. C. A principal wall painting of the period is the Shaḍdanta Jātaka in Cave 9. Some of the caves and sculptures of Pitalkhora, depicting Yaksha figures and scenes from Buddha's life belong to the same period, i. e. the the second century B. C. At Nasik there is a group of twenty-three caves ascribable from the second century B. C. to the second century A. D.[56]

Kanheri was for a long time an important centre of Buddhism in Western India. Some of the Kanheri caves, as is evident from inscriptions, can be attributed to the reign of Gautamīputra Śātakarṇi about 180 A. D. [57] The Chaitya hall of Karle dates from the lst century B. C. An ancient inscription found here describes it as the most excellent rock mansion in Jambudvīpa.

[56] *2500 Years of Buddhism*, pp. 332 ff.

[57] *Ibid.*, p. 334. That Aparaśaila monks lived here during the Sātvāhana period is proved by an epigraph occurring in one of its caves. Ajoy Mitra Shastri, *op. cit.*, p. 97.

Karle seems to have been an important centre of the Mahāsaṅghikas in the second century A. D. as is indicated by two epigraphs of the cave temple here. One of these inscriptions records the gift of the village of Karajika by Gautamīputra Śātakarṇi to the monks of the Valuraka caves for the support of the school of the Mahāsaṅghikas. The other inscription of the time of Śrī Vāsishṭhiputra Śrīpulumāvi records the gift of a nine-celled hall to the school.[58]

Apart from the above, Bhaja, the earliest Chaitya hall, dating from the second century B. C., the caves at Kondane, slightly later in date than Bhaja, and those in Junagadh and other places[59] speak of the continued popularity of Buddhism in Western India from the second century onward.

Buddhist Schools

It may be convenient here to describe in brief the chief Buddhist schools and sects.[60] The Buddhist Saṅgha, as we know, was divided into eighteen schools or sects within a century and a half after Buddha's death. The names of all these schools are mentioned not only in certain Buddhist texts, but also in Śunga, Sātavāhana, Kushana and Ikshvāku inscriptions (second century B. C. to the second century A. D.).

As is well known, the second Buddhist council gave rise to two main schools, viz. the Sthaviravādins and the Mahāsaṅghikas. In course of time, differences arose within each school and more sects came into existence till the total number of such schools as recorded in Buddhist tradition was eighteen.

The Sthaviravādins maintained harmony among themselves for a long time, but dissension arose among them in the third century (after the death of Buddha) and they were in course of time divided into as many as eleven schools, namely the Sarvāstivāda,

[58]Ajoy Mitra Shastri, *op. cit.,* p. 89.

[59]*2500 Years of Buddhism, op. cit.*, p. 326 ff.

[60]For a detailed descripton of the Buddhist schools and sects and their religious views, see N. Dutt, *op. cit.*, Vol. II, pp. 46-206; *2500 Years of Buddhism, op. cit.*, pp. 97-124; Jiryo Masuda, "Origin and Doctrines of Early Indian Buddhist Schools," *Asia Major,* Vol. II, 1925, pp. 6-69; Ajoy Mitra Shastri, *op. cit.*, p. 42 ff.

the Haimavata, the Vātsīputrīya, the Dharmottarīya, the Bhadrayānīya, the Sammitīya, the Channagarika, the Mahīśāsaka, the Dharmaguptika, the Kāśyapīya and the Sautrāntika.

During the second century, following the death of Buddha, dissension assailed the Mahāsaṅghika school as well resulting in its division into schools such as the Ekavyavahārika, the Lokottaravāda, the Kaukkuṭika, the Chaityaśaila, the Aparaśaila, the Uttaraśaila, the Bahuśrutīya and the Prajñaptivāda.

The Sthaviravāda

This represents the orthodox school of Buddhism which accepted the canon compiled in the first council at Rajagriha. The followers of this school considered Buddha a human teacher though endowed with certain supreme qualities.

Its teachings exhort the people to abstain from evil deeds, and lay emphasis on *śīla* (good conduct), *samādhi* (meditation), and *prajñā* (wisdom). Good conduct purifies the mind; *samādhi* brings about its concentration and helps one to understand the real nature of things. On the attainment of *prajñā* (wisdom) we understand the significance of the four noble truths, and the law of dependent origination (the inter-relationship of one with another).

The main philosophy of this school is that all we find in this world is *anitya* (impermanence), *duḥkha* (suffering) and *anātman* (soul-less). All compounded things are composed of two elements, namely *nāmā* and *rūpa*. They constitute what is called five skandhas, i. e. *Rūpa*, *Vedanā*, *Sañjā*, *Saṁskāra* and *Vijñāna*.

The attainment of arhathood is the goal of this school. An arhat understands the true nature of things, and he follows the noble eight-fold path, i. e. the middle path, and strives for *Nirvāṇa*, the state of dispassionateness. From epigraphical records it would appear that during the third and second centuries B. C. this school had its strongholds in Sarnath and Sanchi. Its popularity extended also to the Nāgārjunakoṇḍa region (which was otherwise a main centre of the Śaila schools belonging to the Mahāsaṅghika school) in the third century A. D. The Nāgārjunakoṇḍa Apsidal Temple Inscription No. F (*Epigraphia Indica*, Vol. XX, pp. 166) refers to the Theravāda fraternities of Ceylon who to their credit are said to have converted the people of Kashmīr, Gandhāra, China, Chilata, (Kirata ?), Tosali, Aparānta, Vaṅga, Vanavāsī. the Yavana countries, Drāviḍa, Palaura and the island of Ceylon. Another Nāgārjunakoṇḍa inscription refers to the monastic establishments of the Thera-vādins, Vibhajjavādins, and Mahāvihāravāsins.[61] Vibhjjavāda is another name of the Theravādins, while Mahāvihāra-vāsins were a sub-sect of the Theravādins in Ceylon.

The Mahīśāsakas

The Mahīśāsakas were of two groups, the earlier and later Mahīśāsakas. The earlier group held tenets closer to those of the Theravādins, while the later group to those of the Sarvāsti-vādins.

The earlier Mahīśāsakas seem to have been followers of Purāṇa of Dakkhinagiri (near Rajagriha). That he was a monk of high esteem and considerable importance is evident from the fact that his seven rules relating to food were incorporated in the Vinaya text. The Mahīśasakas assert that after the delibera-tions of the first council were finished, the texts were once more recited for the approval of Purāṇa, who accepted the same after adding his seven rules.

According to the researches of Professor Przyluski, the expan-sion of this school took place 'along the Kausambi-Bharukachha axis'. It seems to have been particularly popular in Mahīsha-maṇḍala and Avantī and ultimately its activities spread to South India and Ceylon. The southward expansion of this school is attested by the Nāgārjunakoṇḍa Pillar inscription and the discovery of the Vinaya text of this school in Ceylon. The Nāgārjunakoṇḍa Pillar inscription in question records the gift of a monastery for the acceptance of the Mahīśāsaka teachers in the eleventh regnal year of Ehuvala by his sister Kodabalisiri, the queen of the Maharaja of Vanavāsa.

Regarding the philosophy of the Mahīshāsakas, only some of their tenets may be mentioned here. They rejected the *sabbam atthi* (everything exists) of the Sarvāstivādins and held that the

[61] *Epigraphia Indica*, Vol. XXXIII, p. 247 ff.

present alone exists. According to the earlier Mahīśasakas, there is no *antarābhava*, i.e. interim existence between this life and the next one. The later Mahīśāsakas, however, believed in the existence of the past. and held that the skandhas, the *āyatanas*, and the *dhātus* always existed in the form of seeds.

The Sarvāstivādins

The Sarvāstivādins seem to have been one of the most popular of all Buddhist sects in ancient India. They also took an active part in preaching Buddhism in Central Asia and China.

The Sarvāstivāda school seems to have originated from the Mahīśāsakas and not from the Theravādins as Vasumitra believes. The Sarvāstivādins are mentioned in a large number of inscriptions which, along with literary evidence, would indicate their range of influence in Mathura, Kashmīr, Gandhāra and also at Tukhara.

The Mathura Lion capital inscription, attributed to *circa* 5-10 A.D. by Sten Konow records the establishment by the chief queen of Mahākshatrapa Rajuvula of the relics of the Śākyamuṇi Buddha, a stūpa and a Saṇghārāma in thc acceptance of the Sarvāstivāda teachers. Again, the Zedda inscription of the eleventh year of Kanishka records the digging of a well in honour of the Sarvāstivādins. The gift of the Bodhisattva images to the Sarvāstivādin teachers is also mentioned in the Kushana inscriptions from Sahet-Mahet (Śrāvastī) and Mathura. The Kaman Buddhist Image inscription refers to the installation of an image of Bhagavat Śākyamuṇi in the Mihira-vihāra as a gift of the monk Nandika for the acceptance of the Sarvāstivāda teachers. Again, the Kurram Relic casket inscription and certain potsherds from Tor Dheri refer to the Sarvāstivāda teachers.[62] It is, however, interesting to note that the inscriptions from Nāgārjunakoṇḍa and Amaravati contain reference to this sect.

According to the Sarvāstivādins, all things exist (compare the expression *sabbham atthi* in the *Saṁyutta-nikāya*). Like the

[62]*Epigraphia Indica,* Vols. II, p. 212; Vol. VIII, pp. 180-111; Vol. IX, p. 141 ff; Vol. XVIII, p. 15 ff.

Sthaviravādins they were realists, but the principal point of difference between the two schools is that the Sarvāstivādins maintain the existence of five *dharmas* in their subtlest forms at all times, whether in the past, present or future, while the Theravādins deny such existence.

The Sthaviravādins attribute a position of unsurpassed importance to the Arhats. But the Sarvāstivādins, like the Vātsīputriyas and the Sammitīyas, held that the Arhats "are subject to retrogression". Further, they did not attribute any transcendental postion to Buddhas and Bodhisattvas as the Mahāsaṅghikas did.

The Haimavatas

The main centre of this school, as the very name would suggest, was the Himalayan region. According to Vasumitra, the Haimavatas branched off from the Sarvāstivādins, while Vinītadeva and Bhavya consider them as a branch of the Mahāsaṅghikas.

During the second century B.C., Sanchi seems to have been an important centre for the activities of this sect as is apparent from some relic casket inscriptions.

The inscription of the steatite Casket No. 1 from Stūpa No. II at Sanchi refers to Sapurisa Kassapagota, who is described as *Śava-hemavatāchariya,* which according to N.G. Majumdar, means the teacher of the whole community of the Haimavatas. The his cirption on the Relic casket found in Stūpa No. 2 at Sonari mentions Gotiputa, the heir of Dudubhisara, as a Hemavata, i.e., a member of the community of the Haimavata. A seal from Sankisa also refers to the Haimavata school.[63]

In common with the Sarvāstivādins, the Haimavatas did not attach any special importance to the Bodhisattvas and considered that "the gods were not capable of living a holy life of Brahmacharya and the heretics could not have miraculous powers".

[63]Marshall, *op. cit.,* pp. 294 ff; Luders List No. 156; *Royal Asiatic Society,* London, 1905, pp. 691; Ajay Mitra Shastri, *op. cit.,* p. 87.

The Vātsīputrīyas

The Vātsīputrīyas, with whom the Sammitīyas were affiliated, were well known for their doctrine of *pudgala*. The main centre of the activities of the school during the early Gupta period seems to have been Sarnath as is attested by an inscription engraved on an Aśokan pillar there. The cardinal doctrine of this school is that besides the elements composing a being there is a *pudgala* (an individuality, a personality, a self) which is indefinable and which persists through all existences. Thus according to some thinkers, they should be treated as a heretical sect.

The Dharmaguptakas

The Dharmaguptakas seem to have branched from the Mahīśāsakas. Like the latter, they held that an Arhat was free from passions and that the heretics were not capable of gaining miraculous powers. Further, they considered a gift to Buddha as of special importance, and they believed in the worship of the stūpas of Buddha.

The main centre of the Dharmaguptakas seems to have been in the north-west of the Indian and Pakistan sub-continent and and from there the tenets of this school went to Iran, Central Asia and China. The Pratimoksha of the Dharmaguptakas was used as the disciplinary guide in all the convents of China.

The Kāśyapīyas

The *Kāśyapīya*s also known as Sthavirīyas, Saddharmavarshakas or Suvarshakas, held doctrines close to those of the Sthaviravādins. According to Tibetan tradition, its founder was one Kāśyapa. Some scholars find a reference to them in the Pabhosa inscription (*circa* first-second century B.C.) which refers to the dedication of a cave (*lena*) to the Kāśyapīya arhats by Āshāḍhasena, son of Gopālīyā Vaihidarī and Rājan Bhāgavata and maternal uncle of the King Bahasati Mita in the 10th year of Udāka.[64] They find mention also in the Bedadi Copper

[64] *Epigruphia Indica*, Vol. II, p. 242.

Ladle Inscription and on the inscribed jars from Palatu Dheri as recipients of some gifts.[65] Bühler considers Sovasaka of the Karle Inscription of the 24th regnal year of the Sātavāhana King Vāsishṭhiputra Pulumāvi as a Prakrit equivalent of Suvarskaka, another name of the Kāśyapīyas. But this view is not accepted by many scholars.

The Kāśyapīyas believed that "the past which has borne fruit ceases to exist, thus partially modifying the position of the Sarvāstivādins for whom the past also exists like the present."

The Sautrāntikas

They seem to have issued from the Kāśyapīya sect. Like the latter, they believed that the *Pudgala* or individuality passes from one life to another. Certain Sanchi inscriptions seem to refer to the teachers of this school as Sutātika and Sutātikini.[66]

Dharmmottarīyas

They are a branch of the Sthaviravādins. The Dharmmottarīyas seem to have been mentioned in two Karle cave inscriptions of the second-century A.D., which record the erection of a pillar with relics by the Bhānaka Satimita (Svātimitra), son of Nanda and disciple of some Sthavira of the community of the Dharmottarīyas from Soparaka, (Surparaka). A Junagadh cave inscription records endowments for Dharmmottarīyas.[67]

Sammitīyas

The Sammitīyas were allied to Vātsīputrīyas and they became popular during the reign of Harshavardhana. They trace their origin to Mahā-Kachchāyana of Avanti. A Kushāna inscription from Mathura refers to the installation of a Bodhisattva image

[65] *Corpus Inscriptionum Indicarum*, Vol. II, p. CXXVII.
[66] *Epigraphia Indica*, Vol. II, p. 195.
[67] Ajoy Mitra Shastri, *op. cit.*, pp. 82-83.

for the acceptance of the Sammitiyas (*Epigraphia Indica*, Vol. II, p. 67).

Bhadrayānīyas

The Bhadrayānīyas are mentioned in the Kanheri cave inscriptions of the time of Gautamīputra Śātakarṇi and two epigraphs from Nasik. One of the Nasik epigraphs records the donation of a cave and a village, Pisājipadaka, on the south-west side of the mount Tiranhu (Trirasmi) by the queen Gotami Balaśrī, to the Sangha of the monks of the Community of the Bhadrayānīyas. The other inscription mentions the command of Vāsiṭhīputra Pulamāvi to his officer Śivakhaṇḍila to give the village of Samalipada to the monks of the Bhadrayānīya school in exchange of the village of Sudarsana.[68]

Very little is known of the doctrines of the Dhammotariyas, Bhadrayānīyas and Channagarika.

The Mahāsaṅghikas, as stated above, originated after the second Buddhist council. They were the first seceders from the parent Saṅga as they formed a separate group after being declared dissidents by the orthodox monks on account of their indulgence in ten points of Vinaya rules.

Because of their revolutionary outlook, they added some new rules to the existing Vinaya adopted in the first council. Again they introduced changes with regard to the arrangement and interpretation of the *Sūtra* and the *Vinaya* texts. They did not accept as Buddha's sayings the Parivāra, the Abhidharma, the Paṭisaṁbhidā, the Niddesa and parts of the Jātākas as Buddha's sayings. All these texts are excluded from the canonical texts of the Mahāsaṅghikas. They made a fresh compilation of the Dhamma and Vinaya and included those texts which were excluded in the first council. They also made some original compilation of which the *Mahāvastu* alone is known to us.

The wide popularity of the Mahāsaṅghikas is reflected in many inscriptions. The earliest epigraph in which the Mahāsaṅghikas are mentioned is the Mathura Lion capital inscription of the time of Mahākshatrapa Soḍāsa. According

[68]Lüders List, Nos. 987 and 124; *Epigraphia Indica*, Vol. VIII, pp. 60-66.

to this epigraph, this sect had a strong opponent in Buddhila, who was an adherent of the Sarvāstivāda School. The Wardak (30 miles to the west of Kabul) Vase inscription of the time of Huvishka shows that Afghanistan was one of the centres of this sect, inasmuch as this epigraph records the enshrinement of a relic of Buddha at the Vagra-Magira Monastery by Kamaguliya, son of Vagra-Magira for the acceptance of the Sarvāstivāda teachers.[69]

On the west, Karla seems to have been an important seat of Mahāsaṅghika activities. The Karla cave inscription No. 19 tells us that King Vāsiṭhiputa Pulamāvi asked his officer to donate the village of Karajika in the Mamala District with all the immunities belonging to the monk's land for the support of the Mahāsaṅghikas. The Inscription No. 20 records the gift of a nine-celled hall to the same sect.[70]

The offshoots of this school, the Chaityakas and the Lokottaravādins, were firmly established in the South, *i.e.* Amaravati and Nāgārjunakoṇḍa. It is well known that some of the Amaravati Rail Pillar inscriptions mention Mahāvinayadharas and Vinayadharas (the monks and nuns expert in Vinaya rules). One Amaravati stone slab inscription refers to the term Samyutta-bhāṇaka. That all these canonical experts belong to the Mahāsaṅghika group is apparent from the fact that such titles as Dīgha-majhima-nikāya-dharasa, digha-majjhimapañcha mātuka-osaka-vāchakānaṁ, dīgha-majjhima-pañcha-mātuka-dèsakānaṁ, and digha-maṇgayaḍhaṛeṇa occur in the Nāgārjunakoṇḍa inscriptions in reference to the monks of the Śaila school.[71] This will confirm the tradition that the Mahāsanghikas had their own *Vinaya*, *Nikāyas* and *Abhidhamma*.

The offshoots of the Mahāsaṅghikas were the Bahusrutīyas, the Rāja-girinivasikas, the Siddhatthakas, the Chetiyakas the Pubba-seliyas, and the Aparamahāvanaseliyas. The Bahusrutīyas are mentioned in the Palatu-dheri jar inscriptions (first

[69]*Corpus Inscriptionum Indicarum,* Vol. II, pp. 48, 170. A Kushana inscription of the time of Vāsudeva refers to the installation of an image of Sākyamuni for the acceptance of this sect.

[70]*Epigraphia Indica,* Vol. VII, p. 64, Vol. VIII, p. 71.

[71]Burgess and Jaggayyapeta, *Buddhist Stupas of Amaravati*, pp. 91, 105 162 ff; *Epigraphia Indica*, Vol. XX. p. 17.

century A.D.) and also in one of the Nāgārjunakoṇḍa detached pillar inscription (No.G) which refers to the construction of a monastery for the Bahuśrutīya teachers by the mother of the King Sri Ehuvula Chāṁtmūla.[72]

The Chaityakas[73] are mentioned in the Nasik Inscription No. 22, which records the gift of a lena or cave by Mugadāsa who was a lay worshipper of the Chaityaka sect. They are mentioned also in the inscriptions of the Junar and Ajanta Caves. An Amaravati Inscription of the time of Vāsiṭhiputa Pulmāvi mentions the gift of a Dharma-Chakra for the acceptance of the Nikāyas of the Chaityakas.[74]

The Rājagriha-nivāsikas and Siddhatthakas are also mentioned in the Amaravati incriptions.

EARLY BUDDHISM AND THE GROWTH OF MAHAYANA

The early or original Buddhism centres round Buddha's teachings, as maintained in the Pali canon. *Śīla* (good conduct), *samādhi* (concentration) and *Prajnā* (wisdom) form the core of Buddha's teachings. Buddha held that existence is suffering. Suffering has a cause. There is a way to overcome it and Buddha alone knows the way. The practice of the noble eightfold path leads to the cessation of suffering, and the attainment of *Nirvāṇa* or emancipation. *Nirvāṇa* is an indescribable state of bliss. The noble eightfold path is the middle path which avoids the two extremes, the one of extreme indulgence and the other of extreme self-mortification.

Buddha believed in *Karma* and rebirth with the majority of Hindu thinkers. He did not encourage the practice of miracles,

[72] Sten Konow, *Corpus Inscriptionum Indicarum*, Vol. II; *Epigraphia Indica*, Vol. XX, pp. 23-4.

[73] Lüders List No. 1130; Burgess, *Notes on Amaravati Stupas*, pp. 27, 41.

[74] N. Dutt describes the special characteristics of Mahāyāna Buddhism as follows: (1) the conception of the Bodhisattva, (2) the practice of the *Pāramitās*, (3) the development of Bodhichitta, (4) the ten stages (*bhūmi*) of spritual development, (5) the goal of Buddhahood, (6) the conception of *trikāya* and (7) the conception of Dharmasunyatā or Dharmsamatā or Tathatā (*Aspects of Mahayana Buddhism and its Relation to Hinayana*, p. 34 ff).

nor was he interested in the origin and end of the universe. He did not consider these metaphysical questions of any relevance to gain knowledge or emancipation.

Buddha's philosophy can be summed up in what is known as *anitya*, *anātman*, and *duḥkha*. Everything we see is impermanent and soulless, and existence is suffering. Except *Nirvāṇa*, which is not made up of any constitutents, everything is temporary, painful and devoid of any rea y.

> What we conveniently call a person or any individual consists of nothing else but name-nonmaterial part, and *rūpa*, material form, both of which are changing every moment. ...The cycle of worldly life is explained by the law of dependent orgination—*pratītya samtupāda*.

> The root of all evil is ignorance or *avidyā*.

> From ignorance as cause arise the aggregates (*sankhārā*), from the aggregates as cause arise consciousness, from consciousness as cause arise name and form (mind and body), from name and form as a cause arise the sphere of the six (senses), from the sphere of the six as cause, contact, from the contact as cause sensation, from sensation as cause, craving, from craving as cause grasping, from grasping as cause becoming, from becoming as cause birth, from birth as cause arise old age, death, grief, lamentation, pain, dejection and despair. Even so is the origination of all mass of pain.[75]

As time passed, new thoughts arose and the religion underwent transformations. The new thinkers of whom Nāgārjuna was the most celebrated, laid emphasis on the supramundane character of Buddha and developed the concept of Bodhisattvas, who though fit to attain *Nirvāṇa*, refuse to do so till all sentient beings were delivered from suffering. With these new schools, not Arhathood but Buddhahood became the goal of the monks. With the deification of Buddha, new Buddhist deities, Avalokiteśvara and others were gradually introduced. The followers of the

[75]E. J. Thomas, *op. cit.*, p. 193.

new school called themselves Mahāyānists, *i.e.* the followers of the greater vehicle[76] throwing open the possibilities of salvation and Buddhahood to all and designated the followers of the orthodox school as Hinayanists, *i. e.* the followers of a smaller vehicle, with whom self-realisation or individual arhathood was of primary concern.[77]

Another aspect of Mahāyānism is the stress on devotion or Bhakti which brought it closer to other important creeds of India.

> It is by that feeling of fervent devotion, combined with the preaching of active compassion that the creed has enlisted the sympathy of numerous millions of people, and has become a factor in the history of mankind of much greater importance than orthodox Buddhism.[77]

It is by its more progressive spirit that it has succeeded finally in absorbing all the sects.

Mahāyāna Buddhism has two important schools of thought, the Mādhyamika and the Yogāchāra. The Mādhyamikas held the middle path or view. But this middle path was apparently different from the middle path preached by Buddha in Benaras. Buddha's middle path (or *pratītyasamutpāda*) had an ethical significance, whereas the middle path advocated by the Mahayanists is a theory of relativity. It advocates neither the theory of *reality nor that of the unreality* of the world, but merely of relativity.

The essence of the Māhāyana philosophy is *Śūnya* or void. Śūnya however does not mean nothingness. It has two aspects, from the positive point of view it means the worldly phenomena as a result of dependent origination; from the negative point of view, it means the *paramartha satya* or the absolute reality without orgination. Thus it avoids the two extremes of existence and non-existence.

The Mādhyamika school was founded by Nāgārjuna or Ārya Nāgārjuna (second century A.D.). The Yogāchāra school

[76]Sir Charles Eliot, *op. cit.*, Vol. II, pp. 3-75.
[77]H. Kern, *op. cit.*, p. 124.
[78]*2500 Years of Buddhism*, *op. cit.*, pp. 121-24.

laid emphasis on *Yoga* as the most important method for attainning enlightenment. *Bodhi* can be attained after all the stages of spiritual progress have been gone through. This school was founded by Maitreya or Maitreyanāth (3rd century A.D.).[78]

BUDDHIST LITERATURE

Before this chapter is closed a few words may be said about the Buddhist literature of the period under review. None of the Buddhist works belong to Buddha's time. Further, all that we find in Buddhist collections were not words or sayings of Buddha only. Some were composed by his disciples.

The oldest of all the Buddhist literatures are the *Tripiṭaka* (Three Baskets). They are the collections of speeches, sayings, songs, narratives and rules of the order (Saṅgha).

The *Tripiṭaka* consists of the Vinayapiṭaka, the Suttapiṭaka and the Abhidhammapiṭaka. The Vinayapiṭaka contains the disciplinary rules to be followed by the monks and nuns of the Sangha. It includes the Suttavibhaṅga (consisting of the Mahāvibhaṅga and the Bhikkunīvibhaṅga); the Khandhakas (consisting of the Mahāvagga and the Chullavagga); and the Parivāra.

The Suttapiṭaka consists of the followings nikāyas, or collections, namely, (*a*) Dīghanikāya, (*b*) Majjhimanikāya, (*c*) Samyuttanikāya, (*d*) Anguttaranikāya and (*e*) Khuddakanikāya.

The Khuddakanikāya contains fifteen books: the Khuddakapāṭha, Dhammapada, Udāna, Itivuttaka, Suttanipāta, Vimāna-Vatthu, Peta-Vatthu, Theragāthā, Therīgathā, Jātaka, Niddesa, Patisambhidā, Apadāna, Buddhavaṁśa and Chariyāpiṭaka.[79]

The Abhiddammapiṭaka has seven books: the Dhammasaṅgaṇī, (compendium of dhammas), Vibhaṅga (classification), Dhātukathā (discourse on the elements), Puggalapaññatti (description of human elements), Kathāvatthu (subjects of discourse), Yamaka and Paṭṭhāna.

The above texts comprise the Pāli scriptures representing the cannon of the Theravādins or Vibhjjavādins. In all probability

[79]M. Winternitz, *op. cit.*, p. 4 ff; Sir Charles Eliot, *op. cit.*, Vol. 1, pp. 277 ff; *2500 Years of Buddhism, op. cit.*, pp. 139 ff.

the Pāli cannon was substantially fixed in the time of Aśoka. Mahinda, brother of Aśoka, carried the canon to Ceylon, where the texts were written during the reign of Vatsagamini (first century B. C.).

The non-canonical Pāli literature includes, among others, the Milindapañha, the Nettipakaraṇa, Buddhadatta's manuals, on Vinaya and Abhidhamma, commentaries on the Pali Tripiṭaka texts including the Jataka ascribed to Buddhaghosha or Dhammapāla and the Ceylones works like the Dīpavaṁsa, Mahāvaṁsa, the Chūlavaṁsa, etc.

Now mention may be made of Buddhist literature in pure and mixed Sanskrit, representing the treatises of the other sects as the Pāli canon does of the Theravāda.

The Mahāvastu, which belongs to the Hīnayāna school, contains legends regarding Buddha's life, Jātakas and other narratives. It is considered a book on *Vinaya* belonging to the Lokottaravādins of the Mahāsaṅghikas. Though the Mahāvastu is a Hinayāna text, it contained many of the features of the Mahāyanist.

The Lalitavistara in mixed Sanskrit deals with the life of Buddha from his birth till his first sermon. It is one of the most important sacred texts of the Mahayanists and it calls itself a *Vaipulya Sūtra*.[80]

Among the Buddhist Sanskrit texts, the works of Aśvaghosha occupy a unique position. As is well known, Aśvaghosha flourished in the reign of Kanishka. He laid stress on Buddha Bhakti which contributed largely to the growth of Buddhism.

Aśvaghosha's works include the *Budahacharita* (the biography of Buddha), the *Saundarānanda* (the story of the conversion of his step-brother, Nanda), both representing ornate poetry, and the Sāriputraprakaraṇa, a nine-act play, the fragments of which have been discovered in Central Asia, besides the *Gaṇḍīstotra* and *Vajrasūchi*. Another poet who flourished during Kanishka's time was Mātricheṭa, whose *Kanikalekha* is a poem of eightyfive verses including some didactic narratives. His other famous hymns are the *Chatuḥsataka stotra* (a hymn of four hundred verses) and the *Satapañchśatika stotra* (a hymn of one hundred

[80]M. Winternitz, *op. cit.*, p. 248 ff,

and fifty verses) fragments of both of which were discovered in Central Asia.[81]

The principal Mahāyāna scriptures of our period include the Prajñāpāramitā, the Saddharmapuṇḍarīka, the Suvarṇaprabhāsa, the Laṅkāvatāra, the Gaṇḍavyūha, the Tathāgataguhyaka, the Samādhirāja, and the Daśabhūmiśvara, etc.

The Prajñāpāramitā contains sūtras on the doctrine of *Śūnyatā*. It is said that originally Buddha expounded the sūtras on the Vulture Beak in Rajagriha. In course of time, they are said to have been lost and rescued from the nether regions by Nāgārjuna. One of the Prajñāpāramitā treatises was translated into Chinese abut 170 A. D.

The Saddharmapuṇḍarīka was composed perhaps in the second century A. D. It is said to contain the doctrine which Buddha delivered to an assembly of Boddhisattvas on the Vulture Peak. It represents developed Mahāyāna Buddhism "with Buddha worship, the cult of relics and image worship and the dedication of Buddhist stūpas and Vihāras." It looks upon the Buddha as an eternal principle; "a god above all gods". The doctrine of *Śūnyatā*, however, does not get much mention here.

The date of the other Mahāyāna scriptures cannot be fixed with certainty, though most were perhaps composed during this period. Of the Avadāna texts the Avadādaśataka seems to be the earliest. It is said to have been translated into Chinese during the early part of the third century A. D. The Divyāvadāna seems to have been composed by different authors in different periods. The major portion of the work was perhaps composed in the second century A.D. The Avadānas introduce a multiplicity of Buddhas and Bodhisattvas and represent Śākyamuṇi as a super-human worker of miracles.

[81] *Ibid.*, pp. 270 ff.

Select Bibliography

Modern Works

V. S. Agarwala, *Hand Book to the Sculptures in the Curzon Museum of Archaeology,* Muttra, Allahabad, 1933; *A Short Guide Book to the Archaeological Section of Archaeological Museum,* Lucknow, Allahabad, 1940.

Aiyappan and **P. R. Srinivasan,** *Guide to Buddhist Antiquities,* Madras Government Museum, 1960.

J. Allan, *Catalogue of Indian Coins (Ancient India) in the British Museum,* London, 1936.

J. N. Banerjea, *The Development of Hindu Iconography,* Vol. I, University of Calcutta, 1941.

P. Banerjee, *The Way of the Buddha* (Publications Division, Government of India), Anonymous work.

R. D. Banerji, *History of Orissa,* Vol. I, Calcutta 1930.

L. D. Barnett, *Hindu Gods and Heroes,* London, 1922.

A. Barth, *Religions of India,* translated into English by Rev. J. Wood, 5th Edition, 1921.

B. M. Barua, *Old Brahmi Inscriptions in the Udayagiri* and *Khandagiri Caves,* University of Calcutta, 1928;

———*Pre-Buddhist Indian Philosophy; Barhuts,* Bks. I-III, Calcutta, 1934-37.

S. Beal, *Buddhist Records of the Western World,* London, 1906.

D.R. Bhandarkar, *Charmichael Lectures on Ancient Indian Numismatics,* Calcutta, 1921; *Asoka,* 3rd Edition, University of Calcutta, 1955; *Some Aspects of Ancient Indian Culture,* Madras, 1940.

R. G. Bhandarkar, *Vaishnavism, Saivism, and Minor Religious Systems*, Strassburg, 1913.

B. C. Bhattacharya, *The Jaina Iconography*, the Punjab Oriental Series, No. XXVI, Lahore, 1939.

Bloomfield, *The Life and Story of the Jaina Savior Parsvanatha*, Baltimore, 1914.

W. Norman Brown, *The Story of Kalaka*, Washington, 1933.

Buhler, *The Indian Sect of the Jainas*, translated and edited by J. Burgess. 1903.

J. Burgess, *The Buddhist Stupas of Amaravati and Jagayyapeta*, London, 1887.

S. K. Chakrabortty, *A Study of Ancient Indian Numismatics*, Calcutta, 1931.

R. P. Chanda, *Archaeology and Vaishnava Tradition*, Memoirs, Archaeological Survey of India, No. 5; *The Indo-Aryan Races*, Part I, Varendra Research Society, 1916.

B. R. Chatterjee, *Indian Influence in Cambodia*, Calcutta, 1928.

H. T. Colebrooke, *Essays on the Religions and Philosophy of the Hindus*, New Edition, Leipzig, 1858.

A. K. Coomaraswamy, *History of Indian and Indonesian Art*, London, 1927.

M'Crindle, *Ancient India as Described in the Classical Literature*, Westminister, 1901.

———*Ancient India as Described by Megasthenes and Arrian*, Calcutta, 1926.

W. Crooke, *An Introduction to the Popular Religion and Folklore in Northern India*, Allahabad, 1894.

A. Cunningham, *Coins of Ancient India*, 1891.

E. T. Dalton, *Descriptive Ethnology of Bengal*, Calcutta, 1872.

S. N. Das Gupta, *History of Indian Philosophy*, Vol. I, London, 1923.

Rhys Davids, *Buddhist India*, Calcutta, 1955.

Paul Deussen, *The Philosophy of the Upanishads*, translated by A. S. Gaden, Edinburgh, 1906.

N. Dutt, *Early Monastic Buddhism*, Vols. I and II, Calcutta, 1941; *Aspects of Mahayana Buddhism and its Relation to Hinayana*, London, 1930.

Sir Charles Eliot, *Hinduism and Buddhism*, London, 1952.

J. N. Farquhar, *The Crown of Hinduism*, London, 1913.

J. Fergusson, *Tree and Serpent Worship* (1868 & 1873 editions), London.

J. F. Fleet, *Corpus Inscriptionum Indicarum,* Vol. III *(Inscriptions of Early Gupta Kings and their Successors),* Calcutta, 1888.

A. Foucher, *Beginnings of Buddhist Art in India,* London, 1908.

Manomohan Ganguly, *Orissa and Her Remains,* Calcutta, 1912.

P. Gardner, *The Coins of the Greek and Scythic Kings of Bactria and India,* London, 1886.

T. A. Gopinath Rao, *Elements of Hindu Iconography,* Vol. I, Part I, Vol. II, Part II, Madras, 1916.

F. S. Growse, *Mathura* (*District Memoir,* 2nd edition), North Western Provinces and Oudh, Government Press, 1880.

A. Grunwedel, *Buddhist Art in India,* translated into English by Gibson, 1901.

M. Hamid, Pandit R. C. Kak, and **R. P. Chanda,** *Catalogue of the Museum of Archaeology at Sanchi,* Calcutta, 1922.

M. Hamid Kuraishi and **A. Ghosh,** *A Guide to Rajgir,* 1939.

Hargreaves, *Hand Book to the Sculpture of the Peshwar Museum,* 1930.

E. B. Havell, *Indian Sculpture and Painting,* London, 1908.

E. W. Hopkins, *The Epic Mythology,* Strassburg, 1915.

————*The Religions of India,* Boston, 1895.

————*The Great Epic of India,* New York, 1901.

E. Hultzsch, *Corpus Inscriptionum Indicarum (Inscriptions of Asoka),* Vol. I, Oxford, 1925.

K. P. Jayaswal, *History of India* (150-550 A.D.), Lahore, 1933.

————*Hindu Polity,* Calcutta, 1924.

————*Manu and Yajnavalkya,* Calcutta, 1930.

A. B. Keith, *The Religion and Philosophy of the Veda,* Lanman, Vol. 31, Harvard Oriental Series, 1925.

P.V. Kane, *History of Dharmasastras,* Vol. II, Part I, Bhandarkar Oriental Research Institute, Poona, 1941.

H. Kern, *Manual of Indian Buddhism,* Strassburg, 1896.

S. Konow, *Corpus Inscriptionum Indicarum,* Vol. II *(Kharoshthi Inscriptions),* Part I, Calcutta, 1929.

A. Macdonell, *The Vedic Mythology,* Strassburg, 1897; *The History of Sanskrit Literature,* London, 1928; and A. B. Keith, *Vedic Index,* two Vols., London, 1927.

N. Macnicol, *The Indian Theism*, Oxford University Press, 1915.

N. G. Majumdar, *Inscriptions of Bengal*, Vol. III, Varendra Research Society, Rajsahi, 1929.

R. C. Majumdar, *Suvarnadvipa*, two parts, Part I, Dacca, 1937; Part II, Calcutta, 1938.

R. C. Majumdar, H. C. Raychaudhury, and **K. K. Dutta,** *An Advanced History of India*, London, 1949.

Sir John Marshall, *Mohenjodaro and the Indus Civilisation*, 3 Vols., London, 1931.

Ajay Mitra Shastri, *An Outline of Early Buddhism*, Varnasi, 1965.

R.K. Mookerjee, *Chandragupta Maurya and His Times*, University of Madras, 1943.

J. Muir, *Original Sanskrit Texts*, Vol. I, 1868 Edition. Vol. II, 1860; Vol. IV, 1863, London.

F. Max Muller, *The History of Ancient Sanskrit Literature*, London, 1860.

F. E. Pargiter, *The Dynasties of the Kali Age*, Oxford, 1913.

B. N. Puri, *India Under the Kushanas*, Bombay, 1960.

Kanakasabhai Pillai, *The Tamils Eighteen Hundred Years Ago*, Madras, 1904.

S. Radhakrishnan, *History of Indian Philosophy*, Vol. I, London, 1923.

R. S. Ranade, *A Constructive Survey of the Upanishadic Philosophy*, Poona, 1926.

E. J. Rapson, *Catalogue of the Coins of the Andhra Dynasty, The Western Kshatrapas, and the Traikutaka Dynasty*, London, 1908, *Cambridge History of India*, Vol. I, 1922.

H. C. Ray Chaudhury, *Political History of Ancient India*, 1st, 2nd and 4th Editions, University of Calcutta. *The Early History of the Vaishnava Sect*, 2nd Edition, Calcutta, 1936.

Lewis Rice, *Mysore and Coorg*, London, 1909.

H. Sarkar and **B. N. Misra,** *Nagarjunakonda*, Delhi, 1966.

S. C. Sarkar, *Educational Ideas and Institutions in Ancient India*, Patna University Readership Lecture, 1928.

F. O. Schrader, *Introduction to Pancharatra and Ahirbudhnya Samhita*, Madras, 1916.

C. J. Shah, *Jainism in North India*, Longman, Green and Co., 1932.

D. C. Sircar, *Select Inscriptions*, Vol. I, University of Calcutta, 1942; *The Successors of the Satavahanas*, University of Calcutta, *1939; Inscriptions of Asoka*, Publications Division, Government of India.

C. Sivaramamurti, *Amaravati Sculptures in the Madras Government Museum*, Madras, 1956.

Sorensen, *Index of Names in the Mahabharata.*

Mrs. Sinclair Stevenson, *The Heart of Jainism*, Oxford, 1915.

K. R. Srinivasan, "Some Aspects of Religion as Revealed by the Early Monuments and Literature of the South," *Journal of the Madras University*, Vol. XXXII, p. 144.

K. R. Subrahmanyam, *Buddhist Remains in the Andhradesa*, Andhra University Series III, 1932.

R. Subrahmanyam, *Sâlihundam*, Hyderabad, 1964.

V. A. Smith, *Jaina Stupas and Other Antiquities of Mathura*, New Imperial Series, Vol. XXI, Allahabad, 1901; *Catalogue of Coins in the Indian Museum*, Vol. I, Calcutta, 1906; *Early History of India*, Oxford, 1919.

E. J. Thomas, *The Life of Buddha as Legend and History*, London, 1952.

Edger Thurston, *Omens and Superstitions of Southern India*, London, 1912.

Madhosarup Vats, *Excavations at Harappa*, 2 Vols., 1940.

J. Ph. Vogel, *Catalogue of Archaeological Museum*, Mathura, 1910; *Indian Serpent Lore*, London, 1926.

Staniland Wake, *Serpent Worship and Other Essays.*

T. Watters, *On Yuan Chwang's Travels in India*, 2 Vols., London, 1904.

Monier Williams, *Sanskrit-English Dictionary*, Oxford, 1898; *Religious Thought and Life in Ancient India*, London, 1883.

M. Winternitz, *History of Indian Literature*, Calcutta, 1927.

Ancient Indian Texts

Rigveda Saṁhitā, with Śāyaṇa's commentary, Vols. I-IV, ed. by F. Max Müller, London, 1890-92.

Rigveda Saṁhitā, English translation by H. H. Wilson in 6 Vols., Poona, 1925-1928.

Atharva Veda Saṁhitā, ed. by Shankar Pandurang Pandit, Vols. I-IV, Bombay, 1895-1898. The English translation of the *Atharva Veda* by W. D. Whitney, Harvard Oriental Series, Lanman, Vols. 7 and 8.

Maitrāyaṇī Saṁhitā, ed. by Dr. Leopold Von Schroeder, Leipzig, 1923.

Vājasaneyī Saṁhitā, ed. by Satyavrata Sama Srami, 3 Vols., Śakābda 1796, Calcutta.

Aitareya Brāhmaṇa, ed. by Pandit Satyavrata Sama Srami, Vols. 1-4, 1895-1906, Calcutta.

Śatapatha Brāhmaṇa, ed. by Dr. A. Weber, Leipzig, 1924 edition.

Śatapatha Brāhmaṇa, English translation by J. Eggeling, *Sacred Books of the East*, XII Part I, Oxford, 1882; XXVI, Part II, Oxford, 1885; XLIV, Oxford, 1894.

Kaushiṭakī Brāhmaṇa, English translation by Keith in his *Veda Brāhmaṇas*, Harvard University Press, 1920.

Taittirīya Āraṇyaka, Anandasrama Press, 1923.

Brihadāraṇyaka Upanishad, Anandasrama Press, 1902.

Chhāndogyopanishad, Anandasrama Press, 1901.

Aitareyopanishad, Anandasrama Press, 1911.

Kenoponishad, Anandasrama Press, 1913.

Muṇḍakopanishad, Anandasrama Press, 1901.

Kaṭhakopanishad, Anandasrama Press, 1914.

Īśavāsyopanishad, Anandasrama Press, 1912.

The Thirteen Principal *Upanishads*, translated into English by R.E. Hume, London, 1921.

Svetāśataropanishad, English translation, *Sacred Books of the East*, Vol. XV, Oxford, 1900.

Śrīmadbhagavadgītā, Gujrati Printing Press, Bombay, 1908.

Bhagavadgītā (English translation), by W. D. P. Hill, London, 1928.

The Sacred Laws of Āpastamba, ed. by Dr. R. Richard Garbe, Vols. I-III, Calcutta, 1882-1902.

Kātyāyana Śrauta-Sūtra, 2 Vols., ed. by Vyakaranacharya Pandit Madan Mohan Pathak, Benaras, 1904.

Baudhāyana Śrauta-Sūtra, ed. by Dr. W. Caland, Calcutta, 1904.

Vāśishṭha Dharma-Sāśtra, *Sacred Books of the East*, Vol. XIV,

Oxford, 1882.
Āpastamba Grihya-Sūtra, Sacred Books of the East, Vol. XXX, 1892.
Āśvalāyana Grihya-Sūtra, Sacred Books of the East, Vol. XXIX, 1886.
Sānkhyāyana Grihya-Sūtra, Sacred Books of the East, Vol. XXIX, 1886.
Pāraskara Grihya-Sūtra, Sacred Books of the East, Vol. XXIX, 1886.
Mahābhārata, Bombay Edition.
Ādi Parva, ed. by V. Sukthankar, Bhandarkar Oriental Research Institute, Poona, 1933.
Āraṇyaka Parva, ed. by V.S. Sukthankar, Bhandarkar Oriental Research Institute, Poona, 1942.
Harivaṁśa, Bombay Edition.
Mahābhārata, English translation by P. C. Roy, Calcutta, 1889-1894.
Rāmāyaṇa, 3 Vols., ed. by T. R. Krishnacharya, T. R. Vyasacharya and T. R. Srinivasacharya.
Mānavadharma-śāstra (The Code of Manu), ed. by J. Jolly, London, 1887.
Vāyupurāṇa, ed. by Panchanana Tarkaratna (Vangavasi edition), Calcutta.
Vishṇu Purāṇa, ed. by Jivananda Vidyasagar, Calcutta, 1882.
Liṅga Purāṇa, ed. by Panchanana Tarkaratna (Vangavasi Edition), Calcutta.
Liṅga Purāṇā, ed. by Jivananda Vidyasagar, Calcutta.
Bhāgavata Purāṇa, Gujrati Printing Press, Bombay, Śakābda, 1824.
Kauṭilya's *Arthaśāstra*, ed. by Shama Sastri, Mysore, 1909.
Kauṭilya's *Arthaśāstra*, English translation by Shama Sastri, Mysore, 1929.
Āvaśyākasūtra of Sudharmā, Agamodayasamiti, Bombay, 1916-1917.
Sthavirāvalī Charita or *Pariśishṭa Parva* of Hemachandra, ed. by H. Jacobi, Calcutta, 1932 Edition.
Vikrama's Adventure (Vikrama Charita), ed. by Edgerton Franklin, Harvard Oriental Series, Vols. 26 and 27, 1926.
Paṭṭāvalīs of Kharatara-gachchha, Indian Antiquary, Vol. XI.

Nirvāṇa Kalikā of Pādalipatāchārya, ed. by M. B. Jhaveri Bombay, 1926.

Gommatsāra (Jivakhanda), ed. by Rai Bahadur J. L. Jaini, Lucknow, 1927.

The Pravachanasāra of Kuṇḍa Kuṇḍa Āchārya, ed. by B. Faddegon, 1935.

Pravachanasāra of Kuṇḍa Kuṇḍa, ed. by A. N. Upadhaya, Bombay, 1935.

Uttarādhyayana-Sūtra, English translation by H. Jacobi, *Sacred Books of the East*, Vol. XIV, 1895.

Darsana Sāra of Devasena, ed. by Nathuram Premi, Bombay, 1918.

Uvāsagadāsāo, ed. by A.F. Rudolf Hoernle, Calcutta, 1885.

The Āchāraṅga Sūtra, English translation by H. Jacobi, *Sacred Books of the East*, Vol. XXII, 1884.

The *Kalpa Sūtra*, English translation by H. Jacobi, *Sacred Books of the East*, Vol. XXII, 1884.

Bhagavatī Sūtra, Agamodaya Samiti, Vol. I-III, Bombay, 1918-1921.

Das Aupapātika Sūtra, ed. by Dr. Barnett, Oriental Translation Fund, 1907.

Yaśatilakachampū of Somadeva Sūri, Kavyamala Series, 2nd Vol., Bombay, 1903.

Vidvadratṇamālā, ed. by Nathuram Premi, Bombay, 1912.

Jātakas, ed. by E.B. Cowell and R.A. Neil, Cambridge, 1886.

Mahāvastu, ed. by Senart, Paris, 1882-97.

Lalitavistara, ed. by R.L. Mitra, Bibliotheca Indica, New Series, No. 473, Calcutta.

Majjhima Nikāya (Pali Text Society's edition), Vol. I, ed. by Trenckner, 1935 edition.

Sāmaññaphalasutta-vaṇṇanā in the *Sumaṅgala vilāsinī*, Buddhaghosha's Commentary on the *Dīgha Nikāya*, ed. by T. W. Rhys Davids and J. E. Carpenter, Part I, pp. 161ff, Pali Text Society Edition, London, 1886.

The Nighaṇṭu and Nirukta, ed. by Lakshman Sarup, University of Punjab, 1927.

Pāṇiniś Ashṭādhyāyī, ed. by Pandit Harishankar Pandeya, Patna, 1938.

Vyākaraṇa Mahābhāshya of Patañjali, ed. by F. Kielhorn, 3

Vols., Bombay, 1892-1909.

Kāśikā of Jayāditya and Vāmana, ed. by Pandit Bala Sastri, Banaras, 1898 edition.

Kāśikā Vivaraṇa Pañchikā of Jinendra Buddhi, ed. by S. C. Chakraborty, Varendra Research Society, Rajasahi, Bengal, 3 Vols., 1913-1925.

Siddhānta Kaumudī of Bhaṭṭoji Dikshit, ed. by Wasudeya Laxman Sastri Pansikar, 1929 edition, Bombay.

Raghuvaṁśa of Kālidāsa, Gujrat Printing Press, 1914 edition, Bombay.

Kumārasambhava of Kālidāsa, ed. by Wasudeva Laxman Sastri Pansikar, 1929 edition, Bombay.

Mālvikāgnimitram of Kālidāsa, ed. by M.R. Kale, Bombay, 1912.

Śūdraka's *Mrichchhakaṭikam*, ed. by Jivanada Vidyasagar, Calcutta, 1891,

Aśvaghosha's Buddhacharitam, *Sacred Books of the East*, Vol. XII.

Bāṇa's *Harshacharitam*, translated by Cowell and Thomas, London, 1897.

Kalhaṇa's Rājataraṅgiṇī or *Chronicle of the Kings of Kashmir*, Vol. I, ed. by M.A. Stein, Bombay, 1892 (Original text).

Kalhaṇa's *Rājatarṅgiṇī*, English translation by Stein, London, 1900.

Sarvadarsana Saṁgraha, English translation by E. B. Cowell and A.E. Gough, London, 1882.

Shaḍguru-śishya Krita Vedārtha Dīpikā Sarvānukramaṇī, Asian Series, Vol. I, Part IV, Oxford, 1886.

2500 years of Buddhism, Publications Division, Government of India.

JOURNALS, PROCEEDINGS, COMMEMORATION VOLUMES, ETC.

Annual Reports, Archaeological Survey of India

Archaeological Survey Reports by Cunningham

Archaeological Survey of India Memoirs

Asia Major

District and Imperial Gazetteers

Encyclopaedia of Religion and Ethics

Epigraphia Carnatica
Epigraphia Indica
Indian Culture
Indian Historical Quarterly
Indische Studien
Indo-Asian Culture
Jaina Antiquary
Journal of Indian Art and Industry, Vol. IV, 1891
Journal of the Bihar and Orissa Research Society
Journal of the Bombay Branch of the Royal Asiatic Society
Journal of thc Department of Letters, University of Calcutta
Journal of the Indian Society of Oriental Art
Journal of the Numismatic Society of India
Journal of the U.P. Historical Society
Journal and Proceedings of the Asiatic Society of Bengal
Lüder's List
Modern Review
Numismatic Chronicles
Pathak Commemoration Volume
Proceedings of Indian History Congress

Index